MARCO POLO

BERLIN

with Insider Tips

What I love about Berlin is the free spirit and tolerance which go to make a true metropolis. Its creativity knows no bounds.

MARCO POLO author
Christine Berger

(see p. 154)

BERLIN

> SYMBOLS

Insider Tip **MARCO POLO INSIDER-TIPPS**
Discovered for you by our author

★ **MARCO POLO HIGHLIGHTS**
Berlin top tips at a glance

SCENIC VIEW

WI-FI HOTSPOT

TRENDY MEETING PLACES

> PRICE CATEGORIES

HOTELS

€€€ over 130 euros
€€ 80–130 euros
€ under 80 euros
Prices are for two people sharing a double room, including breakfast

RESTAURANTS

€€€ over 20 euros
€€ 10–20 euros
€ under 10 euros
Prices are for an average main course, drinks not included

> MAPS

[120 A1] Page numbers and coordinates for the Berlin Street Atlas

[0] Site located outsid map sheet

For your orientation, co-ordinates are also given fo places which are not mark in the Street Atlas. Overvie map of Berlin and surrour ding area on p. 146–147. A plan of the U- and S-Ba networks can be found ins the back cover.

CONTENTS

> SCENES

P. 12–15: Trends, finds, hot spots! MARCO POLO'S on-site author reveals what's going on in Berlin and when

> 24 HOURS

P. 106/107: 24 hours packed with action and one-off experiences! MARCO POLO has put together for you a day in Berlin with a difference!

> LOW BUDGET

Have a great time without breaking the bank. Find out where to enjoy something special and snap up a bargain or two:

> DID YOU KNOW?

ON THE COVER

DISCOVER BERLIN!

Our Top 15 takes you to the most fantastic places and most exciting sites

The highlights are marked on the map on the back cover

1 Fernsehturm and Alexanderplatz
The best panoramic view of the city is to be had from the viewing platform of the television tower, a lofty 203 m above 'Alex', the legendary Alexanderplatz (page 30)

2 Gendarmenmarkt
The finest square in the city with Karl Friedrich Schinkel's Schauspielhaus as well as Deutscher and Französischer Dom (page 32)

3 Pergamonmuseum
Among the highlights of the breath-taking collection are the 113-m-long sculptured frieze, the Pergamon Altar and the decorative tiles of the famous Babylonian Processional Way (page 35)

4 Unter den Linden
From the Brandenburger Tor to the Palast der Republik: Berlin's most historically significant boulevard (page 37)

5 Brandenburger Tor
The landmark with the famous Quadriga today links East and West of the city (page 40)

6 Sony-Center
The light and airy tent-like roof, centre point of the 'new' Potsdamer Platz, impresses from afar (page 43)

7 Reichstagsgebäude
The modern glass cupola atop the venerable old building is a crowd-puller (page 44)

> THE BEST MARCO POLO HIGHLIGHTS

8 Jüdisches Museum Berlin
Two thousand years of Jewish culture in star architect Daniel Libeskind's stunning showcase (page 50)

9 Schloss Charlottenburg
Sophie Charlotte's summer residence: the magnificent splendour of the 18th century set in beautiful palace gardens (page 53)

10 Botanischer Garten
An extravagant abundance of plants in themed gardens and huge, magnificent hothouses (page 54)

11 Sowjetisches Ehrenmal
Monumental sculptures in Treptow on one of the largest Soviet military cemeteries (page 57)

12 Fischers Fritz
Classic cuisine at The Regent hotel: the only top-class restaurant in Berlin with two Michelin stars (page 62)

13 KaDeWe
The legendary delicatessen department of this noble store is a particular customer favourite (page 75)

14 Philharmonie
Music lovers from all over the world rave about Scharoun's architecture and the superb acoustics (page 86)

15 Schloss Sanssouci
Potsdam's world-famous castle and park ensemble boasts a Chinese teahouse, orangerie, sculptures and fountains (page 110)

WHAT A CITY!

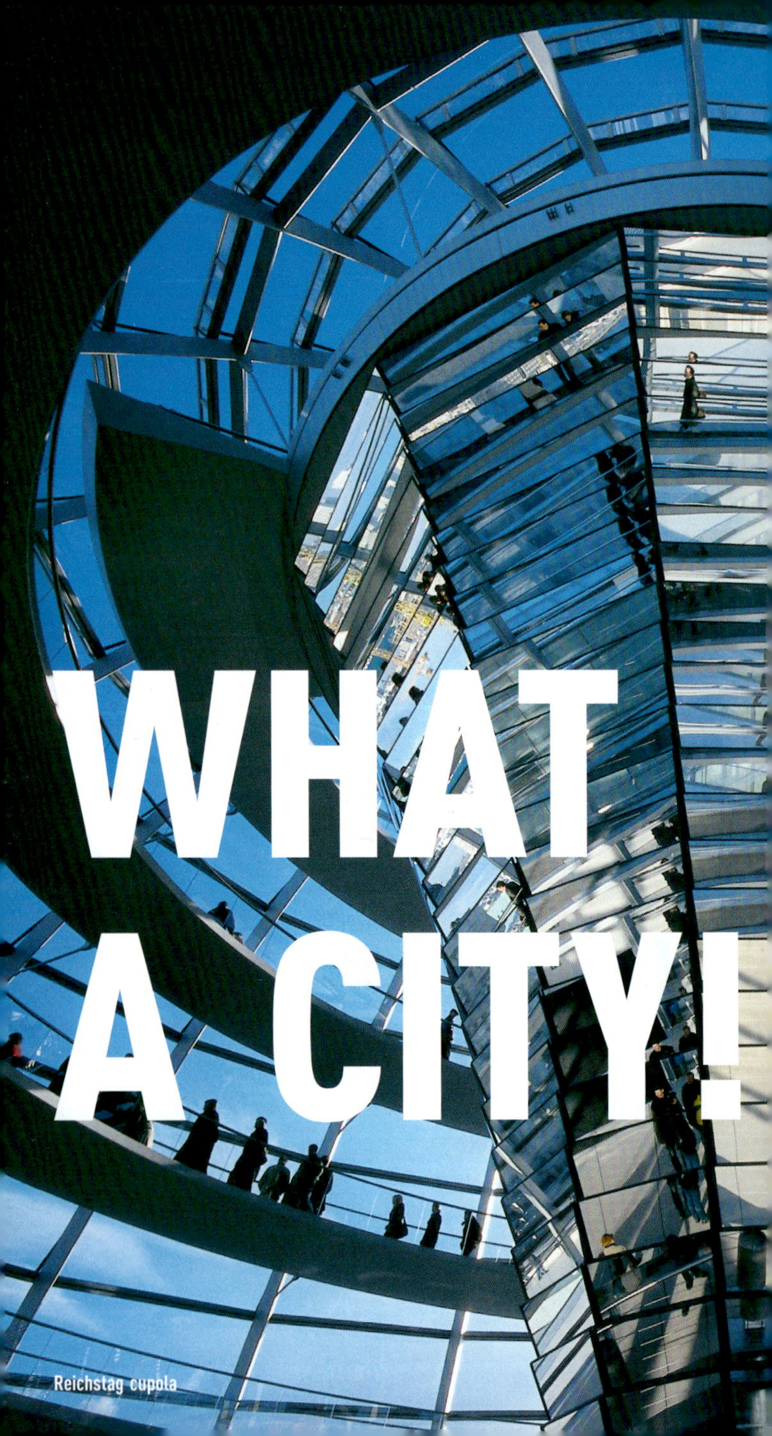

Reichstag cupola

INTRODUCTION

Design capital, city of the Wall, biggest city in Germany, metropolis which never sleeps – there are many reasons for visiting Berlin. You'd be hard put to find a second city anywhere else in the world with so many stories to tell and so many varied faces. The city's charming waterways of Havel, Spree and several canals, the kaleidoscopic museum landscape, buzzing nightlife and host of shopping centres invite you on a unique journey of discovery. Even after a morning's shopping, a lunchtime view of the administrative district from the Reichstag cupola and an afternoon spent marvelling at the Pergamon Altar, you're far from done. In the evening, the stylish club scene or a visit to the Staatsoper beckons. This city never sleeps – you're in for a surprise!

> Points on the compass have always had a greater significance in Berlin than elsewhere: 'Where does the East actually begin? Or where does it end?' A topic which still has the power to fascinate – even the city's residents. For a long time, you didn't need a compass to determine where the East stopped and the West started. The Wall that ran through the divided city from 1961 to 1989 was indicator enough: on the one side East Berlin, capital of the Soviet-influenced German Democratic Republic, and on the other the walled city of West Berlin under the protection of the western Allies France, Great Britain and the USA. Today, over 15 years after the Wall came down, visitors to the city can hardly imagine the effect the different political systems also had on the cityscape. In the eastern part of the city, many of the pre-fabricated concrete-panel housing blocks so typical of the GDR have been renovated. They look so astonishingly modern and comfortable that it's now become chic to live, say, on the eighth floor on Alexanderplatz. Standing at Checkpoint Charlie, the former Allied border crossing in Friedrichstrasse, you'll notice the dominance of luxury shops and boutiques in what was East Berlin. The western end of Friedrichstrasse paints a rather sadder picture, though: state-subsidised apartments and discount stores wherever you look.

> *Tolerant and open to new ideas*

The new, old capital Berlin, with around 3.4 million inhabitants, is still changing. Over many years now, the efforts undertaken to create an architecturally prestigious capital city have been enormous. New buildings are being constructed, old ones restored and renovated. Potsdamer Platz, in the mid-1990s Europe's biggest

Summer in the city – pavement café on Kurfürstendamm

building site, has already established itself as a new centrepoint. The tent-like roof of the Sony Center rates as one of the city's notable landmarks. A new multi-functional arena, the O2-World, opened in 2008 at the Ostbahnhof and will eventually be the hub of a new business and commercial district. Following the demolition of the Palast der Republik, once the seat of the East German Parliament, a replica of the former Stadtschloss is set to take its place in 2014.The architectural success story of the new administrative district makes even the most sceptical residents of Berlin proud. Looking out from the cupola of the Reichstag, you can see Potsdamer Platz to the south, the monumental glass roof of the new main railway station to the north, the Bundeskanzleramt to the west and the offices of the members of parliament to the east.

On the subject of the Reichstag cupola: where in other cities the common people are separated from their representatives by a kind of no-go-area, they can here – literally – climb up into the roof and look down on the debating chamber below. This is populism after the politician's heart, and it's something which gives the capital quite a special flair. Another factor here is that many politicians and members of parliament are not at all reluctant to be seen in public. You'll be surprised at how many famous faces you'll encounter in the surrounding restaurants and cafés. This could only happen in a city such as Berlin, where people are treated first and foremost as normal human beings. Whether or not they are famous is of lesser importance. 'Live and let live' is the predominant motto. People here want to be treated as individuals, and they grant others the same privilege, too.

Tolerant, open to new ideas and often avantgarde; typical adjectives which describe Berlin's attitude to culture. With over 150 concert halls and theatres, three opera houses and around 200 museums and galleries, Berlin boasts a cultural variety rivalled by few other comparable cities. Berlin is also famous for its sizzling nightlife, featuring over 200 clubs, countless bars, cafés and pubs to suit every taste. Since there's no official closing time, most places don't close until the early morning – if at all.

> *Where East and West rub shoulders*

Nowadays, at least 200,000 Russians, Poles and also Ukrainians and Czechs live in the city. Berlin is living proof of the coming together not only of the formerly divided country, but also of Europe as a whole. Berlin belongs to both Eastern and Western Europe – a unique position on the continent. Since many of the Russians and Ukrainians here are of the Jewish faith, the culture of everyday Jewish life has re-established itself. On a walk around the lively district around Oranienburger Strasse in Mitte you'll also find a Jewish grammar school and cafés offering a variety of Jewish specialities clustered round the Neue Synagoge.

Turkish life, on the other hand, dominates the western inner-city districts in particular, most notably Kreuzberg and Wedding. At the weekly markets, Turkish families can be seen buying aubergines and grapes by the crateful, while veiled women haggle over prices and the stallholders cry out their wares. A touch of the Orient and a real experience!

> History at the hub of world politics

Throughout its 775-year history, cultural and economic impulses have often come from newcomers to the city. Whether Huguenots, Bohemians or Silesians, they all found a new home in Berlin at various times over the centuries and left their mark on the city in terms of customs and traditions, not least culinary ones. Take *Bouletten*, the French word for meatballs, which have become a Berlin speciality.

Refugees from religious persecution in particular were drawn to the Spree since the Prussian rulers were known even beyond their national boundaries for their religious tolerance. Under Frederick I the Französischer Dom was built on Gendarmenmarkt in 1701 for the Protestant Huguenots; Catholic St.-Hedwigs-Kathedrale on Bebelplatz was constructed at the end of the 18th century for the Silesians; Europe's largest synagogue was erected in Oranienburger Strasse in 1866.

On more than one occasion in the course of history, Berlin has stood at the very heart of world politics; admonition and remembrance today play a major role in the city. The memory of the Nazi dictatorship, the persecution of the Jews and the terrible consequences of World War II are kept alive in the form of numerous memorials. Naturally enough, the events of recent history have also left their mark. Many of Berlin's young residents and visitors have not experienced the division of the city first-hand. For this reason memorials such as the Dokumentationszentrum Berliner Mauer in Bernauer Strasse or the Alliiertenmuseum in Zehlendorf, are now more important than ever.

A regular, audible reminder of the Berlin Airlift is the droning of the Douglas DC 3, one of the transport planes which kept the western part of the city supplied with food during the Soviet blockade in 1948–49. They are now used for nostalgic sightseeing flights over the city. The four occupying forces are represented by French, English, Russian and American educational facilities and cultural centres, which explains why some Berlin children go to a French music school or a grammar school specialising in Russian. In excess of 400,000 trees, which were planted along the streets to make life in the then walled city more bearable, still stand. There is hardly another comparable city in the world with so many parks and green, open spaces as Berlin! It must be said, though, that the economic effects of the 40-year division of the city are not so easy to deal with. Progress here is slow. Once drip-fed by financial aid of around 14 per cent. The people of Berlin, however, are making the best of things, starting up new, creative businesses and so managing to head the field again and again. There is no

The waters of the Neptunbrunnen play before the Rotes Rathaus

from two political systems and lacking a well-founded, competitive economy, the city is now finding it difficult to stand on its own feet.

> *Berlin: full of surprises ...*

Despite a dramatic rise in job numbers in the service sector, Berlin still has to live with an unemployment rate shortage of ideas elsewhere, but it is here in Berlin that so many ideas actually do become a reality. Like many residents who experience the city on a day-to-day basis, you, too, will be surprised to discover many things you didn't know before as you tour the numerous, highly individual districts of the capital. Berlin is a real surprise package – you never know what you'll find inside, but you'll have a lot of fun unwrapping it!

BERLIN TREND GUIDE

Svenja Brecht steers you through the scene jungle to the hottest finds and coolest hot spots!

Our scene scout

The arts editor on the staff of the booking agency *Ich bin Pop* knows what's new in town in terms of culture, theatre and the like. Always on the lookout for trends, our scene scout is often to be found at art previews or variety theatres. On her travels through Berlin she gets a first-hand look at exciting developments in the capital as she dips into the lively, creative scene.

CREATIVE IMAGE

Art in the no-go area

There are plenty of pretty corners in Berlin; Potsdamer Strasse is not one of them. For years, the prostitution and drug-ridden 'Kiez' (neighbourhood) has battled with its grim image. Now, however, art has taken to this problem street in Berlin. Martin Klosterfelde, from the renowned *Klosterfelde gallery*, has even termed it an "interesting area with a promising future" and recently taken the daring step of moving here from the established district of Mitte *(Potsdamer Strasse 93; www.klosterfelde.de)*. Marianne Wagner, co-founder of the *Freies Museum* at Potsdamer Strasse 91, is confident that the district will become a new centre of creative art in Berlin *(www.freies-museum.com)*. Patricia Kohl and Salome Sommer, too, inspired by the charm of the derelict area, opened their gallery here in a disused bed factory *(Kurfürstenstrasse 13–14; www.sommerkohl.com*, (above)).

SCENES

TRENDY FOOD

From club owner to hip chef

Berlin's most famous party guru, Heinz Gindullis – better known as *Cookie* – knows what Berlin's in crowd likes. For 15 years now, the event manager has been entertaining Berlin's clubbing elite in superlative style. Cookie has now extended his party monopoly and opened a gem of a vegetarian eatery, tucked away behind the *Westin Grand Hotel (Cookies Cream, Behrenstrasse 55–56; www.cookiescream.com)*. The competition has not been idle, though. Hence you can dine in an ambience suffused with a raw, industrial charm at the recently opened Berlin *Sage-Club* restaurant *(Köpenicker Strasse 18–20; www.sage-restaurant.de)*. The owners of the legendary *Rodeo Club*, on the other hand, serve up their hearty, south German fare in a former butcher's shop *(Fleischerei, Schönhauser Allee 8; www.fleischerei-berlin.com)*.

GREEN FASHION

Think green

There's no stopping the 'Lohas' (Lifestyle of Health and Sustainability) movement in Berlin. Eco-supermarkets are well established on the city streets; now the demand is growing for fashion which has been fairly and ecologically produced. Among the trend trailblazers is designer *Carolin Graening*, whose *caro.e* label comes up trumps in terms of transparency of origin and production. Now, the environmentally-conscious fashion designer has opened her own shop in Berlin-Friedrichshain *(Kochhannstrasse 21; www.caro-e.de* (right)). Berlin outlet *Wertvoll* keeps strictly to the fair trade concept with international labels such as *PeopleTree* and *Kuyichi (Marienburgerstrasse 39; www.wertvoll-berlin.de)*. Alongside organic cosmetics, Patrick Bolk's green fashion store *Every day is like Sunday* features young, regional labels, like *Slowmo* or *Fairliebt (Reichenberger Strasse 86; www.everydayislikesunday.de)*.

BERLIN BEATS

House revival

Gone are the days when shell-suit-clad freaks could maintain that monotonous, non-stop techno tracks count as danceable music. At last, the minimal techno era is coming to a well-earned close, and Berlin can start stepping out again. The most popular place of pilgrimage for new lovers of house is Berlin's *Tape Club,* where famous DJs from the international scene come and go *(Heidestrasse 14; www.tapeberlin.de* (above)). At the *Dice Club*, opened in mid-2009 and located in an old 1960s transformer station, house rules the roost *(Voltairestrasse 5; www.dice-club.de).* Parties at the *Maxxim Berlin* are a little more chic, with the dress code fine and sexy *(Joachimsthaler Strasse 15; www.maxxim-berlin.de).*

LOVELY SIGHTS

Berlin puts on a pretty face

In London, Paris and New York, professional make-overs are the norm. Ladies are known to dash in their lunch break to the nearest beauty salon to have their make-up freshened up. Clever Berlin beauticians are following suit. The finest example at the moment is the beauty salon run by *Miriam Jacks* from New York. As well as a 20-minute make-up service, there's also a lash bar with 40 different eyelash styles to choose from *(Jacks Beauty Department, Sredzkistrasse 54; www.jacks-beautydepartment.com* (above)). Things are a little more elegant and sedate at *Fine & Dandy*. On offer here: top-to-toe re-vamps ranging from eyelashes to nails for him and her – with a cup of Earl Grey tea thrown in *(Lychener Strasse 43; www.fineanddandy.de).* Not quite as personal, *Kiehl's* flagship store in Berlin is still a classic address for beauty consulting *(Münzstrasse 14–16; www.kiehls.de).*

SLACKLINING

Berlin balancing act

The latest trend on the Berlin sports scene has young men and women, their faces rigid with concentration, balancing along strips of flexible webbing suspended half a metre above the ground between two trees. This new sporting craze is called slacklining, and its fans are increasingly peopling Berlin's parks. You'll find the necessary equipment in specialist climbing shops, e.g. *Globetrotter (Schlossstrasse 78–82; www.globetrotter.de)* or *Peak-Outdoor (Wilhelminenhofstrasse 88; www.peak-berlin.com)*. Kindred spirits get together online at the Berlin community forum *(www.slackliner-berlin.de)*.

SUPPERTIME

The comeback of the roll

Who needs 5-course menus? Night owls swear by the good old-fashioned sandwich. The queen of the bread-roll spreaders is the *Joseph-Roth-Diele,* boasting 26 different types of bread *(Potsdamer Strasse 78; www.joseph-roth-diele.de)*. The luxury version is to be had from *Quchnia*. Here, your average roll is spruced up with sophisticated toppings, such as mango-curry cream and prawns *(Markgrafenstrasse 35; www.quchnia.de* (above)). Bread specialist *Manufactum brot & butter* bakes its own bread and garnishes it freshly on request with cheese and ham specialities *(Hardenbergstrasse 4–5; www.manufactum.de)*.

NEUKÖLLN

Thriving Kiez

For a long time, Neukölln was to many in Berlin just a problem district with a high crime rate and low education standards. Since more and more creative people are settling here, things have been changing for the better. At the *Heimathafen Neukölln* theatre, younger residents are bringing such topics as integration to the stage *(Karl-Marx-Strasse 141; www.heimathafen-neukoelln.de)*. Let yourself be won over by Neukölln's potential once a month at the *SideSeeing* design market, where young fashion and product designers from the district showcase their treasures *(www.sideseeing-berlin.com* (left)). A paradise for the more daring fashionistas is Barbara Nau's shop-cum-atelier *(Q-Ture, Friedelstrasse 29)*.

> CITY OF NEW IDEAS

Beach bars along the Spree, the Stadtschloss re-born or the world's largest animal home – anything's possible in Berlin

BERLINER SCHLOSS

Destroyed in World War II, its ruins razed to the ground by the East German authorities and now on the brink of re-birth. Since 2006 demolition workers have been tearing down the Palast der Republik, the former cultural centre of the GDR. At some point, the palace façade is to be re-erected. Behind it, the new *Humboldt Forum* will contain the Museums of Non-European Culture, the Berlin regional library and the collections of the Humboldt University.

Above: Federal Ministry of the Interior

DESIGN

In a ceremony in 2006, Unesco awarded Berlin the title 'City of Design', thereby making it the first German representative in a global chain of

BERLIN IN CONTEXT

imaginative and original metropolises initiated by the United Nations Educational, Scientific and Cultural Organization, entitled the 'Creative City Network'. Other cities in this illustrious, international circle include Buenos Aires, also a 'City of Design', and Edinburgh, a 'City of Literature'.

Seven institutions, including two art colleges and three fashion design schools are currently training designers in Berlin, around 5,000 of them according to the senate department for economics. Some 11,700 designers work in the so-called creative industries. A total of 6,700 design companies in Berlin alone generate a turnover of 1.8 billion euros each year – a growing market which is making its presence felt internationally. The branch's most important event is the annual *Designmai Festival* (www.designmai.de) featuring exhibitions and experimental designs.

COURTYARD ARCHITECTURE

Berlin is famous for its courtyard ensembles. Between two and eight houses, one behind the other, interlinked by courtyards and passageways, are not unusual. Not least the Hackesche Höfe in Mitte have established a reputation as fine examples of this particular architectural style. Further highlights of such expert renovation are the Heckmann-Höfe in Oranienburger Strasse, the Sophie-Gips-Höfe in Sophienstrasse and the Kurt-Berndt-Höfe in Neue Schönhauser Strasse. The latter were built for the Metropol Theatre Company in 1912. After its restoration to its former owners, the building was modernised and re-constructed at the end of the 1990s.

FASHION

Trend scouts from big fashion companies from all around the world flock regularly to the city to pick up some inspirational ideas from the imaginative outfits paraded by residents of hip districts like Mitte, Prenzlauer Berg or Friedrichshain. Not least thanks to fashion fairs such as *Durchreise* and *Premium,* fashion design is big news. A number of Berlin designers put together their one-off outfits in backroom ateliers and sell them in the showrooms out front. Admittedly, most Berlin residents prefer a casual look for every day. In some districts, shell suits and flip-flops are considered the height of fashion …

DIALECT

You could say the people of Berlin shoot straight from the lip! They certainly have a reputation for straight talking and can be rather brusque at times. Get on a bus and ask the driver for directions and you're likely to get a stroppy reply along the lines of 'Am I the tourist information office, or what?' Don't take it to heart, but don't expect too much in the way of out-and-out friendliness either. Visitors who already know a little German may notice local variations. Instead of *Brötchen* (bread rolls), people in Berlin eat *Schrippen* for breakfast, and the jam-filled doughnuts called *Berliner* elsewhere are just *Pfannkuchen* (pancakes) to the locals.

(N)OSTALGIA

Even before Wolfgang Becker's film *Goodbye Lenin*, GDR day-to-day culture had already become hip again. Design objects from former 'Volkseigener Betrieb' (the rather quaintly named 'People's Own Factories') are highly sought-after; shops selling Mitropa crockery and GDR furniture are swamped by interested customers. "Plattenbau' Happy Families card games are favourite souvenirs, and those who want to spend the night in an original GDR bed at the Ostel (p. 95) can also have their wish fulfilled. Various tour operators offer so-called 'Ostalgie Tours' to capitalise on this fondness for all things East German. There are two sides to every coin, of course, and the current wave of sentimentality should be tempered perhaps by a visit to the Stasi prison at Hohenschönhausen *(Gensler-Genslerstrasse 66 | guided tours daily 11 am and 1 pm, Sat&Sun also 3 pm)* to recall vividly the darker side of the regime.

AQUATIC CITY

Hardly a city in Europe can boast so many lakes, rivers and canals as 'Athens on the Spree'. A total of around 500 km of waterside are an ideal place to live, stroll or sunbathe! Restaurants and clubs with an aquatic perspective are plentiful around the Oberbaumbrücke in Friedrichshain. Beach bars with loungers on the banks of the Spree and, of course, any number of lidos are an open invitation to relax – with water quality rated from good to excellent. A particular highlight is the over 100-year-old lido at Wannsee, Europe's largest inland bathing area. Fine sand and typical North German roofed wicker beach chairs give guests that real seaside feeling *(Apr–Oct. daily 10am–6 pm, summer until 8 pm | Admission 4 euros | www.strandbadwannsee.de | S 1, 7 | Nikolassee).*

SCIENCE

Not many people realise that Berlin is one of the most important scientific locations in Europe: 200,000 scientists, technicians and students from all over the world teach, study and carry out research at four universities, the Charité Universitätsmedizin (University Hospital), eight universities of applied sciences, three art academies, 18 private universities and over 60 research institutes. The Long Night of Science each year in June gives an interesting insight into the achievements of these institutions.

GET YOUR FILL OF CULTURE, SPORT & FUN

Don't wait for the summer – Berlin likes to party all year round

> In recent years, numerous events have developed into real crowd-pullers. For example the Long Night at the Museums, which gets thousands up and moving twice a year. Shuttle buses transport visitors from one museum to the next, and despite the large crowds everyone has a lot of fun. The people of Berlin love crowds anyway, whether at the Carnival of Cultures or Christopher Street Day; the more the merrier!

SPECIAL EVENTS

January/February

Six-Days Race: Cycle races with a funfair atmosphere in the Velodrom; Prenzlauer Berg, Landsberger Allee; *Tel. 44 30 44 30; www.sechstagerennen-berlin.de*

Grüne Woche: Fine foods from all over the world on the Exhibition Grounds near the Funkturm; Charlottenburg; *info: Tel. 303 80; www.gruenewoche.de*

Long Night at the Museums: Visit van Gogh & Co. at the witching hour; *info: Tel. 24 74 98 88; www.lange-nacht-der-museen.de*

February

★ *Berlinale:* International Film Festival: Ten days of hustle and bustle around German and international stars and their latest films; *info: Tel. 25 92 00; www.berlinale.de*

March

International Tourism Fair (ITB): On the Exhibition Grounds near the Funkturm; Charlottenburg; *Tel. 303 80; www.itb-berlin.de*

May

Theatertreffen: Important productions from German-language countries grace Berlin's stages; *info: Tel. 25 48 92 33; www.berliner-festspiele/theatertreffen.de*

International Air Show: The fascination of flight every 2 years at Schönefeld airport (2010, 2012); *www.ila-berlin.de*

DFB Cup Final: Football's seasonal high-

> FESTIVALS AND EVENTS

light at the Olympic Stadium; *info: Tel. 896 99 40*

June/July

Carnival of Cultures: Inter-cultural carnival parade; *www.karneval-der-kulturen.de*

Christopher Street Day: Highlight for gays and lesbians with parade; *www.csd-berlin.de*

Long Night of Science: Teaching institutions and research institutes showcase their work; *www.langenachtderwissenschaften.de*

Classic Open Air on Gendarmenmarkt: Festive setting, catchy melodies; Mitte; *info: Tel. 308 78 56 85; www.classicopenair.de*

sider Tip *Sandsation Festival:* Sand sculpture artists in action at the Humboldthafen. *Europaplatz/Invalidenstrasse | Tiergarten | www.sandsation.de*

August

Second *Long Night at the Museums*

Internationale Funkausstellung: Entertainment and electronics trade fair every two years on the Exhibition Grounds near the Funkturm; Charlottenburg

September

real-Berlin-Marathon: Over 40,000 participants start at the Brandenburg Gate; *info: Tel. 30 12 88 10; www.berlin-marathon.com*

Berlin Music Festival: Two weeks of classical music at its finest; *www.berlinerfestspiele.de*

Jüdische Kulturtage: Theatre, architecture, music and readings; *www.juedische-kulturtage.org*

September/October

International Literature Festival: Features interviews with authors, readings and other events; *www.literaturfestival.com*

November

Jazzfest Berlin: An institution for international greats of the trade; *info: Tel. 25 48 91 00; www.jazzfest-berlin.de*

> A CITY RE-INVENTS ITSELF

Berlin is changing at breakneck speed: new museums, streets, buildings – even the locals come in for a surprise or two

> Even the people of Berlin don't recognise their own city. Those who haven't set foot in a district for a few months suddenly find new buildings where there was previously wasteland; they drive across bridges which weren't there before; they respectfully enter newlyopened museums. No other city in Europe is changing so quickly!

The building boom has long since caught on in the western part of the city. New hotels are springing up and run-down buildings, such as the famous Kranzlereck on Kurfürstendamm, have been unceremoniously torn down and replaced by modern architecture. The administrative district captivates the imagination of the observer with its light, airy structures, and crowds of visitors queue up in front of the Reichstag and its cupola.

There is still plenty of scope for visions and new ideas. At the Ostbahnhof, for example, is a huge new

Above: High-rise blocks on Potsdamer Platz

SIGHT SEEING

arena and the Stadtschloss is due to be re-built in 2016 – the Palast der Republik has already been demolished to make room for it. The new main railway station opened in 2006 and rates as the largest in Europe. The majority of the trains run underground. The station was designed by the Hamburg architect Meinhard von Gerkan.

Bit by bit the inner city is revealing its handsome face; whoever walks through the renovated Brandenburger Tor today can hardly imagine that for many years Pariser Platz behind it was just a desolate open space. Hence, many guests see a city which, in its present form, didn't exist ten years ago – and they don't even realise. It's all down to the skill of the architects, whether at Potsdamer Platz or on Friedrichstrasse, who have actually managed to integrate post-modern architecture into the existing

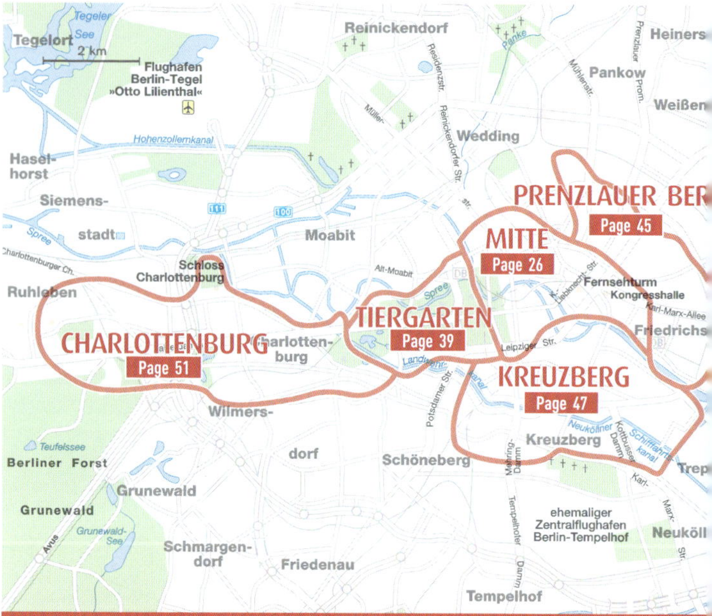

The map shows the location of the most interesting districts. There is a detailed map of each district on which each of the sights described is numbered.

cityscape, and only a few ridicule the fact that Berlin still has no skyscrapers. The locals prefer to keep things in proportion, and there simply isn't enough financial clout around to sustain a business centre like that in Frankfurt am Main.

Culture, however, takes pride of place in Berlin. With over 200 museums, collections and archives, Berlin's museum landscape almost defies description. There is such a broad palette of painting, day-to-day culture, technology and local history on show, that it would take months to get even a rough idea of the whole picture. And that picture is changing all the time.

Berlin has never lacked courage when it comes to breaking new cultural ground. Which other city boasts a museum specially built for an altar? The Pergamonmuseum, opened in 1930, is one of the most popular museums in the city, attracting some 1 million visitors per year. Its success radiates across the entire Museumsinsel (Museum Island).

The ensemble of five museums contains art treasures comparable only to those in the Louvre in Paris or the Hermitage in St. Petersburg. It was Crown Prince Frederick William's idea to create this centre for art and history. The *Altes Museum* (Greek and Roman antiquities),

Neues Museum, Bodemuseum, Nationalgalerie (19th century European and German painting and sculpture) and *Pergamonmuseum* (Greek and Roman antiquities, near-eastern art, Islamic art, central archive and library) were built between 1825 and 1930. The Neues Museum was reconstructed to plans by British architect David Chipperfield and since 2009 has housed, among other things, the collection of the Ägyptisches Museum which had previously been on temporary display at the Altes Museum. The *Bodemuseum* with its striking cupola shows exhibits from the Museum of Byzantine Art and the Sculpture Collection. The 'Royal Museum', founded by Frederick William III, has evolved into the *Stiftung Preussischer Kulturbesitz* (Foundation of Prussian Cultural Heritage) to which the National Museums in Berlin belong. These include the National Library, State Archive, the Ibero-American Institute and the

MARCO POLO HIGHLIGHTS

★ **Fernsehturm and Alexanderplatz**
The finest view across the city in the old centre (page 30)

★ **Gendarmenmarkt**
Most beautiful square in the city studded with historical gems (page 32)

★ **Hackesche Höfe**
Europe's largest courtyard complex, beautifully restored (page 32)

★ **Pergamonmuseum**
The Pergamon Altar versus Babylon's Processional Way (page 35)

★ **Unter den Linden**
Magnificent boulevard with a string of historic buildings (page 37)

★ **Brandenburger Tor**
Berlin's spruced up landmark shines once again (page 40)

★ **Gemäldegalerie**
Botticelli, Dürer, Rembrandt: 1,400 paintings from six centuries (page 42)

★ **Sony-Center**
Urban centre on Potsdamer Platz (page 43)

★ **Reichstagsgebäude**
Super view from the top of the exciting glass dome (page 44)

★ **Deutsches Technikmuseum**
The world of technology – see it, touch it! (page 49)

★ **Jüdisches Museum Berlin**
Gripping exhibition of Jewish culture in Libeskind's 'flash of lightning' (page 50)

★ **Schloss Charlottenburg**
Baroque architecture of the 18th century set in splendid palace gardens (page 53)

★ **Botanischer Garten**
42 hectares of nature at its most exotic (page 54)

★ **Sowjetisches Ehrenmal**
Monumental kitsch to honour the Russians who fell in Berlin (page 57)

State Institute for Music Research and the Musikinstrumentenmuseum. The latter is located at the Kulturforum in Tiergarten, the Western counterpart of the Museumsinsel.

Admission to the National Museums of Berlin costs between 4 and 8 euros. Special exhibitions, such as at the Neue Nationalgalerie, are considerably more expensive. Information on all museums, guided tours and special exhibitions is available from the Museumsinformation office: *Tel. 24 74 98 88* or on the Internet at *www.museumsportal-berlin.de*.

MITTE

> The treasures of the Museumsinsel are acclaimed the world over as art-historical highlights, the television towerwith its viewing platform at 203 m is a crowd-puller in fine weather and a photograph of the ultimate city landmark, the Brandenburger Tor, is a must for many visitors to the city. In the whole city, Mitte has by far the most sights on offer. A stroll along the boulevard Unter den Linden is a journey of discovery to the historical heart of the city. The Humboldt-Universität, for example, where famous scientists such as Albert Einstein or Rudolf Virchow taught, or the Zeughaus containing the Deutsches Historisches Museum. Between Gendarmenmarkt, Nikolaiviertel and Neue Synagoge there's a lot going on in the evenings, too.

Countless restaurants, bars and clubs aim to please until well into the night. Shoppers should head for the area around the Hackescher Markt. This is where Berlin designers have their ateliers and shops. To the north of the Neue Synagoge you'll find mainly modern art on sale: the dense array of international galleries is most impressive.

Marking the cultural heart of Mitte: the Berliner Dom on Museumsinsel

1 BERLINER DOM [123 E3]

Built between 1894–1905, Berlin Cathedral was severely damaged in World War II. It was not until the mid-1990s that the interior was sufficiently restored to hold services. Of the previous cathedral building only the altar frieze depicting the 12 Apostles, the font and two candelabras survive. The crypt houses the Hohenzollern tomb with some 90 sarcophagi, some of them richly decorated. From the cupola, you have a spectacular view of the Museumsinsel and the Schloss construction site! *Apr–Sept: Mon–Sat 9 am–8 pm, Sun noon– 8 pm; Oct to Mar: Mon–Sat 9 am to 7 pm, Sun noon–7 pm | Admission: 5 euros | Prayers Mon–Sat noon–12.30 pm, Mon to Fri 6 pm–6.30 pm, Services Sun 10 am, 6 pm, Several guided tours daily | Am Lustgarten | S-Bahn Hackescher Markt | Bus 100 | Schlossplatz*

Insider Tip

2 DDR-MUSEUM [123 E3]

For those directly affected, this look back at everyday life in the GDR probably arouses ambivalent feelings:: food shortages, unfashionable jeans, nudist holidays, the typical 'Erika' typewriter and music by Karat or City, which can be recalled to mind via headphones. Some 400 sqm of GDR day-to-day history. *Daily 10 am to 8 pm, Sat until 10 pm | Admission: 5,50 euros | Karl-Liebknecht-Strasse 1/Spreepromenade | www.ddr-museum.de | S-Bahn Hackescher Markt*

Insider Tip

3 DENKMAL DER BÜCHERVERBRENNUNG [134 B3]

On Bebelplatz by the Staatsoper (State Opera) a monument by Israeli artist Micha Ullman commemorates the burning of works by Erich Kästner, Bertolt Brecht, Kurt Tucholsky, and many more authors who had fallen foul of the Nazis, on 10 May 1933. The monument, which has been incorporated into a former tram tunnel, is conceived as an empty library with room for around 20,000 books. Visitors look down through a glass plate set into the floor onto the empty, white shelves below. *Mitte | Unter den Linden | Bus 100 | Staatsoper*

4 DEUTSCHE GUGGENHEIM BERLIN [122 C3]

Exhibitions of internationally acclaimed modern art. Joint project of the Deutsche Bank and the Solomon R. Guggenheim Foundation. *Daily 10 am–8 pm, Thurs until 10 pm | Admission 4 euros | Unter den Linden 13 | www.deutsche-guggenheim.de | U6 | Französische Strasse*

5 DEUTSCHES HISTORISCHES MUSEUM [123 D3]

The heart of the permanent Historical Museum display, re-opened at the Zeughaus in 2006, are the so-called 'period rooms', through which visitors can 'wander' down German history from its beginnings to the present day. Ieoh Ming Pei's extension hosts changing exhibitions. *Daily 10 am–6 pm | Admission 5 euros | Zeughaus (old building) | Unter den Linden 2 | www.dhm.de | S-Bahn Hackescher Markt*

6 DOKUMENTATIONSZENTRUM BERLINER MAUER [128 A4–5]

A piece of the original Wall still stands; observation slits give a

MITTE

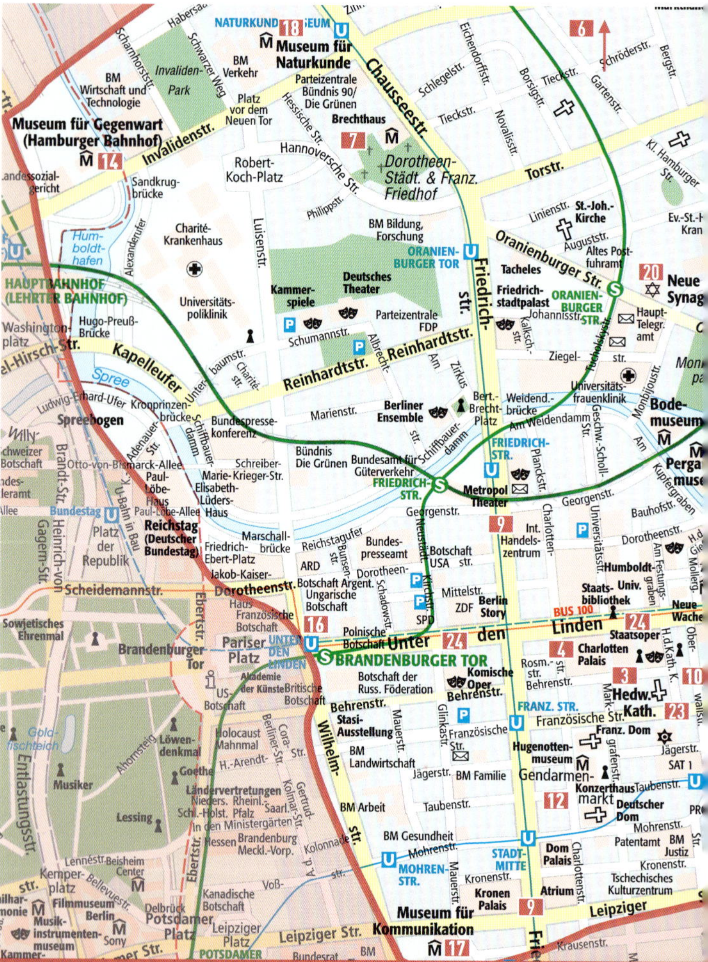

SIGHTSEEING IN MITTE

1 Berliner Dom
2 DDR-Museum
3 Denkmal der Bücherverbrennung
4 Deutsche Guggenheim Berlin
5 Deutsches Historisches Museum
6 Dokumentationszentrum Berliner Mauer
7 Dorotheenstädtischer Friedhof
8 Fernsehturm and Alexanderplatz
9 Friedrichstrasse
10 Friedrichswerdersche Kirche
11 Gedenkstätte Stille Helden
12 Gendarmenmarkt

- 13 Hackesche Höfe
- 14 Hamburger Bahnhof
- 15 Karl-Marx-Allee
- 16 Madama Tussauds Berlin
- 17 Museum für Kommunikation
- 18 Museum für Naturkunde
- 19 Museumsinsel
- 20 Neue Synagoge
- 21 Nikolaiviertel
- 22 Rotes Rathaus
- 23 St.-Hedwigs-Kathedrale
- 24 Unter den Linden

glimpse of 'the other side'. In this way, visitors can begin to imagine what the division of the city felt like. The Berlin Wall Documentation Centre illustrates daily life in the shadow of the Wall on Bernauer Strasse, part of the district of Wedding. *Tues–Sun 9.30 am–7 pm; winter: 10 am–5 pm | Free Admission | Bernauer Strasse 111 | www.berliner-mauer-dokumentationszentrum.de | S1, 2 | Nordbahnhof*

7 DOROTHEENSTÄDTISCHER FRIEDHOF [128 A6]

Many great names of the artistic and cultural world have been laid to rest here, most recently former German President Johannes Rau. Heinrich Mann, Bertolt Brecht, Helene Weigel, Anna Seghers, Karl Friedrich Schinkel, Johann Gottlieb Fichte and Georg Wilhelm Friedrich Hegel are also buried here. Within the bounds of the cemetery lie the remains of the French Cemetery, established in 1780 for the Huguenot refugees. Its fine stock of trees makes it an idyllic place in which to escape the hectic pace of the big city. *Chausseestrasse 126 | U 6 | Museum für Naturkunde*

8 FERNSEHTURM AND ALEXANDERPLATZ ★ [123 F2–3]

The second-highest television tower in Europe, the 'Tele-asparagus' is the symbol of the city, alongside the Brandenburger Tor. It was built in 1966–69 and, at 365 m, the tower and its glazed sphere are visible from almost every inner-city district. On clear days, the viewing platform at 203 m is packed with people. Thanks to a new text message service, visitors no longer have to queue to get in, but are informed when it's their turn to be whisked up to the platform in just 40 seconds! The restaurant above the viewing platform rotates twice every hour around its own axis. In fine weather you can see up to 40 km away. *(Nov–Feb: daily 10 am–midnight; Mar–Oct: 9 am–midnight | Admission: 10 euros, VIP ticket: 19.50 euros (no waiting time) | Panoramastrasse 1a).*

Named after the Russian Tsar Alexander I, *Alexanderplatz* at the foot of the television tower (on the other side of the railway line) has been used since 1805 as both parade ground and market place. Today, its generous proportions attract shoppers

> WATERBORNE IN BERLIN

By pleasure boat though the city

The most comfortable way to explore the historic Mitte or the administrative district is by passenger boat. Numerous craft ply the Spree. There are landing stages, for example, on the Museumsinsel, Friedrichstrasse or at the Haus der Kulturen der Welt. A round trip from Mitte via Kreuzberg to Charlottenburg and back to Mitte along the Spree and Landwehrkanal is an interesting option. The three-hour tour not only lets you see almost all the city's sights, but the guide on board gives you plenty of insights into everyday life in Berlin. *Information on departure times and prices: Tel. 536 36 00 | www.sternundkreis.de*

and visitors to the tower in particular. Following renovation of the square, the refurbishment of the Kaufhof department store and the move by C&A into Peter Behrens' *Berolinahaus* (built in 1929, now a listed building), the square has changed

Weltzeituhr at the foot of the Fernsehturm

completely. Only the Weltzeituhr (World Time Clock) and the Brunnen der Völkerfreundschaft (Fountain of International Friendship) hark back to the East German past.

Close to the Rotes Rathaus (Red Town Hall) stands the *Neptunbrunnen:* as if to get a better view, sea god Neptune stands atop a huge shell, holding his trident – hence the nickname 'pitchfork pond'. At his feet recline four female figures personifying the rivers Oder, Weichsel, Rhine and Elbe. When William II was presented with the fountain, a creation by Reinhold Begas, he had it erected in front of the Stadtschloss. Following its restoration in 1969 it was moved to its present location. *Alexanderplatz | Bus 100 | Spandauer Strasse U-/S-Bahn Alexanderplatz*

9 FRIEDRICHSTRASSE [122 C1–6]

As early as the 1920s Friedrichstrasse was committed to the pursuit of pleasure! Theatres, revues and bars lined its 3.5-km route from north to south through the district of Mitte. Before the collapse of Communism, the Wall cut the street in two. The famous Checkpoint Charlie was the border crossing-point. Today nothing but a few piled-up sand sacks and a customs clearance hut bear witness here to the old days. Chic office buildings and shops, such as *Quartier 206* with its exclusive boutiques, tower up. The *Galeries Lafayette* department store is an architectural highlight. The *Friedrichstadtpalast (S. 87)* was also famous in the GDR for its revues. *U-/ S-Bahn Friedrichstrasse*

10 FRIEDRICHSWERDERSCHE KIRCHE [123 D4]

Schinkel's work rates as one of the major examples of German Neo-Gothic architecture. Built in 1824–

30, the church's interior contains sculptures from the early 19th century. Here the main emphasis is on the Classicist style, with works by Johann Gottfried Schadow or Christian Daniel Rauch. *Daily 10 am–6 pm | Free admission | Werderscher Markt | U 2 | Hausvogteiplatz*

11 GEDENKSTÄTTE STILLE HELDEN [123 E2]

Impressive archive which uses multimedia technology to present the biographies of Jews and their rescuers during the Third Reich. *Daily 10 am to 8 pm | Free admission | Rosenthaler Strasse 39 | S-Bahn Hackescher Markt*

>LOW BUDGET

- Visitors to all National Museums of Berlin enjoy free admission on Thurs for the last four hours of opening.
- The spectacular view from the cupola of the Reichstag [122 A2] doesn't cost a cent. There are big crowds, though, so you should be prepared for a long wait to get in.
- One of the cheaper sightseeing trips covering many important sights is a journey with bus number 100 from Bahnhof Zoo to Alexanderplatz. It takes you past the Siegessäule, Schloss Bellevue, Reichstag and the Brandenburger Tor.
- There's a fantastic view across the city from the roof of the *Park Inn Hotel* [123 F3] on Alexanderplatz *(daily 2 pm–10 pm; winter: noon to 6 pm | Mitte | Alexanderplatz 7).* Admission to the panorama terrace on the 39th floor: only 3 euros.

12 GENDARMENMARKT ★ [122 C4]

With its 18th- and 19th-century buildings, it rates as the most beautiful square in the city. Flanked by the Französischer Dom and the Deutscher Dom (the French and German Cathedrals) is the *Schauspielhaus*, built by Karl Friedrich Schinkel in 1818–21, which today serves as a concert hall. The *Französischer Dom* was devastated in the last war and re-built in 1983. It was constructed in 1701–05 for the city's 8,000-strong Huguenot community. An exhibition inside the cathedral illustrates the life of these newcomers to the city. The 70-m-high tower was only added in 1780–85. Since completion of renovation work in 2005, visitors have been able once again to enjoy the fine views over the Gendarmenmarkt *(Tues–Sun noon–5 pm | Tower daily 9 am–7 pm | Gendarmenmarkt 5).* The *Deutscher Dom*, built at the other end of the square at the same time as its French counterpart, is no longer in use as a church, but houses an exhibition on German history. *U6 | Stadtmitte*

13 HACKESCHE HÖFE ★ [123 D1]

The *Hackesche Höfe*, built in 1905–07 and famous for their labyrinthine network of courtyards, are now home to a number of restaurants, cinemas, galleries, a variety theatre and several boutiques. Neighbouring Sophienstrasse, with its traditional craftsmen and small retailers, was home to many Jews before the war, a fact illustrated by the partly reconstructed *Neue Synagoge* (New Synagogue) in Oranienburger Strasse. *S-Bahn Hackescher Markt*

14 HAMBURGER BAHNHOF [133 E1]
Railway station turned museum, showing art from the last 60 years in 13,000 sq m of exhibition space. Part of the collection was lent to the museum by private collector Erich Marx, and centres on works by Andy Warhol, Cy Twombly, Robert Rauschenberg, Roy Lichtenstein, Anselm Kiefer and Joseph Beuys. Exhibits from the Flick collection also feature in special shows. *Tues–Fri 10 am to 6 pm, Sat 11 am–8 pm, Sun 11 am to 6 pm | Admission: 8 euros | Invalidenstrasse 50 | www.hamburgerbahnhof.de | S 5, 9, 75 | Hauptbahnhof*

Insider Tip

15 KARL-MARX-ALLEE [135 D–F 2–3]
Germany's longest historical monument points towards Moscow, and not only in architectural terms. Examples of Socialist Realism, also called Stalinist 'wedding-cake' style, line the magnificent 90-m-wide avenue built in 1952–60. As a result of the war, only ruins remained of the former Frankfurter Strasse. The two towers at the Frankfurter Tor, modelled on the cathedral domes on Gendarmenmarkt, still stand as landmarks on this impressive avenue, along which up to 300-m-long and nine-storey-high residential blocks stand. These buildings were constructed largely from the remains of bombed-out houses. It was here, on 17 June 1953, that the worker's revolt broke out and was subsequently bloodily put down. *Friedrichshain | U 5 | Frankfurter Tor*

Always popular meeting places: the pubs and cafés at the Hackesche Höfe

16 MADAME TUSSAUDS BERLIN [122 B3]
The famous wax museum close to the Brandenburger Tor shows around 80 life-size figures, including Berlin's current Lord Mayor Klaus Wowereit, Johnny Depp, Madonna, The Beatles, goalkeeper Oliver Kahn and Chancellor Angela Merkel. *Daily 10 am–7 pm | Admission: 19 euros | Unter den Linden 74 | www.madametussauds.com | S 1, 2, 25 | Brandenburger Tor*

Insider Tip **17 MUSEUM FÜR KOMMUNIKATION** [122 B5]
The Museum of Communication rates as the oldest postal museum in the world. Since renovation in 1996–2000, visitors have been treated to a fascinating display featuring a computer gallery, interactive exhibits, robots, Philip Reis' first telephones and the world's most famous postage stamps, the Red and Blue Mauritius. *Tues–Fri 9 am–5 pm, Sat&Sun 10 am–6 pm | Admission: 3 euros | Leipziger Strasse 16 | www.museumsstiftung.de/berlin | U 2, 6 | Stadtmitte*

18 MUSEUM FÜR NATURKUNDE [133 F1]
The Natural History Museum, with over 25 million zoological, palaeontological, mineralogical and geological exhibits, is a world-beater. Now completely restored, the famous, genuine skeleton of a brachiosaurus brancai (Insider Tip) – 23 m long and 13 m high – is quite a sight! Hundreds of prepared animal specimens illustrate the broad variety of Germany's native animal kingdom. *Tues–Fri 9.30 am to 5 pm, Sat&Sun 10 am–6 pm | Admission: 6 euros | Invalidenstrasse 43 | www.naturkundemuseum-berlin.de | U 6 | Naturkundemuseum*

19 MUSEUMSINSEL [123 D–E 2–3]
All museums *Tues–Sun 10 am–6 pm | Nationalgalerie and Pergamonmuseum Thurs until 10 pm | S-Bahn Hackescher Markt*

The steps of the Pergamon Altar in the Pergamonmuseum are a favourite spot for a breather!

The *Altes Museum* (Old Museum) is home to art and sculptures from Ancient Greece and Rome. The Etruscan treasures, the heart of the collection, will go on display after the building is renovated. Until then the Greek exhibits are to be found in the newly fitted-out main floor. Stone sculptures and figures made of clay and bronze, friezes, vases, gold jewellery and silverwork are arranged by theme.

Berlin is justly proud of its freshly-renovated *Bodemuseum* containing collections of sculptures, Byzantine art (featuring images from the early Middle Ages to the end of the 18th century) and the coin collection of 500,000 rare specimens.

Now fully renovated, the *Nationalgalerie* (Old National Gallery) is one of Berlin's finest museum buildings, housing valuable paintings and sculptures from the 19th century. By studying the works of Menzel, Schadow and Blechen, for example, visitors gain an insight into building styles, fashions and the general spirit of imperial times in the city.

The ★ *Pergamonmuseum* was built in 1910–30 to house the Pergamon Altar. Discovered in Turkey in the 19th century, the altar took 20 years to re-construct. The 113-m-long sculptured frieze is considered a masterpiece of Greek art and depicts gods and giants in combat. The adjacent exhibition room contains the magnificent market gate from Miletus, a prime example of Roman architecture dating back to 130 AD. The museum also houses unique collections of Islamic and near-eastern art, including the superb 30-m-long Babylonian Processional Way with its decorative lion images.

As of autumn 2009, the *Neues Museum* has been home to the over 3,000-year-old bust of the Egyptian queen Nefertiti and the collection of Egyptian artefacts belonging to the Stiftung Preussischer Kulturbesitz (Foundation of Prussian Cultural Heritage). The museum, one of the finest in the city, was re-built to plans by David Chipperfield. The partially restored murals are a particularly impressive feature inside the building which was built by Friedrich August Stüler in 1843–1855, severely damaged in World War II, and then stood empty for 60 years.

20 NEUE SYNAGOGE [123 D1]

When it was consecrated in 1866 it was the world's largest synagogue with 3,200 seats. Today, the New Synagogue on Oranienburger Strasse serves as a place of prayer and an exhibition venue. Once past the security checks, the visitor is confronted by the glass panel giving onto the former interior, today a huge open space covered with gravel. Thanks to the intervention of a courageous policeman, an arson attack was prevented on the night of

Renovated cupola of the Neue Synagoge in Oranienburger Strasse

the Nazi pogrom on 9 November 1938. In 1943, however, a bombing raid did in fact destroy the building almost completely. The façade and the golden dome, accessed via some steps, were renovated in 1988. *Mar–Oct: Sun/Mon 10 am to 8 pm, Tues–Thurs 10 am–6 pm, Fri 10 am to 5 pm (Mar, Oct Fr only until 2 pm), Nov–Feb: Sun–Thurs 10 am–6 pm, Fri 10 am to 2 pm | Admission: 3 euros, dome: 1.50 euros | Oranienburger Strasse 30 | S 1, 2, 25 | Oranienburger Strasse*

21 NIKOLAIVIERTEL [123 E–F4]

The Nikolaiviertel around the Nikolaikirche to the southeast of Alexanderplatz is considered to be the cradle of the city; it was here that the first houses were erected in the 13th century. At first sight, today's buildings appear to date from the 18th and 19th centuries; most of them are, in fact, from the 1980s. *U2 | Klosterstrasse*

22 ROTES RATHAUS [123 F3]

The red brick façade of the Red Town Hall, built in 1861–70 on Alexanderplatz, is visible from afar. The building itself is in the style of the Italian High Renaissance, while the bell tower resembles that of Laon cathedral in France. Along the entire façade at first-floor level is a frieze consisting of 36 panels, depicting the history of Berlin. Badly damaged in World War II, the Town Hall became the seat of the East Berlin municipal authorities in 1958. With reunification in 1990, the Red Town Hall took up the reins of the united city once again. *Rathausstrasse 15 | Tel. 902 60 | www.berlin.de | U-/S-Bahn Alexanderplatz*

23 ST.-HEDWIGS-KATHEDRALE **[123 D4]**
At the beginning of the 18th century a mere 700 Catholics lived in Berlin. As little as 30 years later, there were around 10,000 – people seeking refuge in liberal Berlin from the Silesian wars. For this reason, the foundation stone for a new church was laid in 1747, though it was not until 30 years later, in 1773, that the baroque Cathedral of St. Hedwig could finally be used. It was designed by architect Jean Legeay in collaboration with the royal master builder Johann Boumann the Elder, who modelled it on the Pantheon in Rome. Badly damaged in World War II, the cathedral was re-built in 1952–63. *Mon to Sat 10 am–5 pm | Bebelplatz | U 2 | Hausvogteiplatz | Bus 100 | Staatsoper*

24 UNTER DEN LINDEN ★ **[122–123 B–D3]**
The spiritual and cultural significance of the avenue between the Branden-

> BLOGS & PODCASTS

Interesting weblogs and files on the Internet

- > ***http://mayda3000.blogspot.com*** – 'Why would a Californian move to Berlin?' Read his avantgarde look at what's going on in the city to find out.
- > ***www.isarsteve.de*** – British ex-pat living in Berlin whose blog also has interesting sections entitled 'Around and About Berlin' and 'Forbidden Places', a closer look at spots which were inaccessible to Westerners during the Wall era.
- > ***www.npr.org/blogs/nprberlinblog*** – Run by a US radio station broadcasting in Berlin. Radio staff and guests contribute their own take on the city.
- > ***http://stilinberlin.blogspot.com*** – A lot of information for fashion victims. Photo blog shows you what Berlin is wearing and the streets the looks originated on.
- > ***www.spottedbylocals.com*** – To-do tips for various European cities, including Berlin, from people who really know their way around.
- > ***www.spiegel.de*** – The English-language site of the top German news magazine has excellent up-to-the-minute reports and background articles on all aspects of German life, politics and culture. There's even an online pub quiz!
- > ***www.dw-world.de*** – Germany's international broadcaster has a very interesting English site packed with information for visitors and new residents. Broad-based overview of national and international events.

MARCO POLO does not take any responsbility for the contents of the blogs & podcasts.

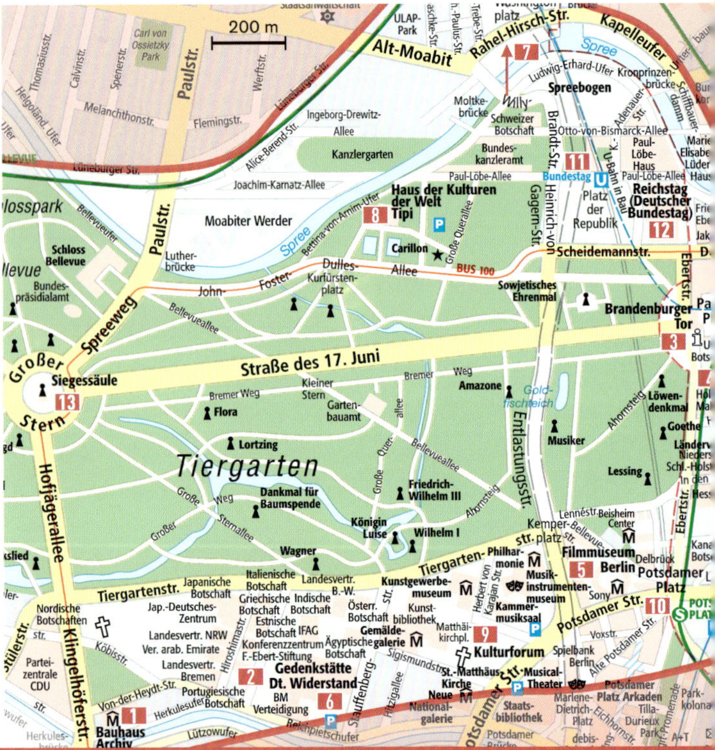

SIGHTSEEING IN TIERGARTEN

1 Bauhaus-Archiv
2 Botschaftsviertel
3 Brandenburger Tor
4 Denkmal Juden Europas
5 Filmmuseum Berlin
6 Gedenkstätte dt. Widerstand
7 Hauptbahnhof
8 Haus der Kulturen der Welt
9 Kulturforum
10 Potsdamer Platz
11 Regierungsviertel
12 Reichstagsgebäude
13 Siegessäule

burger Torand the Berliner Dom is as great today as ever, not least because of the Museumsinsel. The *Kronprinzenpalais*, (the Crown Prince's Palace), the *Zeughaus* (Arsenal), the *Staatsoper* (State Opera) and the current *Humboldt-Universität* were erected here ins the 18th century. At the end of the 19th century the *Berliner Dom* was added in the Wilhelmine style. The boulevard was devastated in World War II and the remaining buildings have been restored, with the exception of the Stadtschloss, the ruins of which were demolished by East Berlin's city council in 1950.

The *Palast der Republik* was built on the banks of the Spree in place of the former Hohenzollern Palace. Nicknamed rather derisively 'Palazzo Prozzi' ('protzen' in German means to show off), it served the GDR as an important cultural centre. Following its demolition, the Stadtschloss is due to be re-built on the same site. *Mitte | S 1, 2, 25 | Brandenburger Tor.*

TIERGARTEN

> Favourite park for joggers, administrative district and shopping centre – as far as districts go, they don't come more varied than Tiergarten. The view from the cupola of the Reichstag is the best to be had, looking across to the tent-like roof of the Sony Center on Potsdamer Platz and towards the Quadriga, the chariot adorning the top of the Brandenburger Tor. To the west, the golden statue of the goddess Victoria glistens from the top of the Siegessäule. This green oasis, which gives the district its name, offers recreation for stressed city dwellers and cultural highlights such as the summer concerts in the Englischer Garten or Indian pop bands in the Haus der Kulturen der Welt.

1 BAUHAUS-ARCHIV [133 D5]

Superb collection illustrating the history of the Bauhaus movement: furniture, paintings and design by the likes of Ludwig Mies van der Rohe and Walter Gropius, who also designed the museum building in 1964. *Wed–Mon 10 am–5 pm | Admission: Sat–Mon 7, Wed–Fri 6 euros | Klingelhöfer Strasse 14 | www.bauhaus.de | Bus 100 | Lützowplatz*

Pavement café on Unter den Linden looking towards the Brandenburger Tor

2 BOTSCHAFTSVIERTEL [132 C5]

Numerous embassies have returned to the area south of the Tiergarten. Before World War II this was the traditional home of the diplomats, although only the renovated embassies of Japan and Italy bear witness to this time. Architectural highlights are the diplomatic missions of Sweden, Norway, Iceland, Denmark and Finland. They share a five-part complex, the so-called 'Nordic Embassy Buildings', which includes the shared 'Felleshus', a restaurant and exhibition rooms. The Mexican Embassy next door, on the other hand, is avant-garde, boasting an 18-m-high foyer, roof garden and striking façade. All of these embassies set great store by offering a cultural programme for the general public. They regularly stage exhibitions, concerts or readings. *Botschaft der Nordischen Länder | Rauchstrasse 1 | Tel. 505 00 | www.nordischebotschaften.org | Felleshus Mon–Fri 10 am–7 pm, Sat&-Sun 11 am–4 pm. | Botschaft der Vereinigten Staaten von Mexiko | Klingelhöfer Strasse 3 | Tel. 269 32 30 | www.mexiko.diplo.de | Exhibition hall Mon–Fri 9 am–1 pm | Bus 100 | Nord-Botschaften*

3 BRANDENBURGER TOR ★ [122 A3]
When the archetypal Berlin landmark, the Brandenburg Gate, was unveiled on 3 October 2002 after years of restoration work, it was cheered by around one million spectators. The people of Berlin are extremely fond of their landmark, which incidentally never actually functioned as a gateway. The 20-m-high monument has stood on Pariser Platz since 1791, built to plans by architect Carl Gotthard Langhans, who took the propylaea of the Acropolis in Athens as his model. The goddess of victory, driving four horses is seen as a bringer of peace. Following his successful campaigns, Napoleon humiliated the Germans by taking the Quadriga back to Paris with him in 1806. Not until eight years later was it returned to its rightful place, perched aloft once more following the Wars of Liberation. Victoria was crowned with the Iron Cross, laurel wreath and the Prussian eagle as a sign of remembrance of the struggle against Napoleon. After World War II the Brandenburger Tor (Brandenburg Gate) was left severely damaged. The Quadriga was re-formed according to the old plaster models – a joint project undertaken by the city councils of East and West Berlin. At the request of the GDR government, the Iron Cross and the Prussian eagle were omitted, and the victory goddess was handed a staff with a wreath of oak leaves instead. It was only after reunification that the old symbols were restored to their

> TAKE IT EASY!

Floating weightless on the water

The *Liquidrom* in the Tempodrom [133 F6] is a hit, not least thanks to its unique architecture. Enjoy the fabulous sensation of floating weightless in the grotto-like saltwater pool, listening to the gentle sound of music underwater and watching as the play of colour and light transforms the water into a rainbow. In the evenings, pool-side DJs provide the musical backdrop, with styles ranging from classic to downbeat. A nice treat: the sauna with steam bath or a Balinese herbal-stamp or hot-stone massage.
Sun–Thurs 10 am-midnight, Fri&Sat 10 am–1 am | Day ticket: 22.50 euros | Kreuzberg | Möckernstrasse 10 | Tel. 258 00 78 20 | www.liquidrom-berlin.de | U 1, 7 | Möckernbrücke

Walk-in monument: Denkmal für die ermordeten Juden Europas

exalted position. *Mitte | Pariser Platz | S 1, 25 | Brandenburger Tor*

4 DENKMAL FÜR DIE ERMORDETEN JUDEN EUROPAS [133 F4]

New York architect Peter Eisenman's Holocaust Memorial to the Jewish victims of Nazi Germany comprises 2,700 concrete pillars (stelae) of differing heights. They are arranged in a grid formation on a 19,000-sq-m site. It is possible to walk into the structure, its wave-like shape taking on a different appearance depending on the perspective of the observer. There is an information centre underneath the site. *Wilhelmstrasse/Behrenstrasse | U-/S-Bahn Potsdamer Platz*

5 FILMMUSEUM BERLIN [122 A4–5]

Costumes, film excerpts and much more illustrate the history of German film. Modern animation techniques, special effects and virtual worlds are also showcased. The adjoining Television Museum lets you rediscover past series and quiz shows! *Tues–Sun 10 am–6 pm, Thurs until 8 pm | Admission: 6 euros | Potsdamer Strasse 2 | www.filmmuseum-berlin.de | U-/S-Bahn Potsdamer Platz*

6 GEDENKSTÄTTE DEUTSCHER WIDERSTAND [133 D5]

An exhibition vividly depicts how individuals and groups resisted the Nazi dictatorship in the years 1933 to 45, using the limited means at their disposal. *Mon–Fri 9 am to 6 pm, Thurs until 8 pm, Sat&Sun 10 am to 6 pm | Free Admission | Stauffenbergstrasse 13 | www.gdw-berlin.de | U 2 | Mendelssohn-Bartholdy-Park*

7 HAUPTBAHNHOF [133 E2]

Europe's largest railway station has been erected to plans by the Hamburg architects Gerkan & Partner. Glass and steel predominate in this magnificent, multi-storey structure, featuring numerous shopping arcades and underground tracks running from north to south. Over 1,000 trains arrive here every day. *Europaplatz | S-Bahn Hauptbahnhof*

8 HAUS DER KULTUREN DER WELT [133 E3]

Opened in 1957 for the 'Interbau' construction fair, the former congress hall aroused a lot of attention abroad due to its daringly arched roof construction and at home earned itself the nickname 'pregnant oyster'! Since 1989 the 'House of World Cultures' has achieved international renown for its cultural festivals and country-specific events. *John-Foster-Dulles-Allee 10 | www.hkw.de | Bus 100 | Haus der Kulturen der Welt*

9 KULTURFORUM [133 E 4–5]

All museums: *Admission: 8 euros | www.smb.museum | U-/S-Bahn Potsdamer Platz*

The ★ *Gemäldegalerie* (Picture Gallery), opened in 1998, contains some of the most important works of 13th to 18th-century European art. Some 72 galleries and exhibition rooms house 1,400 paintings covering various styles and epochs. Italian painting of the 14th to 18th centuries and 15th- to 16th-century Dutch works. *Tues–Sun 10 am–6 pm, Thurs until 10 pm | Stauffenbergstrasse 40*

The *Kunstgewerbemuseum* (Museum of Arts and Crafts) is a Baroque treasure trove. Delft faïence objects and Baroque glassware are just two outstanding features of the collection. You'll also find European porcelain – Meissen and KPM in particular –, decorative pieces and tableware from Rococo through Classicist to Art-Nouveau, gold- and silverwork plus costumes and silks. *Tues–Fri 10 am to 6 pm, Sat&Sun 11 am–6 pm | Tiergartenstrasse 6*

Around 800 items from the collection of over 3,000 European instruments from the 16th to 20th centuries are on display at the *Musikinstrumentenmuseum* (Museum of Musical Instruments). The collection of wind

Berlin's new rail junction in steel and glass: the Hauptbahnhof

instruments dating back to the first half of the 17th century is unique, as is the Bach cembalo. You may even try out certain instruments, and every Saturday at noon there is a demonstration of the 70-year-old Wurlitzer cinema organ. *Tues–Fri 9 am–5 pm, Thurs until 10 pm, Sat&Sun 10 am–to 5 pm | Admission: 4 euros | Tiergartenstrasse 1*

The *Neue Nationalgalerie* (New National Gallery), located in a building designed by Ludwig Mies van der Rohe, is devoted to 20th-century European paintings and sculptures, from the modern classics right up to the art of the 1960s. On display are works by artists such as Kirchner, Picasso, Klee, Feininger and Dix. *Tues–Fri 9 am–6 pm, Thurs until 10 pm, Sat&Sun 11 am to 6 pm | Potsdamer Strasse 50*

10 POTSDAMER PLATZ [122 A4–5]

On the western edge of Potsdamer Platz, whose original buildings were completely destroyed during World War II, a totally new district has sprung up, with shopping centres, cinema complexes, musical theatres, a casino, hotels and a film museum. The tent-like roof over the ★ *Sony Center* is particularly impressive. Whatever the weather you can stroll around, sit by the fountain or take a seat on the terrace of one of the numerous cafés. Inside the *Daimler-Chrysler building* Europe's fastest lift propels visitors up to the viewing platform *(daily 11 am to 8 pm | 5 euros)* at a height of 93 m. *Mitte | www.panoramapunkt.de | U-/ S-Bahn Potsdamer Platz*

11 REGIERUNGSVIERTEL [122 A–B 2–3]

Modern parliament buildings are grouped close to the Reichstag (Parliament), straddling the Spree, in an ensemble known as the 'Federal Band'. The *Bundeskanzleramt* (Federal Chancellery) to the northwest was designed by architects Axel Schulte and Charlotte Frank who were also responsible for the overall concept of the administrative district. Due to its box-like form, the bright, white Chancellery, which was completed in 2001, earned the nickname the 'Chancellor's washing machine'. In front of the entrance stands the 5.5-m-high steel sculpture *Berlin* by the Spanish-Basque artist Eduardo Chillida, who died in 2002. Its four interlocking arms symbolise German unity. To the north of the Reichstag is the *Paul-Löbe-Haus*, named after the Reichstag president from 1924–32. It contains primarily 550 rooms for 275 members of parliament and their staff. On the opposite side of the Spree stands its counterpart, the *Marie-Elisabeth-Lüders-Haus*, facing eastwards. It is home to the parliamentary library, the third-largest of its kind in the world. Also of interest in architectural terms are the so-called *Ministergärten* (ministerial gardens), a grouping of federal state offices to the northeast of Potsdamer Platz.

Grass-roots democracy: enjoying the summer at the Reichstag

12 REICHSTAGSGEBÄUDE ★ [122 A2]
Built to plans by Paul Wallot in 1884–94, the seat of parliament has turned into a real crowd-puller since the glass cupola was added in the mid-1990s. Visitors are prepared to face long queues, depending on the time of day, to take the lift up to the roof and then follow the spiral-shaped walkway up to the top of the dome or go out onto the roof terrace and take a seat in the restaurant, *Käfer*. From the top there is a fabulous view across the new administrative district, the main station and the rest of Berlin – a spectacular sight, particularly after nightfall. One floor below, the members of the German Parliament, the Bundestag, began meeting here again in 1999 and can be observed through the glass ceiling of the debating chamber. Following the huge fire of 1933 and the fight for Berlin at the end of World War II, the devastated building was re-built in 1961–72. It then housed an exhibition of German history which can now be seen at the Deutscher Dom. In 1990 the Bundestag held its inaugural session in a new, united Germany. In order to better suit its new

purpose, the building was completely gutted and renovated according to plans by British architect Sir Norman Foster, who crowned it with the new glass dome. *Dome and viewing platform daily 8 am–midnight | last adm. 10 pm | Deutscher Bundestag visitor information service (guided tours and visits to parliamentary sessions) Tel. 22 73 21 52 | Platz der Republik | Bus 100 | Reichstag*

13 SIEGESSÄULE [122 C4]

This 67-m-high national monument once graced the square in front of the Reichstag. In order to create more space for his Imperial capital 'Germania', Hitler had the golden statue of Victoria, lovingly known as 'Goldelse', moved to the Grosser Stern roundabout in the middle of the Tiergarten. The Victory Column was erected in 1864–73 according to plans by Heinrich Strack to commemorate victory over the Danes. The viewing platform affords a fine view of the city. *Apr–Oct: Mon–Fri 9.30 am to 6.30 pm, Sat&Sun 9.30 am–7 pm; Nov–Mar: Mon–Fri 10 am–5 pm, Sat&Sun 10 am–5.30 pm | Admission: 2.20 euros | www.monument-tales.de | Strasse des 17. Juni | Bus 100 | Grosser Stern*

PRENZLAUER BERG/FRIEDRICHSHAIN

> Nowhere will you find so many organic ice-cream parlours, and the playgrounds are so full in summer, you're tempted to think you're in China. No wonder – the districts of Prenzlauer Berg and Friedrichshain are among the places in Europe with the highest proportion of children. Young people are definitely in the majority here, not least because of the buzzing nightlife. The profusion of bars, value-for-money restaurants, clubs and pubs is unrivalled in the city. Low rents attract many students to Friedrichshain. Prenzlauer Berg, on the other hand, is the choice of high-earning academics. Many residents of both districts flock at the weekend to the Volkspark Friedrichshain to go roller-blading, walking or for a game of beach volleyball.

1 EASTSIDE GALLERY [136 A4]

The world's largest open-air gallery extends between the Ostbahnhof and the Oberbaumbrücke. Some 118 artists from 21 countries have immortalised themselves on a 1,316-m-long section of the Berlin Wall. Among the most famous works are *Brotherly Kiss* by Dimitri Vrubel and *Berlin–New York* by Gerhard Lahr. *Friedrichshain | Mühlenstrasse | www.eastsidegallery.com | U-/S-Bahn Warschauer Strasse*

2 KULTURBRAUEREI [129 D4]

The former Schultheiss brewery has successfully established itself as the cultural centre in the district. A large cinema with several screens, concert and event venues plus a multitude of clubs, restaurants and retail outlets inject life into this 25,000-sq-m courtyard ensemble day and night. The yellow brick building – typical for Berlin – was built in 1890–1910 to plans by the head of the royal building department Franz Schwechten, who also designed the Kaiser-Wilhelm-Gedächtnis-Kirche. *Prenzlauer Berg | Knaackstrasse 75–97 | U 2 | Eberswalder Strasse*

3 MAUERPARK [128 C3]

Plenty of dogs and even more adults and children populate daily the wide, open meadows of this park on the former border area. To this day, aspiring graffiti artists can still hone their skills on a remaining section of the Wall. Star attractions are the huge swings in the south of the park and children's farm at the northern end. Insider Tip On Sundays in summer, DJs provide a musical backdrop! *Prenzlauer Berg | Eberswalder Strasse | U2 | Eberswalder Strasse*

Insider Tip 4 MOLECULE MEN [136 B5]

The *Molecule Men* have stood in front of the 'Treptowers', the twin towers of the Allianz concern, since 1999. These impressive 30-m-high figures by American artist Jonathan Borofsky, rooted in the waters of the Spree, are intended to symbolise a peaceful coming together of the districts Friedrichshain, Treptow and Kreuzberg. *Treptow | Eichenstrasse | S-Bahn Treptower Park*

5 VOLKSPARK FRIEDRICHSHAIN [135 E–F1–2]

At the 52-ha *Volkspark Friedrichshain* in the north, kids let off steam on the halfpipe, while their parents relax with their younger brothers and sisters at the *Märchenbrunnen* Insider Tip (Fairy Tale Fountain).

It's not just children who love the fountains which first spouted water in 1913. Nine archways encircle stone ponds with fountains, statues from the

Hugging or wrestling? The Molecule Men stride across the Spree in Treptow

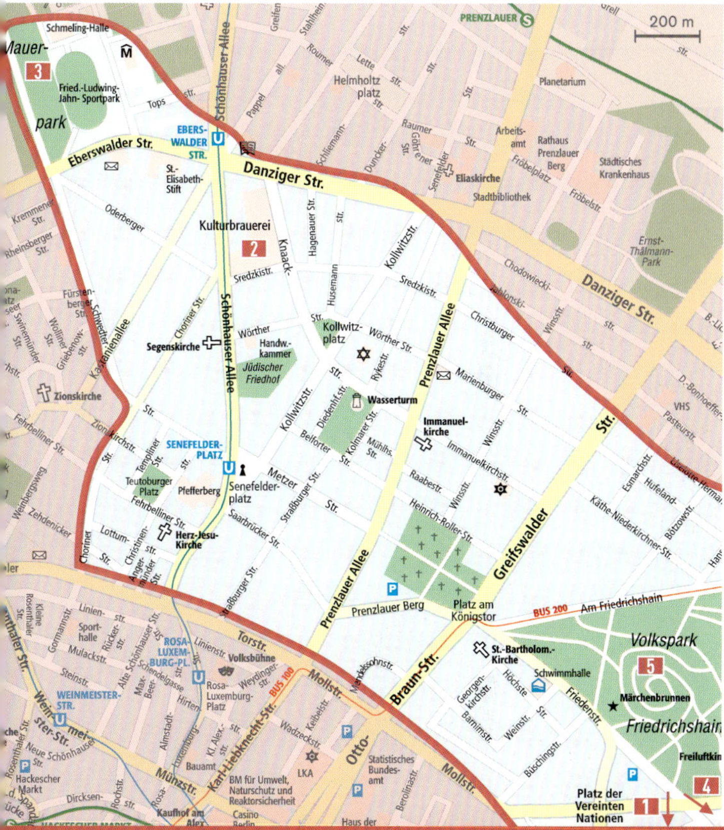

SIGHTSEEING IN PRENZLAUER BERG/FRIEDRICHSHAIN

1 Eastside Gallery
2 Kulturbrauerei
3 Mauerpark
4 Molecule Men
5 Volkspark Friedrichshain

famous Grimm's fairy tales and animal figures. The fountain has a delightful kitschy flair which makes it a magnet for families, courting couples and the permanently young-at-heart in need of a break. *Am Friedrichshain | U-/S-Bahn Warschauer Strasse*

KREUZBERG

> There's a real exotic feel to things here: Turkish life permeates the streets, especially in the northeast of the district – with Turkish mens' cafés, vegetable shops, markets and bakeries. In between there's no end of bars, restaurants and clubs for the German-Turkish bohemians who know how to enjoy life. Many young people live in the 'Kiez' (neighbourhood) around Oranienstrasse; the selection of bars and pubs is correspondingly large. Well-to-do academics prefer the Paul-Lincke-Ufer, living and working in lofts. Directly opposite, there's a large market every Tuesday and Friday. The many Turkish stallholders and customers make for an atmosphere straight out of the bazaar.

1 BERLINISCHE GALERIE [134 B6] Insider Tip

The new Museum of Modern Art, Photography and Architecture dazzles

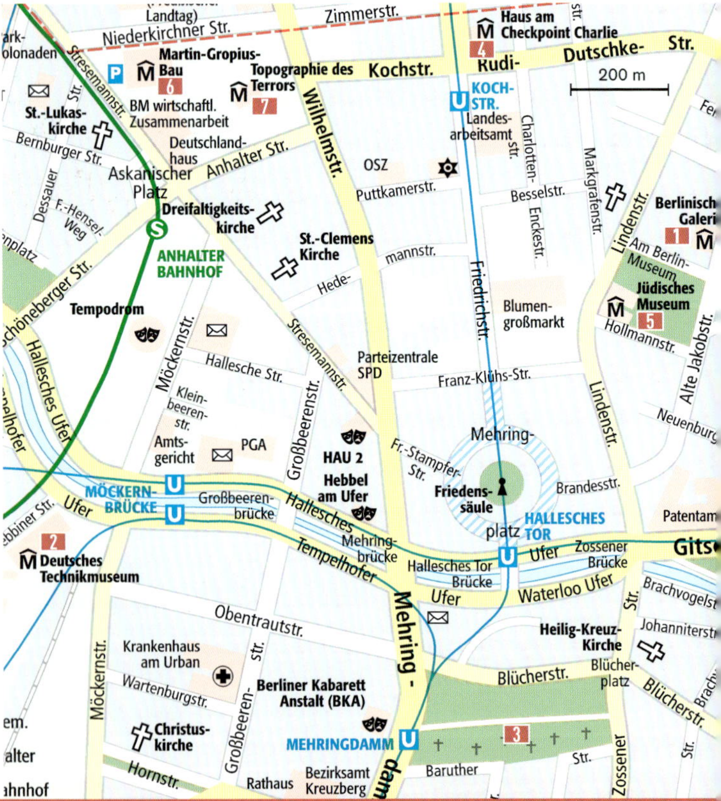

SIGHTSEEING IN KREUZBERG

1 Berlinische Galerie
2 Deutsches Technikmuseum
3 Friedhöfe am Halleschen Tor
4 Haus am Checkpoint Charlie
5 Jüdisches Museum Berlin
6 Martin-Gropius-Bau
7 Topographie des Terrors

Multicultural charm and alternative touch: blocks of flats and cycle shop in Kreuzberg

with its works by the 'Neue Wilden' around Rainer Fetting, alongside expressionists such as Erich Heckel and Ernst Ludwig Kirchner. New functionalism is represented by Otto Dix and George Grosz. *Wed–Mon 10 am–6 pm | Admission: 6 euros | Alte Jakobstrasse 124–128 | www.berlinischegalerie.de | U 1, 6, 15 | Hallesches Tor*

2 DEUTSCHES TECHNIKMUSEUM ★ [141 F2]

The Museum of Technology's collection of historical vehicles, tools and inventions is fascinating. You'll need more than a day to take in the huge engine shed with its historical traction engines, the 1,500 exhibits in the shipping section or the aviation section. The 250 experiments in the hands-on *Spectrum* section give an exciting insight into technical operating principles. *Tues–Fri 9 am to 5.30 pm, Sat&Sun 10 am–6 pm | Admission: 4.50 euros | Trebbiner Strasse 9 | www.dtmb.de | U 1, 2, 15 | Gleisdreieck*

3 FRIEDHÖFE AM HALLESCHEN TOR [142 A–B 2–3]

Well known for its splendid chapels and the mausoleum-like graves of rich families, the cemetery is becoming more and more dilapidated. A number of people in the city have agreed to sponsor graves in order to preserve what is left of this magnificent graveyard. Among the most famous 'residents' are E.T.A. Hoffmann, Adelbert von Chamisso and the Mendelssohn-Bartholdy family. *Daily 8 am until dusk | Mehringdamm | U 6 | Mehringdamm*

4 HAUS AM CHECKPOINT CHARLIE [122 C6]

Permanent exhibition dedicated to the building of the Wall and the division of the city. It documents various successful and unsuccessful escape attempts and the equipment used to make them, including a mini U-boat and a hot-air balloon. *Daily 9 am–10 pm | Admission: 12.50 euros | Friedrichstrasse 43 | www.mauer-museum.com | U 6 | Kochstrasse*

5 JÜDISCHES MUSEUM BERLIN ★ [134 B6]

Two thousand years of Jewish culture are showcased in the spectacular Jewish Museum designed by New York architect Daniel Libeskind. The aim is to create an emotional link between the visitor and the exhibits by means of multimedia technology, lighting effects and the bizarre form of the exhibition rooms. A central theme is the history and persecution of the Jews in Germany from the early Middle Ages to the present. *Mon 10 am–10 pm, Tues–Sun 10 am to 8 pm | Admission: 5 euros | Lindenstrasse 9–14 | www.jmberlin.de | U 1, 6, 15 | Hallesches Tor*

6 MARTIN-GROPIUS-BAU [133 F5]

Built in 1877-81 to plans by Martin Gropius, a great-uncle of Walter Gropius, and originally conceived as an arts and crafts museum, the magnificent building with its fine relief sculptures now serves as the splendid setting for changing exhibitions on the subject of art and history. *Wed–Mon 10 am–8 pm | Admission charge depending on exhibition | Niederkirchner Strasse 7 | www.gropiusbau.de | S-Bahn Anhalter Bahnhof*

7 TOPOGRAPHIE DES TERRORS [134 A5]

This open-air exhibition on the site of the former SS and Gestapo headquarters documents the atrocities which were planned here. The walls are hung with huge portraits of executed politicians and members of the Resistance, among others. A new documentation centre is due to be

Not just an architectural highlight: Jüdisches Museum

opened here in 2010. *Oct–Apr: daily 10 am–6 pm; May to Sept: 10 am to 8 pm | Free Admission | Niederkirchner Strasse 8 | www.topographie.de | S 1, 25 | Anhalter Bahnhof*

CHARLOTTENBURG/ WILMERSDORF

> Shopping centre, gourmet territory and El Dorado for culture vultures – a joint venture mounted by the districts of Charlottenburg, between KaDeWe and Schloss Charlottenburg, and Wilmersdorf, to the south of the Ku'damm. The abundance of restaurants around Savignyplatz is rife for the record books; in the pretty Schlosspark joggers and museum visitors dodge each other gracefully. The Ku'damm is still the traditional shopping street for the comfortably-off; younger shoppers window-shop and hunt for cheap gear, overlooked by the Gedächtniskirche. Boasting the Theater des Westens, the Schaubühne, the Deutsche Oper and the Schillertheater, Charlottenburg competes with the stages in the East of the city. Wilmersdorf has plenty of traditional and specialist shops to offer.

1 FUNKTURM [130 B5]

Modelled on the Eiffel Tower in Paris, its far smaller Berlin counterpart, erected on the Messegelände (exhibition grounds) in 1926, was long rated the symbol of modern Berlin. In the days of the Wall especially, the 138-m-high 'Langer Lulatsch' ('beanpole'), as it was nicknamed, was of great symbolic significance for the people of West Berlin. There is a restaurant at 55 m and 71 m above that is the viewing platform. The transmitter at the top of the tower is used for police radio. Since the tower is often closed for maintenance work, it is advisable to ring before your visit. *Mon 10 am–8 pm, Tues–Sun 10 am–11 pm | Admission: 4.50 euros | Charlottenburg | Messedamm | Tel. 30 38 19 05 | S-Bahn Messe Nord | U 2 Kaiserdamm*

2 KAISER-WILHELM-GEDÄCHTNISKIRCHE [121 D–E4]

Like a finger raised to admonish, the blackened, ruined tower of the church points heavenwards. Erected in 1891–95 in memory of William I, it was almost completely destroyed in World War II. The church authorities decided to leave at least the tower standing. Next to it Egon Eiermann's modern octagonal place of worship, erected in 1958–61, is constructed from thousands of blue glass blocks. On the ground floor of the old tower is an exhibition illustrating the history of the church. *Daily 9 am–7 pm, Church concerts: Sat 6 pm | Charlottenburg | Breitscheidplatz | www.gedaechtniskirche-berlin.de | U-/S-Bahn Zoologischer Garten*

3 KURFÜRSTENDAMM [138–140 C–A 1–2]

Before the Wall came down this was West Berlin's top shopping boulevard and the epitome of metropolitan flair. Today, it's mostly Japanese and Russian tourists who shop in its boutiques. In recent years, a number of 1960s eyesores have disappeared;

their replacements include the new Kranzlereck, containing offices, shops and a café. The 3.5-km-long riding path was laid out in 1883–86 and is still lined with numerous opulent houses dating back to the turn of the 20th century. *Charlottenburg | U 1, 9 | Kurfürstendamm*

4 MUSEUM BERGGRUEN [130 C3]

Art dealer Heinz Berggruen put together this unique collection focusing on works by Pablo Picasso and Paul Klee. Under the title 'Picasso and his Time', the exhibition over three floors of this magnificent Stüler building shows fascinating early works as well as paintings, sculptures and works on paper. *Tues–Sun 10 am to 6 pm | Admission: 8 euros, Thurs 2 pm–6 pm free admission | Charlottenburg | Schlossstrasse 1 | www.smb.museum | S 41, 42 | Westend*

5 OLYMPIASTADION [146 C3]

Germany's second-largest stadium seats around 75,000 spectators. Built to plans by Werner March for the

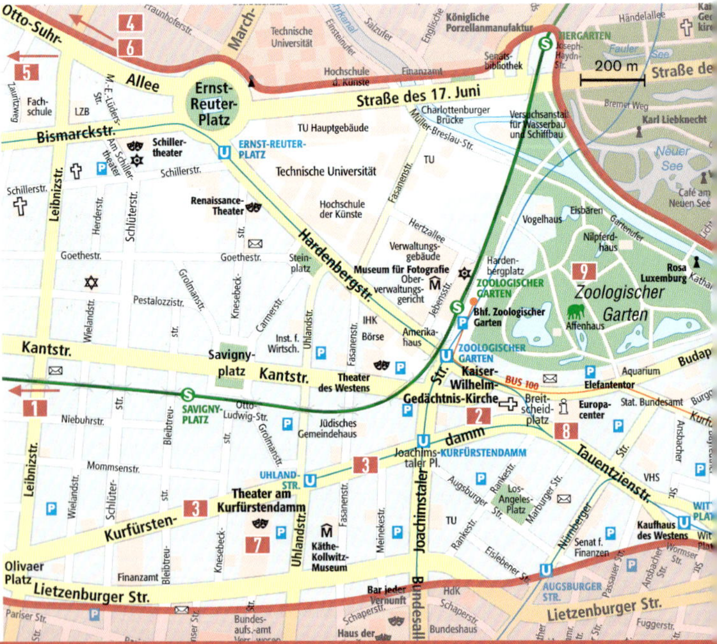

SIGHTSEEING IN CHARLOTTENBURG/WILMERSDORF

1 Funkturm
2 Kaiser-Wilhelm-Gedächtniskirche
3 Kurfürstendamm
4 Museum Berggruen
5 Olympiastadion
6 Schloss Charlottenburg
7 The Story of Berlin
8 Weltkugelbrunnen
9 Zoologischer Garten

Olympic Games in 1936, today it is home to the professional footballers of Hertha BSC. The Nazi architecture is showing its age, and for this reason the stadium underwent thorough renovation in the run-up to the World Cup in 2006. All spectator seats are now covered over. *Daily 9 am–7 pm; winter: until 4 pm | Admission: 4 euros | Tours of the stadium daily 11 am, Apr–Oct also 1 pm, 3 pm, Jun–Aug 5 pm | 8 euros | Charlottenburg | Olympischer Platz 3 | Tel. 254 69 00 | Tel. 25 00 23 22 | www.olympiastadion-berlin.de | U 2 | Olympiastadion*

6 SCHLOSS CHARLOTTENBURG ★ [130–131 C–D 1–2]

The over 300-year-old summer residence of Electress Sophie Charlotte is impressive not only because of its French-style landscaped garden with box-hedges standing smartly to attention, but is also a fine example of the palatial architecture of the 17th and 18th centuries. The private apartments of Frederick I and his wife are open to the public. At the far end of the park is the mausoleum of Queen Luise, wife of Frederick William III. *Altes Schloss Apr–Oct: Tues–Sun 10 am–6 pm (Nov–Mar: until 5 pm), New Wing Apr–Oct: Wed–Mon 10 am to 6 pm (Nov–Mar: until 5 pm), Belvedere Apr–Oct: Tues–Sun 10 am to 6 pm (Nov–Mar: noon–4 pm), Mausoleum Apr–Oct: Tues–Sun 10 am–6 pm (Nov–Mar: noon to 5 pm), Belvedere (KPM porcelain collection), Neuer Pavillon (art works and crafts of the Romantic period) Tues–Sun 10 am to 5 pm | Charlottenburg | Spandauer Damm | Admission, castle only: 6 euros, Combined ticket: 10 euros, Belvedere, Neuer Pavillon, Mausoleum: 3 euros each | Tel. 32 09 11 | www.spsg.de | Bus 145 | Luisenplatz*

Schloss Charlottenburg: golden Fortuna dances atop the cupola

7 THE STORY OF BERLIN [130 C5]

Passing through 24 themed rooms, the visitor is transported back in time on a journey through Berlin's history. High-tech and multimedia exhibits appeal to young people in particular. *Daily 10 am–8 pm, last adm. 6 pm | Admission: 9.80 euros | Charlottenburg | Kurfürstendamm 207 | www.story-of-berlin.de | U 1 | Uhlandstrasse*

8 WELTKUGELBRUNNEN [121 E4]

In 1983, Berlin sculptor Joachim Schmettau administered a dose of art in the form of a now highly popular fountain on Breitscheidplatz. In the shadow of the Gedächtniskirche and the Europacenter, its sheer size earned it the nickname 'Wasserklops'. Yet this granite sphere, which is broken up by a series of arches, is in no way ungainly or inelegant, but impresses by the interplay of trickling streams, statues and cascades. *Charlottenburg | Breitscheidplatz | U-/S-Bahn Zoologischer Garten*

9 ZOOLOGISCHER GARTEN [121 E–F 3–4]

The 160-year-old zoo is Germany's oldest and boasts the most species in the world, namely 13,700 animals from over 1,388 species. The aquarium and crocodile house are real highlights. *Daily 9 am–7 pm; winter: until 5 pm | Admission: zoo 12 euros, incl. aquarium: 18 euros | Charlottenburg | Budapester Strasse 5 | www.zoo-berlin.de | U-/S-Bahn Zoologischer Garten*

OTHER DISTRICTS

ALLIIERTENMUSEUM [144 A3]

The Allies' Museum tells the story of the western powers and Berlin between 1945–94. Impressive presentation of the Berlin Airlift of 1948–49. One of the transport planes, the so-called 'Rosinenbomber' ('raisin bombers') is on display outside. *Thurs–Tues 10 am–6 pm | Free admissionZehlendorf | Clayallee 135 | www.alliiertenmuseum.de | U 3 | Oskar-Helene-Heim*

BOTANISCHER GARTEN ★ [144 C3]

The botanical world united on a 43-ha site: Siberian prairie grass, Japanese cherry trees and German garden vegetables. Highlights are the huge hothouses which include giant water lilies, bamboo and palms; the orchid house and cactus collection are superb. *Daily 9 am until dusk | Admission: 5 euros | Steglitz | Entrance: Unter den Eichen | Königin-Luise-Strasse | www.bgbm.org | S 1 | Botanischer Garten*

Orang-utan at the zoo: take it easy, man!

BRÜCKE-MUSEUM [144 A1]

Idyllic location in the Grunewald for the world's most comprehensive collection of works by the group 'Die Brücke', founded in 1905 in Dresden. Includes Ernst Ludwig Kirchner, Karl Schmitt-Rottluff, Erich Heckel, Max Pechstein and Emil Nolde. *Wed–Mon 11 am–5 pm | Admission: 4 euros | Dahlem | Bussardsteig 9 | www.bruecke-museum.de | Bus 115 | Pücklerstrasse*

FLUGHAFEN TEMPELHOF [142 A–B5]

At a length of over 1,200 m and boasting 5,000 offices, the airport at Tempelhof rates as the largest office complex in Europe, harking back to the monumental architecture of the Nazi era. It was opened in 1936 on the occasion of the Olympic Games and was intended not only as a crossing of international air routes, but also as the seat of the Aviation Ministry. Since 2008, the airport has been closed to air traffic. A landscape garden is set to be completed on the freed-up site by 2017. The airfield is accessible to the public in the daytime since May 2010. *Guided tours of the buildings: Mon–Fri 4 pm, Fri also 1 pm, Sat& Sun 11 am and 2 pm | 15 euros | Tempelhof | Platz der Luftbrücke | www.flughafen-berlin-tempelhof.com | U 6 | Platz der Luftbrücke*

Insider Tip **GÄRTEN DER WELT** [147 E3]

Europe's largest Chinese garden (2.7 ha) features a rocky landscape with waterfalls, a lake spanned by bridges and typical pavilions. The tea ceremony at the 'Berghaus zum Osmanthussaft' is not to be missed. The site also includes Japanese, Islamic and Balinese gardens and a maze. *Daily 9 am–dusk | Admission, park only: 2 euros | Guided tours (Apr–Oct): 3 euros/1.50 euros | Tel. 512 94 98 | Tea ceremonies: 5 euros | Tel. 0179-394 55 64 by arrangement | Marzahn | Eisenacher Strasse 99 | U 5 | Cottbusser Platz | then bus 195 | Erholungspark Marzahn*

GASOMETER SCHÖNEBERG [141 D5] Insider Tip

The landmark in Berlin's southwest boasts a very special viewing platform. You just need to get up there – and you'll need a good head for heights! Visitors who do manage the 80-m climb up narrow, open-mesh walkways and 456 iron steps are rewarded with a fabulous view. The walk around the gasometer on an open-mesh platform gives an unobstructed view of the ground below! *Apr–Oct: Thurs&Fri 3.30 pm, Sat& Sun noon, 2 pm, 3.30 pm and 5 pm | Admission: 25 euros | Schöneberg | Torgauer Strasse 12–15 | Tel. 01805/ 44 70 | www.climb-berlin.com | S-Bahn Schöneberg*

GLIENICKER PARK [146 B4]

A wonderful place to stroll, as in the days when Electors and princesses held hands under the oak trees and enjoyed the view across the Havel! Laid out at the beginning of the 19th century by Lenné and Schinkel, the 116-ha landscaped park features a well-tended stock of trees, italian pavilions, pergolas and arcades. Schinkel's round temple, designed in 1835, is a real gem. The *Glienicker Brücke* (Glienicke Bridge) towards Potsdam at the southern end of the park was the scene of exchanges of agents during the Cold War. *Wannsee | Königstrasse | Bus 316 | Glienicker Brücke*

GRUNEWALD [144 A1–2]
Before the Wall fell, Grunewald was the largest piece of woodland in West Berlin and hence its No. 1 recreation area. Today, things have quietened down, even at weekends. A number of lakes, such as the *Teufelssee* (Devil's Lake) and the River Havel are just right for a swim. At the Teufelssee you'll find the *Ökowerk (Tel. 300 00 50)*, an ecological information centre featuring a nature garden, bee hives and children's survival courses The 16th-century *Jagdschloss Grunewald* (Hunting Lodge) on the banks of the lake houses a valuable painting collection and a hunting museum *(mid-May–Oct: Tues–Sun 10 am to 6 pm; otherwise Sat&Sun 10 am–4 pm)*. The 120-m *Teufelsberg* (Devil's Mountain) to the north was created out of 21 million cubic metres of rubble from the war-torn city. At the weekends it's a popular spot with kite fans. *Grunewald | S 7, 9 | Grunewald*

The white castle on the Pfaueninsel

HAUS DER WANNSEEKONFERENZ [146 C4]
It was on 20 January 1942 in this villa overlooking the Wannsee lake that government officials and the SS discussed the practicalities of the planned total eradication of the Jews. A exhibition on the ground floor relates the events of the conference, the run-up to it and its terrible consequences. *Daily 10 am to 6 pm | Wannsee | Am Grossen Wannsee 56 | Tel. 805 00 10 | www.ghwk.de | S-Bahn Wannsee | then bus 114 | Haus der Wannseekonferenz*

JÜDISCHER FRIEDHOF WEISSENSEE [147 D3]
Over 115,000 Berlin Jews are buried here, making this the largest Jewish cemetery in Europe. Established in 1880, its brick buildings and the burial grounds were designed by architect Hugo Licht. A plaque at the entrance commemorates the six million Jews murdered by the Nazis. Publishers Samuel Fischer and Rudolf Mosse and the artist Lesser Ury are just some of the more prominent personalities who lie here. Male visitors to the cemetery must cover their heads; caps may be hired for a small fee. *Apr–Oct: Sun–Thurs 8 am–5 pm, Fri 8 am–3 pm; Nov–Mar: until 4 pm, Fri until 3 pm| Weissensee | Herbert-Baum-Strasse 45 | Tram 12 | Albertinenstrasse*

PFAUENINSEL [146 B4]
Originally, the idyllic, 67-ha Peacock Island was home to a zoo which was

put together by Frederick William III at the beginning of the 19th century. Today only the peacocks which roam free around the park hark back to its earlier purpose. The touchingly kitschy white castle could be straight out of a film set. It was built for the mistress of Frederick William II, Wilhelmine Enke. Take a look at the *Meierei* (dairy) with its splendid hall in the style of a neo-Gothic church *(Sat&Sun 11 am to 3.30 pm | Admission: 2 euros). Wannsee | Pfaueninselchaussee | Ferry: Nov to Feb: daily 10 am–4 pm; Mar&Oct: 9 am–5 pm; Apr&Sept: 9 am–7 pm; May–Aug: 8 am–9 pm | 2 euros | Castle: Apr–Oct: Tues–Sun 10 am to 5 pm | Admission: 3 euros | www.spsg.de | Bus 218 | Pfaueninsel*

SOWJETISCHES EHRENMAL ★ [136 C6]

In the centre of the Treptow Park lies one of the biggest Soviet military cemeteries in Germany. Not only the gravestones in memory of around 7,000 fallen troops are impressive, but also the monumental 12-m-high bronze sculpture of a soldier bearing the German child he has rescued, and the similarly large granite sculpture *Mother Russia*. The memorial was built in 1947–49. *Treptow | Alt-Treptow 1 | S-Bahn Treptower Park*

Insider Tip

STASIGEFÄNGNIS HOHENSCHÖNHAUSEN [147 E3]

Grey buildings, high walls and barbed wire give some idea of how political prisoners must have felt during their incarceration here in solitary confinement. Eyewitnesses guide visitors through the buildings, leaving them in no doubt that people underwent psychological torture here during the GDR era. *Hourly guided tours: Mon to Fri 11 am–3 pm, Sat&Sun 10 am to 4 pm | Admission: 5 euros | Hohenschönhausen | Genslerstrasse 66 | Tram 6 | Genslerstrasse*

Sowjetisches Ehrenmal in Treptow

TIERPARK FRIEDRICHSFELDE [147 E3]

The zoo with around 8,000 animals is particularly fascinating due to its location in the spacious palace gardens once designed by Lenné. You can also visit the Schloss, which was built in 1690. *(Tues–Sun 10 am to 6 pm). Daily 9 am–6 pm; winter: until 5 pm | Admission: 11 euros | Lichtenberg | Am Tierpark 125 | www.tierpark-berlin.de | U 5 | Tierpark*

> GOURMET METROPOLIS AND SNACK CITY

From Currywurst to sushi – Berlin caters to all tastes

> Berlin is heaven on earth for lovers of fine foods. The restaurant spectrum reaches from Michelin-rated restaurants serving international cuisine to superb specialist Turkish or Russian eateries.

Alpine cooking is a particular favourite on the Spree, featuring classic dishes such as *Wiener Schnitzel*, *Tafelspitz* (soured boiled rump of beef) and potato salad. The so-called lounge-restaurants are very popular, too. Here, you can even eat lying down! If you want to enjoy some top-class food without breaking the bank, you should eat at lunchtime. Most gourmet restaurants offer attractive lunch menus at relatively reasonable prices – and of the same quality as in the evening!

Of course, the city also offers good, value-for-money, down-to-earth cooking. Simple dishes made from fresh, regional ingredients are appreciated by locals and visitors

Above: Margaux restaurant

FOOD & DRINK

alike. Nourishing soups, too, are popular, hence the specialist soup restaurants which are now a permanent fixture on the culinary landscape, offering different varieties every day. Countless 'Italian' restaurants are on hand for a quick bite between meals. Quite a few are actually Turkish-owned, and Italian is the last language you'd hear in the kitchen! In most cases, though, pizza and pasta are of good quality. It's only the salads which are a bone of contention; tasteless greenhouse lettuce and packet dressings are unfortunately widely encountered. As far as Turkish food is concerned, the number of restaurants in proportion to the Turkish population of 160,000 is astonishingly low. On the other hand, stands selling doner kebab (Turkish unleavened bread filled with meat and salad) can be found on every corner, even in the eastern part of the city. The fact that

CAFÉS & BREAKFAST

Stop for a breather in the conservatory: Café im Literaturhaus

this Turkish speciality – like the Currywurst – originated in Berlin is known only to few.

And then there are the Russians – represented not only by their own clubs and bars, but also increasingly by Russian gastronomic culture. bœuf stroganov, *borschtsch* or *pelmeni* suit, particularly if 'oiled' beforehand with vodka!

Asian cuisine, too, is as popular as ever, although many Chinese restaurants are by no means of the same high standard as 'the real thing' back home. Modern Asian food, such as lemongrass soup or chicken Paeng, goes down very well, especially where the restaurateur has turned his back on the kitschy, pseudo-Asian interiors of the past. There's many a restaurant owner who owes his success to a timely switchover to 'pan-Asian' cuisine, i.e. Asian dishes with an American or European note. Eating, after all, is not just about satisfying hunger – it's an event, particularly in a major city like Berlin!

CAFÉS & BREAKFAST

CAFÉ EINSTEIN ★ [141 D1]

Traditional, Vienna-style coffee house in the villa which once belonged to silent-movie star Henny Porten. The other branch is more modern *(Mitte | Unter den Linden 42)*. What both have in common is a set of famous-name regulars and a good menu which includes *Tafelspitz* (soured boiled rump of beef) and excellent cakes. *Daily from 9 am| Tiergarten | Kurfürstenstrasse 58 | Tel. 261 50 96 | U 1, 2, 15 | Kurfürstenstrasse*

CAFÉ LIEBLING [129 D3]

Cosy corner café on Helmholtzplatz with newspapers and exotic hot drinks made with fresh ingredients, such as orange-ginger-mint tea. Small, but delicious choice of cakes and also soup at lunchtime. *Daily from 9 am | Prenzlauer Berg | Raumerstrasse 36a 36a | corner of Dunckerstrasse | Tel. 41 19 82 09 | Tram 12 | Raumer Strasse*

CAFÉ IM LITERATURHAUS [120 C5]
A little refreshment in the conservatory of this pretty villa works wonders after some window-shopping on the Ku'damm: coffee, delightful cakes and freshly prepared light meals! *Daily 9.30 am–1 am | Charlottenburg | Fasanenstrasse 23 | Tel. 882 54 14 | U 1 | Uhlandstrasse*

CAFÉ STEINER [140 C2]
Delicious drinking chocolate, bread and cakes and 12 types of muesli are on offer at this classic café with its Biedermeier interior. There's also a huge selection of breakfast specialities and tempting gateaux, pastries and various teas in the afternoons. *Tues–Sun 8 am–10 pm (breakfast until 10 pm) | Schöneberg | Motzstrasse 30 | Tel. 23 63 09 00 | U 1, 2, 3 | Nollendorfplatz*

DACHGARTENRESTAURANT KÄFER IM DEUTSCHEN BUNDESTAG [122 A2]
The only parliament building in the world which can boast a restaurant on its roof – complete with sensational view and Käfer's usual standard of quality. Here, guests can feast to their heart's content. In summer, also on the terrace. Tip: If you book a table, you don't have to queue for the lift to the viewing platform, but can use a side entrance. *Daily 9 am–4.30 pm, 6.30 pm–midnight, breakfast until 10.30 am | Mitte | Platz der Republik | Tel. 226 29 90 | www.feinkost-kaefer.de | U-/S-Bahn Friedrichstrasse*

MANOLO [129 D4]
The city-dweller's idea of happiness? Sitting at one of the busiest junctions in town enjoying a caffè latte with cake or a fruit salad and watching the world go by. The good selection of newspapers and cosy coffee-house architecture with comfy leather seats make for a pleasant self-service stopover. Have a listen to tales by Berlin authors at the CD player near the entrance. *Daily 7 am–8 pm, in summer: until 9 pm | Prenzlauer Berg | Schönhauser Allee 45 | corner of Danziger Strasse | Tel. 24 62 79 58 | U 2 | Eberswalder Strasse*

MARCO POLO HIGHLIGHTS

★ **Café Einstein**
Superb coffee, polite service and cosy, Viennese coffee-house charm (page 60)

★ **Tadschikische Teestube**
The stuff of fairy tales: seated on colourful cushions to enjoy Middle-Eastern specialities (page 63)

★ **Fischers Fritz**
Haute Cuisine not just for fish-lovers (page 62)

★ **Margaux**
The chef pampers his guests with dishes with a distinctly French flavour (page 62)

★ **Horváth**
Unpretentious gourmet cuisine with that little bit extra – in the heart of Kreuzberg (page 65)

★ **Restaurant im Fernsehturm**
Coffee with a view – not to be topped! (page 68)

OXYMORON [134 C2]
This fine café-restaurant with Art Nouveau charm in the Hackesche Höfe ist definitely worth a visit. Abundant breakfast menu; sophisticated Mediterranean cuisine at lunchtime and in the evening. *Daily from 8 am | Mitte | Rosenthaler Strasse 40–41 | Tel. 28 39 18 86 | www.oxymoron-berlin.de | S-Bahn Hackescher Markt*

SANKT OBERHOLZ [128 C5]
Trendy scene café with Wi-Fi connection and tennis umpires' chairs at the entrance. From up here guests have a good view of one of the busiest junctions in the city. Large selection of coffee specialities. *Mon–Fri 8 am to 1 am, Sat&Sun 9 am–midnight | Rosenthaler Strasse 72a | Mitte | Tel. 24 08 55 86 | www.sanktoberholz.de | U 8 | Rosenthaler Platz*

> GOURMET RESTAURANTS

Culinary adventures, perfect service

FACIL [132 B5]
You can dine outside in summer on the 5th floor of The Mandala Hotel. The glass roof is simply pushed to one side: sea bass or bread salad with quails, accentuated by sun or moon. Menus from 85–100 euros. *Mon to Fri noon–3 pm, 7 pm–11 pm | Tiergarten | Potsdamer Strasse 3 | Tel. 590 05 12 34 | www.facil.de | U-/S-Bahn Potsdamer Platz*

FISCHERS FRITZ ★ [122 C4]
Chef Christian Lohse, with two stars to his name, pampers his guests in the elegant surroundings of The Regent Berlin hotel. Dishes include fillet of turbot in a saffron-crustacean jus and Povençale potato puree. Three-course menu at lunchtime for 39 euros. *Daily noon–3 pm, 6.30 pm to 10.30 pm | Mitte | Charlottenstrasse 49 | | Tel. 20 33 63 63 | www.fischersfritzberlin.de | U 6 | Französische Strasse*

MARGAUX ★ [122 B3]
Inspired by Château Margaux, plenty of gold leaf, gourmet shrine in top location. Michael Hofmann regularly earns himself a Michelin star for his French-style delicacies. Exclusive wine list. Main courses: approx. 35 euros. *Mon–Sat 7 pm–10.30 pm | Mitte | Unter den Linden 78 | Tel. 22 65 26 11 | www.margaux-berlin.de | S 1 | Brandenburger Tor*

MA TIM RAUE [134 A3]
Asian-inspired gourmet restaurant in the Hotel Adlon. Celebrity chef Tim Raue serves delicacies from, for example, Hong Kong. A white terra cotta horse from the Han dynasty dominates the centre of the restaurant. Menus from 90–128 euros. *Tues–Sat 12.30 pm–2 pm, 7 pm–10 pm | Mitte | Budapester Strasse 2 | | Tel. 301 11 73 33 | www.ma-restaurants.de | S 1, 2, 25 | Brandenburger Tor*

VAU [122 C4]
Up-to-the-minute, restrained ambience with Thonet cantilever chairs and modern art – in keeping with Kolja Kleeberg's superb, no-nonsense menus. Main courses: approx. 38 euros. *Mon to Sat noon–2.30 pm, 7 pm–10.30 pm; closed: Sun | Mitte | Jägerstrasse 54–55 | Tel. 202 97 30 | www.vau-berlin.de | U 6 | Französische Strasse*

VAU: a star in Berlin's culinary heaven

TADSCHIKISCHE TEESTUBE ★ [123 D3]
The atmosphere at the Tadzhik tea room is straight out of the Arabian Nights: lots of cushions, wall hangings and the typical tea rituals from Tadzhikistan. Russian specialities, too. *Mon–Fri 5 pm–midnight, Sat& Sun 3 pm–midnight | Mitte | Am Festungsgraben 1 | Tel. 204 11 12 | U-/S-Bahn Friedrichstrasse*

THEODOR TUCHER [133 F3]
Located directly next to the Brandenburg Gate, this tastefully decorated literary café lets you browse through the latest books, sunk into cosy armchairs up in the gallery. When you've 'read up' an appetite you can try a typical German dish one floor below. *Daily 9 am–1 am | Mitte | Pariser Platz 6a | Tel. 22 48 94 64 | S 1 | Brandenburger Tor*

BEER GARDENS

CLÄRCHENS BALLHAUS [128 B6]
In summer it's hard to drag yourself away from the idyllic courtyard garden. Friendly waiters serve organic buletten, pizza or cakes with consummate ease! *Daily from 10 am | Mitte | Auguststrasse 24 | Tel. 282 92 95 | www.ballhaus.de | S-Bahn Oranienburger Strasse | €*

Insider Tip **DECKSHAUS [135 D4]**
In the heart of the historical port, sit on the deck of the sternwheel tug, the 'Jeseniky' and tuck into sprats, meatballs and young herrings. A wonderful spot to sit back and relax over a beer, listening to the gentle splash of the Spree waters. *Tues–Sun (summer: also Mon) from noon | Mitte | Märkisches Ufer 1z | Tel. 0174/871 51 07 | www.deckshaus.de | U 2 | Märkisches Museum | €*

FREISCHWIMMER ▶▶ [136 B5]
Idyllic setting on the banks of the Flutgraben. Especially busy in hot weather, due to the cool drinks and inspiring summer menu. Younger guests in the majority. Canoe and kayak rental. Insider Tip *Summer: Mon–Fri from 2 pm; Winter: from 6 pm, Sat&Sun from 10 am | Kreuzberg | Vor dem Schlesischen Tor 2 | Tel. 61 07 43 09 | U 1 | Schlesisches Tor | €*

SCHOENBRUNN [129 E6]
Families and the trendier residents of Prenzlauer Berg enjoy the pizzas, pasta and antipasti here. Ideal after a walk through Friedrichshain. *Daily 10 am–1 am; winter: until 8 pm |*

Friedrichshain | Am Schwanenteich 1 | Tel. 46 79 38 93 | www.schoenbrunn.net | Tram 10 | Kniprodestrasse/corner of Danziger Strasse | €

CLASSICS

HENNE [135 D5]

Insider Tip

A classic when it comes to dining on all possible variations of crispy chicken. Families, students, intellectuals and long-time residents gnaw at chicken drumsticks and down a cool beer. Often full, so be prepared to wait. *Tues–Sat from 7 pm, Sun from 5 pm | Kreuzberg | Leuschnerdamm 25 | Tel. 614 77 30 | www.henne-berlin.de | U 8, 15 | Kottbusser Tor |* €

PRATER [128 C4]

Traditional venue for raising a glass or two with a hearty dish from the grill. On sunny days families and students like to come to the large beer garden for supper. *Mon–Sat from 6 pm, Sun from noon, beer garden Apr–Sept: daily from noon | Prenzlauer Berg | Kastanienallee 7–9 | Tel. 448 56 88 | U 2 | Eberswalder Strasse |* €–€€

WELTRESTAURANT MARKTHALLE [143 E1]

A byword for *Sauerbraten,* goulash and the like. No frills, classic eatery for the '68 generation and their heirs. *Daily 10 am–3 am | Kreuzberg | Pücklerstrasse 34 | Tel. 617 55 02 | www.weltrestaurantmarkthalle.de | U 1, 15 | Görlitzer Bahnhof |* €–€€

ZUR LETZTEN INSTANZ [135 D3]

Time-honoured Berlin culinary tradition, bringing you dishes entitled 'Kreuzverhör' (cross-examination) or 'Anwaltsfrühstück' (solicitor's breakfast) – conclusive evidence of this cosy restaurant's proximity to the law courts! *Mon–Sat noon–1 am | Mitte | Waisenstrasse 14–16 | Tel. 242 55 28 | www.zurletzteninstanz.de | U 2 | Klosterstrasse |* €–€€

Horvath: pretty terrace on the Landwehrkanal

FOOD & DRINK

RESTAURANTS €€€

BOCCA DI BACCO [122 C3–4]

Ravioli with bass in prawn cream or loin of lamb in a herb crust satisfy businessmen and politicians alike. Exquisite wine list. Book in advance. *Mon–Sat noon–midnight, Sun 6 pm–midnight | Mitte | Friedrichstrasse 167–168 | Tel. 20 67 28 28 | www.boccadibacco.de | U 6 | Französische Strasse*

HORVÁTH ★ [143 D2]

The atmosphere is not especially formal, but the fresh ingredients and culinary compositions bestow an air of true greatness. Head chef Torsten Lehmann puts real class on the plate: whether fillet of halibut au gratin with pumpkin puree or roast fillet of beef with a ragout of root vegetables in red wine sauce – the guest is sure of a delicious feast. *Tues–Sun 6 pm–1 am | Kreuzberg | Paul-Lincke-Ufer 44a | Tel. 61 28 99 92 | www.restaurant-horvath.de | U 1, 8 | Kottbusser Tor*

LOCHNER [132 C5]

Light, no-frills interior goes down well with the light, gourmet menu. The roast saddle of Irish lamb with red-wine shallots and leek and herb crêpes is sheer poetry, as the monkfish on ox-cheek ravioli with spinach. Sound choice of wines. *Tue–Sun from 6 pm | Tiergarten | Lützowplatz 5 | Tel. 23 62 44 70 | U 1, 15 | Nollendorfplatz*

RESTAURANTS €€

AIGNER [122 C4]

Refined German and Austrian cuisine: a Sauvignon Blanc is served along with the Palatinate vineyard salad with fillet of brook char, followed by blood-sausage dumplings on Riesling-*Sauerkraut* accompanied by a 2005 cuvée Horcher – a product of the restaurant's own vineyard. *Daily noon–2 am | Mitte | Französische Strasse 25 | Tel. 203 75 18 50 | www.aigner-gendarmenmarkt.de | U 2 | Französische Strasse*

BANDOL SUR MER [134 B1]

French restaurant with country-style cuisine. Whether it's a stew of beef and black salsify or sea bass with endive, value for money is guaranteed. The menu is chalked on blackboards around the walls! *Daily 6 pm–2 am, kitchen open until midnight | Mitte | Torstrasse 167 | Tel. 67 30 20 51 | U 8 | Rosenthaler Platz*

BIEBERBAU [140 A5] Insider Tip

It's the clever addition of Mediterranean touches to German dishes which makes the menu stand out. Knuckle of pork with truffles, pikeperch with taglierini, rounded off with a selection of cheeses à la Maître Philippe. Delicious! *Daily 6 pm–midnight | Wilmersdorf | Durlacher Strasse 15 | Tel. 853 23 90 | www.bieberbau-berlin.de | U-/S-Bahn Bundesplatz*

ENGELBECKEN [130 C5]

Cosy setting and honest-to-goodness food: Weisswurst (veal sausage), roast pork with dumplings and red cabbage, Leberkäs (a kind of meatloaf) with sweet mustard and a pretzel. For the anti-meat faction, there's gnocchi in sage butter plus delicious cakes. Everything goes down a treat! The meat comes from species-appropriate husbandry. *Mon to Sat 5 pm–1 am, Sun noon–1 am |*

Charlottenburg | Witzlebenstrasse 31 | Tel. 615 28 10 | www.engelbecken.de | U 2 | Sophie-Charlotte-Platz

ENTRECÔTE [134 B5]
Steak-lovers can't go wrong here. French specialities, also from Aberdeen Angus cattle, calves' kidneys in Madeira sauce are presented in pleasant, 5-m-high rooms by the friendly, attentive staff. *Mon–Fri noon–midnight, Sat 6 pm–midnight | Schützenstrasse 5 | Mitte | U 2, 6 | Stadtmitte*

> SPECIALITIES

Savour typical Berlin cooking!

Berliner Weisse – A typical ladies' drink, the kind of thing men turn their noses up at! Who else would add a shot (Schuss) of raspberry or woodruff syrup to their wheat beer? The ladies of Berlin love it.

Buletten – Meatballs made of minced beef on offer at just about every butcher's and with curry at every snack bar. Boulette means 'little ball' in French and harks back to the arrival of the Huguenots 300 years ago.

Currywurst – a *Bratwurst* covered in plenty of ketchup and curry powder and sold on every street corner. It was invented over 50 years ago by sausage-stand owner Herta Heuwer.

Doner kebab – Doner kebab – Turkish unleavened bread filled with grilled lamb and salad. A speciality which is just as much a part of the Berlin landscape as the *Currywurst*.

Eisbein – Salted knuckle of pork, served with mushy peas, sauerkraut and potatoes. But one might need at least one Korn (corn schnapps) to aid the digestive process ...

Kasseler – Smoked pork ribs which owe their good name to a Berlin butcher named Kassel and not the town of the same name, as you might think. Tradition dictates a portion of sauerkraut on the side.

Quark mit Leinöl – Quark with linseed oil and a pinch of salt, served with jacket potatoes – a combination which can be found on the menu of many Berlin households. Simple, but tasty!

Schmalzstulle – Stullen (simple, open sandwiches) are back in fashion again, ideally spread with something down-to-earth like dripping sprinkled with salt. Mmm ...

Schokolade – If you've a sweet tooth, you should try Berlin chocolate. Hamann and Fassbender & Rausch produce superb quality and have done for many decades.

FOODORAMA [143 B3]
At Germany's first carbon-neutral restaurant the beef is always organically produced. The furniture is made from renewable materials, biogas is used to cook with and the lights are powered by green electricity. Japanese-style atmosphere. *Daily from 10 am | Kreuzberg | Bergmannstrasse 94 | Tel. 69 00 11 11 | U 6, 7 | Mehringdamm*

HOSTARIA DEL MONTE CROCE [142 B3]
Italy in the rear courtyard, just like in Emilia-Romagna. The feasting starts at 7.30 pm. You sit at long tables and enjoy the 9-course menu, which changes every four weeks, with as much wine as you can drink, directly from the cask. Book a table! *Tues–Sat 7.30 pm–midnight | Kreuzberg | Mittenwalder Strasse 6 | Tel. 694 39 68 | www.hostaria.de | U 7 | Gneisenaustrasse*

LUTTER & WEGNER IM WEINHAUS HUTH [133 F5]
Wiener Schnitzel and *Sauerbraten* (braised beef) are the favourite dishes of the regulars in this small restaurant with its own wine shop. What's more, it's in the oldest building on Potsdamer Platz. *Daily 11 am–1 am | Tiergarten | Alte Potsdamer Strasse 5 | Tel. 25 29 75 24 | U-/S-Bahn Potsdamer Platz*

NOCTI VAGUS [135 D1]
'Dark restaurant', with show programme, which sharpens the taste buds in an intriguing manner. While the eyes cease to be of use in the complete darkness, the senses of taste and smell are heightened. The chef aims to steer his guests onto new olfactory pathways: saddle of rabbit in plum-wine sauce or strawberries with green pepper. *Mon from 6 pm, Tue–Sun from 8 pm | Mitte | Saarbrücker Strasse 36–38 | Tel. 74 74 91 23 | www.noctivagus.de | U 2 | Senefelderplatz*

PARIS-MOSKAU [134 C2]
Down-to-earth gourmet cuisine tastes good in this half-timbered house which managed to survive the rebuilding of the administrative district. Dishes include pike perch from the River Havel on 'Himmel und Erde' (mashed potato and apple) with fried black pudding. *Mon–Fri noon–3 pm and daily 6 pm–1 am | Tiergarten | Alt-Moabit 141 | Tel. 394 20 81 | www.paris-moskau.de | S-Bahn Hauptbahnhof*

Chef's special

RESTAURANT IM FERNSEHTURM [123 F3]
The café rotates on its own axis twice every hour. Over veal roulade with a typical mushroom gravy you can enjoy the sensational view across the city at a height of 207 m. Tip: if you reserve a table at the café in advance, you don't have to queue at the entrance of the television tower to get in! *Daily 10 am–midnight | Mitte | Panoramastrasse 1a | Tel. 242 33 33 | www.berliner-fernsehturm.de | U-/S-Bahn Alexanderplatz*

SAN NICCI [122 C2]
Lovers of fine Italian cooking feast on pasta and meat dishes in the Admiralspalast building. *Daily 10 am–midnight | Mitte | Friedrichstrasse 101 | Tel. 306 45 49 80 | www.san-nicci.de | U-/S-Bahn Friedrichstrasse*

SARAH WIENER [133 E–F1]
Alpine cooking using fresh ingredients is to be had in the side wing of the Hamburger Bahnhof museum. Pretty terrace on the bank of the Nordkanal. Branches in *Chausseestrasse 8 (Mitte)* and in the Akademie der Künste on *Pariser Platz* next to the Brandenburger Tor. *Tues–Fri 10 am–6 pm, Sat 11 am–8 pm, Sun 11 am–6 pm | Mitte | Invalidenstrasse 50–51 | Tel. 70 71 36 50 | www.sarahwiener.de | S-Bahn Hauptbahnhof*

SCHNEEWEISS [136 C3]
The name is an ode to the interior decor, since almost the only colour to be found here in on the plates! The crispy, golden-yellow *Wiener Schnitzel* positively beams at the guest and the goat's cheese and *Spätzle* (south German noodle variation) give a touch of southern culinary flair. *Daily 11 am–1 am | Friedrichshain | Simplonstrasse 16 | Tel. 29 04 97 04 | www.schneeweiss-berlin.de | U-/S-Bahn Warschauer Strasse*

UMSPANNWERK OST [136 A2]
At the old transformer station, wine, cocktails and beer flow instead of electricity, to wash down *Wiener Schnitzel* or gnocchi. Huge dining hall with 7-m-high ceiling and kitchen which is open to view. *Daily from 11.30 am | Friedrichshain | Palisadenstrasse 48 | Tel. 42 80 94 97 | www.umspannwerk-ost.de | U 5 | Weberwiese*

> LOW BUDGET

- Pizza-like pastry delicacies from the *Foccaceria* (1.50 euros each) garnished with scrumptious toppings quell those hunger pangs quickly. *Daily from 11 am | Fehrbelliner Strasse 24* [128 C5] *| Mitte | Tel. 44 03 27 71 | U 8 | Rosenthaler Platz*
- At lunchtime you get haute cuisine at low prices at *Restaurant 44 (kitchen open: daily noon–2.30 pm, 6 pm to 10.30 pm | Augsburger Strasse 44* [121 D5] *| Tel. 220 10 22 88 | U 9, 15 | Kurfürstendamm).* Degustation menu at lunchtime: 33 euros (three courses) or 22 euros (two courses).
- *Vöner & Wagenburger* in Friedrichshain is Berlin's only vegetarian snack bar. *Mon–Fri 11.30 am–10.30 pm, Sat&Sun 1.30 pm–10.30 pm | Boxhagener Strasse 56* [136 C4] *| S-Bahn Ostkreuz*

FOOD & DRINK

Good and reasonably priced: La Focacceria

RESTAURANTS €

BABA ANGORA [131 F5]
Refined Turkish cuisine, most notably lamb dishes, grilled vegetables and tempting desserts. Cosy atmosphere conjured up by candlelight and comfy benches. *Daily from noon | Charlottenburg | Schlüterstrasse 29 | Tel. 323 70 96 | www.babaangora.de | S-Bahn Savignyplatz*

GASTHAUS LENTZ [131 D5]
A classic which entices not only the '68 generation out of the surrounding apartments. Good choice of wines and a fine selection of draught beers, including *Kölsch*, the typical Cologne variety. *Buletten* or *Landjäger* sausages can be ordered any time, even chicken wings or Swabian *Maultaschen soup* are on the menu. *Daily 9 am–2 am | Stuttgarter Platz 20 | Charlottenburg | Tel. 324 16 19 | S-Bahn Charlottenburg*

GNADENBROT ▶▶ [140 C2]
Goulash, roast meats and fried potatoes: that's the recipe for success of this city-centre eatery. Its proximity to the Schöneberg gay scene is unmistakable. Self-service. *Daily from noon | Schöneberg | Martin-Luther-Strasse 20a/corner of Motzstrasse | Tel. 21 96 17 86 | www.raststaette-gnadenbrot.de | U 4 | Victoria-Luise-Platz*

NÖ! WEINGALERIE [134 A4] Insider Tip
Small, but excellent restaurant with the chance to participate in a wine tasting. The guest chooses five wines, accompanied by cheese and grape sticks and baguette bread, all for 15 euros. *Mon–Fri noon–1 am, Sat 7 pm–1 am | Mitte | Glinkastrasse 23 | Tel. 201 08 71 | www.cafe-noe.de | U 2, 6 | Stadtmitte*

SASAYA [129 D3]
Cheerful service and value-for-money meals. The quality of the raw fish dishes also attracts Japanese guests. *Thur–Tues noon–2.30 pm, 6 pm to 10.30 pm | Prenzlauer Berg | Lychener Strasse 50 | Tel. 44 71 77 21 | U 2 | Eberswalder Strasse*

TOCA ROUGE [134 B1] Insider Tip
Crazy atmosphere with a defamiliarised image of Mao over the entrance. The food is a mixture from all parts of Asia. The 'Crazy Orange Chicken' is scrumptious! *Mon–Fri noon–midnight, Sat&Sun 5 pm–midnight | Mitte | Torstrasse 195 | Tel. 84 71 21 42 | S 1, 2 | Oranienburger Strasse*

> FROM CLASSY TO CRAZY

There are shopping streets and arcades all over Berlin, not just in the centre

> Berlin has more shopping streets than you can count. Don't go looking for the shopping centre; there isn't one. Why? Because each district has its own retail hot spot.

In Mitte, for example, it's Friedrichstrasse with lots of exclusive addresses. In the Galleries Lafayette, say, or at Quartier 206, the clientele is just as international as the brand names on sale there. On Alexanderplatz, on the other hand, shoppers are tempted by Germany's biggest branch of the Kaufhof department chain and the Alexa shopping centre. The pride of Charlottenburg's business world is the Kurfürstendamm, packed with designer boutiques, and Tauentzienstrasse, where department stores such as Wertheim, Peek & Cloppenburg and KaDeWe draw the customers. Schlossstrasse in the south is the preferred haunt of the residents of Zehlendorf and Steglitz.

Above: Quartier 206

SHOPPING

And then there are the many smaller streets with their resourceful and imaginative retailers, for example, Goltzstrasse in Schöneberg, well-known for its fashion boutiques and furniture shops. Reuterstrasse in Neukölln is home to more junk shops and second-hand boutiques than anywhere else in the city. The area around the Hackesche Höfe in Mitte, too, is famous for its fashion and design boutiques.

ANTIQUES AND ANTIQUARIAN BOOKS

BERLINER ANTIKMARKT [122 C2]

At Friedrichstrassestation some 35 antique dealers under the S-Bahn archways offer antique dolls, toys, watches, jewellery and paintings. The teddy bear shop, *Bärenstark*, also has antique specimens. *Wed–Mon 11 am–6 pm | Mitte | Georgenstrasse 190–203 | Tel. 208 26 55 | www.berliner-antikmarkt.de | U-/S-Bahn Friedrichstrasse*

BEAUTY

Connoisseurs of a 'wee dram' are hard put to choose at 'Whisky & Cigars'

DÜWAL **[120 B3]**
Lovers of old books will surely appreciate the selection at this well-known dealer's. Mountains of valuable works! *Mon–Fri 3 pm–6 pm, Sat 11 am–2 pm* | *www.duewal.de* | *S-Bahn Savignyplatz*

Insider Tip **PLATTEN PEDRO** **[125 D6]**
Berlin's largest source of second-hand records, including some 200,000 singles. From folk music to hard rock, everything the collector's heart desires. *Mon–Fri 10.07 am–5.52 pm, Sat 10 am–3.30 pm* | *Charlottenburg* | *Tegeler Weg 102* | *www.platten-pedro.de* | *U 7* | *Mierendorffplatz*

BEAUTY

BEAUTY AND NATURE **[132 B6]**
Products from Dr. Hauschka, Weleda or Lavera are in stock in Germany's first department store devoted to natural cosmetics. Two floors of high-quality products and special beauty and massage treatments; there's even a perfume bar where you can have your own private scent put together. *Mon–Fri 10 am–8 pm, Sat 10 am–6 pm* | *Schöneberg* | *Nürnberger Strasse 55 (Ladenpassage Ellington Hotel)* | *Tel. 79 01 65 86* | *www.beautyandnature.de* | *U-Bahn Wittenbergplatz*

THE ENGLISH SCENT **[139 E1]**
Known for its highly original British scents, to be found in hardly any other perfumery in Berlin. Almost all the perfumes are from English suppliers to the Crown. Comprehensive advice is on hand if you're not sure which scent suits you best. *Mon&Tues, Thurs&Fri 10 am–2 pm, 3 pm to 6.30 pm, Wed from 2 pm, Sat 10 am to 3 pm* | *Charlottenburg* | *Niebuhrstrasse 11* | *www.english-scent.de* | *S-Bahn Savignyplatz*

DELICATESSEN

CONFISERIE MELANIE **[120 B3]** Insider Tip
Over 4,000 sweets and other delicacies, crammed into Eberhard Päller's small shop. Alongside violet mustard,

milk grappa and seaweed jelly, the hand-made chocolates are surely the cult objects of the future: how about garlic, horseradish or asparagus flavour? *Mon–Wed, Fri 10 am–7 pm, Sat 10 am–2 pm | Charlottenburg | Goethestrasse 4 | U 2 | Ernst-Reuter-Platz*

GOLDHAHN & SAMPSON [129 D–E3]
Studying the selection of spices is like taking a round-the-world trip. Cookery courses take place in the rear of the shop. Small, but fine selection of wines and spirits. *Mon–Sat 10 am–8 pm | Prenzlauer Berg | Dunkerstrasse 9 | www.goldhahnundsampson.de | U 2 | Eberswalder Strasse*

Insider Tip

KERNKRAFT BERLIN [136 C4]
Paradise for squirrels and other nut-lovers! High shelves are full of wasabi and chilli peanuts, chocolate-covered almonds and many other titbits from all over the world. If you favour something softer, take a bite of the dried fruits or buy a little candied ginger. Try before you buy, too! *Mon–Fri 10 am–7 pm, Sat 11 am to 4 pm | Friedrichshain | Neue Bahnhofstrasse 3 | www.kernkraft-berlin.de | S 5, 9, 75 | Ostkreuz*

WHISKY & CIGARS [123 E1]
Cosy shop where you can sample hand-rolled cigars from Cuba, the Dominican Republic and Honduras, while relaxing in one of the club chairs and clutching a glass of one of 1,000 different whiskies in the other hand! On offer are mostly Scottish malts, classy bourbons and also blended whiskies and rum. *Mon–Fri 11 am–7 pm, Sat 11 am to 6 pm | Mitte | Sophienstrasse 8–9 | www.whiskycigars.de | U 8 | Weinmeisterstrasse*

THIS & THAT

AUS BERLIN ▶▶ [123 F2]

Insider Tip

Products from over 400 Berlin designers and manufacturers bring colour to this otherwise nasty pre-fabricated block opposite Kaufhof. From decorated fishermen's oilskins to

MARCO POLO HIGHLIGHTS

★ **KaDeWe**
The delicatessen department is an experience in itself (page 75)

★ **HUGO Store**
Light show, mirrors, bamboo: an incredibly sensual shopping experience (page 75)

★ **Quartier 206**
Classy atmosphere, good selection and no hustle and bustle (page 75)

★ **Trippen**
Wooden shoes as cult objects and a showroom like a gallery (page 76)

★ **Sterling Gold**
Five decades of magnificent ball gowns for retro fans (page 77)

★ **Markt am Maybachufer**
Large Turkish families buying vegetables by the crateful amid the competing cries of the traders (page 77)

lovesickness pills, there's something for everyone. The popular Gorbaschov brand of vodka, produced in nearby Reinickendorf, is also on the shelves here. *Mon–Sat noon–7 pm | Mitte | Karl-Liebknecht-Strasse 17 | www.ausberlin.de | U-/S-Bahn Alexanderplatz*

KPM WELT [132 A–B3]
Porcelain from the Königliche Porzellan Manufaktur is not merely sold here, but stunningly showcased in open workshops, guided tours and special exhibitions. *Daily 10 am to 6 pm | | Admission: 8 euros, Guided tours (10 euros): Sat&Sun 3 pm | Tiergarten | Wegelystrasse 1 | www.kpm-berlin.de | S 7, 9, 75 | Tiergarten*

LUXUS INTERNATIONAL [128 C4]
Some 120 Berlin designers present their latest creations and imaginative ideas in this small shop. From cuddly *Döner kebab* to football-hater badges – it's all here! Bestsellers include the Currywurst stand 'Happy Families' game! *Mon–Sat 11 am–8 pm | Prenzlauer Berg | Kastanienallee 101 | U 2 | Eberswalder Strasse*

All sorts of handy – and crazy – second-hand stuff on offer at Berlin's flea markets

FLEA MARKETS

AM MAUERPARK ▶▶ [128 C3–4]
Berlin's biggest flea market doesn't just have loads of junk and retro furniture. Lots of young designers, too, sell their first collections here, mostly printed T-shirts, jewellery and fashionable bags. Trendy shoppers also like to hang out in the diverse

beach bars on the site. *Sun 9 am–5 pm | Prenzlauer Berg | Eberswalder Strasse | U 2 | Eberswalder Strasse*

BOXHAGENER PLATZ [136 C3]
Small square with idyllic flea market, whose low prices attract much student custom from the neighbourhood. The cafés round about are an ideal place from which to observe the occasional traders in action. *Sun 9 am–4 pm | Friedrichshain | Boxhagener Platz | U 5 | Samariterstrasse*

TRÖDELMARKT AM 17. JUNI [121 E2]
The most famous flea market in the west of the city. Many professional antique and record dealers ask horrendous prices – but then, isn't haggling fun? *Sat&Sun 10 am–5 pm | Charlottenburg | Strasse des 17. Juni | S-Bahn Tiergarten*

DEPARTMENT STORES

DUSSMANN [122 C3]
The so-called 'culture store' offers CDs, DVDs, videos, books, games and software on four floors. Plenty of special offers entice browsers. In the music department you can listen to extracts from your favourite titles. *Mon–Sat 10 am–midnight | Mitte | Friedrichstrasse 90 | www.kulturkaufhaus.shop-asp.de | U-/S-Bahn Friedrichstrasse*

GALERIES LAFAYETTE [122 C4]
Shopping El Dorado with excellent delicatessen department, international fashions and exciting architecture. *Mon–Sat 10 am–8 pm | Mitte | Französische Strasse 23 | U 6 | Französische Strasse*

KADEWE ★ [121 E5]
The 7,000-sq-m delicatessen department alone makes the Kaufhaus des Westens worth a visit. From artichokes to zucchini, you'll find (almost) everything. The range of designer-fashion labels is overwhelming. *Mon–Thurs 10 am–8 pm, Fri 10 am to 9 pm, Sat 9.30 am–8 pm | Schöneberg | Tauentzienstrasse 21–24 | U 1, 2, 3| Wittenbergplatz*

FASHION

HUGO STORE ★ [134 C2]
The completely mirror-clad changing rooms can be opened and closed at the push of a button. Outside, on the store front, a relief depicting the streets of Berlin is drenched in coloured light by a scanner. Finally, the view of the inner courtyard is enhanced by a bamboo grove. In case you hadn't already guessed, the Hugo Boss young collection is showcased here. *Mon–Sat 11 am–8 pm | Mitte | Rosenthaler Strasse 49 | www.hugoboss.com | U 8 | Weinmeisterstrasse*

NIX [123 D1] Insider Tip
Discreet colours, quality fabrics and simple cuts are the key to the success of designer Barbara Gebhardt. A Nix coat or skirt is equally suited to everyday demands as to a visit to the opera. *Mon–Sat 11 am–7 pm | Mitte | Oranienburger Strasse 32 | www.nix.de | S 1, 2, 25 | Oranienburger Strasse*

QUARTIER 206 ★ [122 C4]
Elegant designer outlets including Cerrutti, Yves Saint-Laurent, rive gauche, Strenesse, Gabriele Strehle and Gucci. The 'Department Store'

has bargains, too. *Mon–Fri 10.30 am to 7.30 pm, Sat 10 am–6 pm | Mitte | Friedrichstrasse 71 | U 6 | Französische Strasse*

Insider Tip

THATCHERS [128 C4]
Black and white, transparent fabrics plus shades of grey are the ingredients for Thatchers' classic fashions with a twist. The evening wear and cocktail dresses are the cream of the label: seductive, original and ingenious. Branch also in the Hackesche Höfe in Mitte. *Mon–Fri noon–8 pm, Sat noon–6 pm | Prenzlauer Berg | Kastanienallee 21 | www.thatchers.de | U 2 | Eberswalder Strasse*

>LOW BUDGET

- For retro fans: From radios to egg cups, *Arm & Sexy* in Neukölln has 1930s to 1960s stuff for everyone – not just the 'poor and sexy'! *Mon–Fri 2 pm–7 pm, Sat noon–5 pm | Reuterstrasse 62* [143 E4] *| www.arm-and-sexy.de | U 7 | Hermannplatz*
- *The Marc O'Polo-Outlet* – the bargain-hunter's idea of bliss. *Mon–Fri 10 am–8 pm, Sat 10 am–6 pm | Kaiserdamm 7* [130 C4] *| U 2 | Sophie-Charlotte-Platz*
- Cheap jeans and shirts from last season on offer at *Maassen 10*. *Mon–Fri 10 am–7 pm, Sat 10 am to 5 pm | Maassenstrasse 10* [141 D2] *| U 1, 2 | Nollendorfplatz*
- *Logo An- und Verkauf* has cheap, new and second-hand CDs and records: indie, pop, rock, hip-hop. *Mon–Fri noon–7 pm, Sat 11 am–4 pm | Bergmannstrasse 10* [142 A3] *| U 7 | Zossener Strasse*

SHOES

JÜNEMANNS PANTOFFEL-ECK [123 F1]

Insider Tip

Genuine felt slippers like Grandma used to wear, piled high to the ceiling of this tiny showroom-cum-workshop. The products from this 100-year-old family business have achieved cult status. *Mon, Wed&Fri 9 am–5 pm, Tues&Thurs 9 am to 6 pm | Mitte | Torstrasse 39 | www.pantoffeleck.de | U 2 | Rosa-Luxemburg-Platz*

LUCCICO [128 C6]
Unusual design and good craftsmanship paired with good value-for-money keep the people flocking to this location. Branches, too, at Oranienburger Strasse 23 (outlet) and Bergmannstrasse 8. *Mon–Fri noon–8 pm, Sat 11 am–4 pm | Mitte | Weinmeisterstrasse 12 | www.luccico.de | U-Bahn Weinmeisterstrasse*

TRIPPEN ★ [123 E2]
The showroom, where each of these top-quality designer wood and leather shoes sits in a back-lit compartment, is more like a gallery than a shop. *Mon–Fri 11 am–8 pm, Sat 10 am to 8 pm | Mitte | Rosenthaler Strasse 40–41 | Hackesche Höfe | Hof IV | www.trippen.com | S-Bahn Hackescher Markt*

SECOND-HAND

MADONNA [120 A4]
Exquisite designer and top-label fashions – and plenty to choose from, too. Versace coats, Jil Sander pullovers or Chanel suits look as good as new. There's a branch at Mommsenstrasse 43 selling designer fashion for men. *Mon–Fri noon–7 pm, Sat 11 am to*

4 pm | Charlottenburg | Mommsenstrasse 57 | S-Bahn Charlottenburg

STERLING GOLD ★ [123 D1]

Dazzling selection of glittering, sequined ball gowns and evening dresses, plus cashmere coats. *Mon–Fri noon–8 pm, Sat noon–6 pm | Mitte | Oranienburger Strasse 32 | Heckmann Höfe | www.sterlinggold.de | S 1, 2, 25 | Oranienburger Strasse*

MARKETS

sider Tip **KARL-AUGUST-PLATZ** [131 E5]

Specialities from all over Europe are what make this market a gourmet's paradise: alpine cheeses, organic carrots, fresh pasta and home-made jam. *Wed 8 am–1 pm, Sat 8 am–2 pm | Charlottenburg | Karl-August-Platz | U 7 | Wilmersdorfer Strasse*

MARKT AM MAYBACHUFER ★ [143 E3]

Also known as the 'Turkish Market', this is where grapes, tomatoes, aubergines change hands by the crateful, while the Turkish stallholders curry favour with passers-by. The young, chic generation of Turks with German passports go for antipasti and organic cheese. *Tues&Fri noon to 6.30 pm | Kreuzberg | Maybachufer | U 8 | Schönleinstrasse*

Even wholesalers had to start somewhere: flower seller on the Maybachufer

WINTERFELDTMARKT ▸▸ [141 D2]

It's very much the done thing within the Schöneberg gay and academic communities to take a stroll over the market. Afterwards it's time to observe the comings and goings at one of the surrounding cafés. *Wed 8 am–2 pm, Sat 8 am–4 pm | Schöneberg | Winterfeldtplatz | U-Bahn Nollendorfplatz*

> PARADISE FOR NIGHT OWLS

First the theatre, then to a bar and afterwards dancing – and that till the small hours

> The night in Berlin is not just for sleeping: you can dance into the small hours, prop up the bar for ages over a beer, listen to a concert, take in a play at the theatre, watch a film – fun for locals and visitors alike.

Night owls would be hard put to find a bigger selection of clubs, bars and cultural venues in any other city in the world. In Berlin, 200 clubs, around 30 cabarets and variety theatres, more than 130 cinemas plus countless pubs and bars vie for custom. In Mitte the number of licences granted for bars and clubs had to be restricted, in order to enable residents to get a good night's sleep. And every year in summer, the same old arguments over noise levels flare up between tenants who live above pubs and their clientele who like to sit and chat outside until all hours! Up to now, the Berlin pub landlords have generally got their way, since even the weariest neigh-

Above: The Newton in Charlottenstrasse

ENTER TAINMENT

bour perks up at some point. And then what does he do? He goes down to the pub for a beer, of course!

BARS

GAINSBOURG ★ [120 C4]

Decorated in the style of a typical American bar, the haunt of Charlottenburg bohemians, who sip the excellent cocktails while listening to the music of the bar's French namesake. Pretty terrace. *Daily from 5 pm; summer: from 4 pm | Charlottenburg | Savignyplatz 5 | Tel. 313 74 64 | S-Bahn Savignyplatz*

KUSCHLOWSKI ▶▶ [143 E3]

Living room-cum-bar with open fire. Vodka to be had in various forms, for the simple reason that the owner is Russian. *Daily from 8 pm | Neukölln | Weserstrasse 202 | Tel. 0176/ 24 38 97 01 | www.kuschlowski.de | U-Bahn Hermannplatz*

NEWTON [122 C4]
The nudes photographed by maestro Helmut Newton, who died in 2004, tend to distract attention somewhat from the well-mixed drinks! Alongside cocktails, you'll find oysters and champagne. A cigar lounge with humidor awaits connoisseurs of tobacco. *Sun–Thurs 10 am–3 am, Fri& Sat 10 am–4 am | Mitte | Charlottenstrasse 57 | Tel. 20 29 54 21 | www.newton-bar.de | U 6 | Französische Strasse*

The nightlife at Adagio is more like 'molto furioso'

RIVA [134 C2]
Guests sit at an oval bar under the curving S-Bahn archway, and the wine rack is built to resemble the Titanic. For aesthetes with a taste in fine cocktails. *Daily from 6 pm | Mitte | Dircksenstrasse 142 | Tel. 24 72 26 88 | www.riva-berlin.de | S 9, 75 | Hackescher Markt*

SCHALL & RAUCH [128 C2]
Pub, restaurant, guest house and café all rolled into one, where the gay scene likes to meet up for a whisky or a cappuccino. Guests can choose between more than 100 cocktails to sip at the 17-m-long bar or at tables made of Canadian maple. *Daily 8 am–2 am | Prenzlauer Berg | Gleimstrasse 23 | Tel. 443 39 70 | www.schall-und-rauch.de | U-/S-Bahn Schönhauser Allee*

SOLAR ★ [142 A1]
It's fun to sip a cocktail on the 16th floor and gaze out over the city, especially since the ride up the façade in the glass-walled lift provides the first tingle of excitement! Incidentally, you can also eat here – Mediterranean – but not dance, however. *Daily from 6 pm | Kreuzberg | Stresemannstrasse 76 | Tel. 0163/765 27 00 | www.solar-berlin.de | S 1, 26 | Anhalter Bahnhof*

STRANDBAR MITTE [134 B2]
In the summer months young and old get together beside the Spree to order cocktails, coffee or beer at this self-service eatery, relaxing in loungers or on genuine sand and enjoying the view of the Museumsinsel. *May to Sept: daily from 10 am | Mitte | Monbijoustrasse 3 | www.strandbar-mitte.de | S 1, 25 | Oranienburger Strasse*

VICTORIA BAR [141 D2]
Known for its cocktail seminars, but well worth a visit on normal evenings, too, for its restrained, unpretentious interior and pleasant clientele from the Schöneberg media and business world. *Daily from 6.30 pm | Schöneberg | Potsdamer Strasse 102 | Tel. 25 75 99 77 | www.victoriaabar.de | U 1, 2, 15 | Kurfürstenstrasse*

Insider Tip **WEINBAR RUTZ** [128 A6]
Around 1,001 different wines are stored along the walls. The wine list is as copious as an atlas, and a sommelier is on hand to guide you through it. Excellent menu. *Mon to Sat from 4 pm | Mitte | Chausseestrasse 8 | Tel. 24 62 87 60 | www.rutz-weinbar.de | U 6 | Oranienburger Tor*

CLUBS

ADAGIO [133 E5]
Huge night club below the theatre on Potsdamer Platz. Boredom doesn't stand a chance amid the Baroque décor with five bars and large dance floor. *Sat 10 pm–5 am | Tiergarten | Marlene-Dietrich-Platz 1 | Tel. 258 98 90 | www.adagio.de | U-/S-Bahn Potsdamer Platz*

A TRANE [120 B–C3]
No frills, modern jazz club puts on a good live programme – every day. Concerts are packed, admission prices reasonable. *Daily from 9 pm | Charlottenburg | Bleibtreustrasse 1/ corner of Pestalozzistrasse | Tel. 313 25 50 | www.a-trane.de | S-Bahn Savignyplatz*

BERGHAIN/ PANORAMABAR ★ ▶▶ [136 A3]
Impressive techno-electro club, now with fans from all over the world. Night owls between 20 and 40 amuse themselves over two floors of a disused thermal power station with 18-m-high ceilings and 're-fuel' at

MARCO POLO HIGHLIGHTS

★ **Gainsbourg**
American-style bar with first-rate cocktails (page 79)

★ **Solar**
Club on the 16th floor with great view over Berlin (page 80)

★ **Berghain/Panoramabar**
Trendy techno-electro club in disused thermal heating plant (page 81)

★ **Tausend**
Cool interior, top-notch drinks and DJs (page 82)

★ **Bar jeder Vernunft**
Top-notch show acts, variety and cuisine in the beautiful 'Spiegelzelt' (page 83)

★ **Philharmonie**
Outstanding acoustics at 'Circus Karajan' (page 86)

★ **Staatsoper Unter den Linden**
The magnificence of yesteryear, combined with fresh interpretations (page 87)

★ **Theatre**
The diversity of the theatre scene is breathtaking (page 88)

one of four bars. It also features art on the walls and chilled atmosphere. *Fri&Sat from midnight | Admission: 12 euros | Friedrichshain | Am Wriezener Bahnhof | S-Bahn Ostbahnhof*

Insider Tip

HAFENBAR [128 A5]

Amusing interior: ship's ropes, aquariums and loads of portholes. ABBA parties, 'Schlager' and rock music for dance freaks between 20 and 50. Cocktails and *Korn (schnapps)* quench the thirst! *Fri (from 9 pm, German 'Schlager' hits) & Sat (from 10 pm, mixed sounds) | Admission: 8 euros | Mitte | Chausseestrasse 20 | Tel. 282 85 93 | http://hafenbar-berlin.de | U 6 | Naturkundemuseum*

>LOW BUDGET

- Students from the Hanns Eisler Music Academy regularly give free concerts – a chance to experience the virtuosi of tomorrow. *Neuer Marstall | Schlossplatz 7 | or Charlottenstrasse 55* [134 A4] *| Tel. 203 09 21 01 | www.hfm-berlin.de | U 2 | Stadtmitte or Hausvogteiplatz*
- Reduced cinema tickets are to be had on Tuesday at the *Cinestar Centers* (see listings magazines for addresses); admission: approx. 5 euros.
- There's free admission to the *Sageclub* for 'Rock at Sage'. *Thurs 7 pm–10 pm | Köpenicker Strasse 76* [135 D4] *| Tel. 278 98 30 | www.sage-club.de | U 8 | Heinrich-Heine-Strasse*
- At the *frannz-Club*, admission for the indie-poprock-Thursday costs just 4 euros. *Schönhauser Allee 36* [129 D4] *| Tel. 726 27 93 33 | www.frannz.de | U 2 | Eberswalder Strasse*

PURO [121 E4]

Sky lounge on the 20th floor of the Europa-Center with dance floor and Japanese-feel interior for the over-thirties. Great view over the city! *Tues–Sat from 9 pm | Admission: 10 euros | Charlottenburg | Tauentzienstrasse 11 | Tel. 26 36 78 75 | www.puro-berlin.de | U 1, 2, 3 | Wittenbergplatz*

QUASIMODO [121 D4]

Traditional jazz club featuring concerts by well-known musicians. From Defunkt to Jasper van't Hof, almost every big-name funk, soul or jazz act has played here. *Tues–Sat from 9 pm | Admission: 5–25 euros | Charlottenburg | Kantstrasse 12a | Tel. 312 80 86 | www.quasimodo.de | U-/S-Bahn Zoologischer Garten*

SPINDLERE & KLATT IN DER HEERESBÄCKEREI [136 A4]

A touch of Asia at this club-restaurant with lounge atmosphere in an old warehouse. You can even eat lying down, a fact which leads some revellers to crash out snoring on the sofas the later it gets! Fine terrace on the Spree. *Mid-May–mid-Sept: daily; winter: Wed–Sun; kitchen open from 8 pm; club: Fri&Sat from 11 pm | Admission: 8 euros | Kreuzberg | Köpenicker Strasse 16–17 | Tel. 69 56 67 75 | www.spindlerklatt.com | U 1 | Schlesisches Tor*

TAUSEND ★ [134 A2]

Expertly mixed drinks and a quietly elegant interior straight out of a James Bond film – with a wall installation in the form of a giant eye. DJs from the dub and electro scene provide the

At the Bar jeder Vernunft

background beats. *Thurs–Sat from 10 pm | Admission: 12 euros | Mitte | Schiffbauerdamm 11 | Tel. 41 71 53 96 | www.tausendberlin.com | U-/S-Bahn Friedrichstrasse*

TRESOR [135 D4]

Former power station sees international techno DJs spinning the decks. A 30-m-long tunnel leads to the dance floor in the cellar. Tough, industrial vibe and noise levels not for those of a sensitive disposition! Young, international clientele. *Wed, Fri&Sat from 11 pm | | Admission: 12 euros | Mitte | Köpenicker Strasse 59–73 | Tel. 890 64 20 | www.tresorberlin.de | U 8 | Heinrich-Heine-Strasse*

WATERGATE [136 A5]

Last chance for a bop before the Spree. High-earning 25- to 40-year-olds groove to the drum 'n' bass and soul rhythms in this stylish, modern location. *Wed, Fri&Sat from midnight | Admission: 12 euros | Kreuzberg | Falckensteinstrasse 49 | Tel. 61 28 03 95 | www.water-gate.de | U 1 | Schlesisches Tor*

WEEKEND [135 D2]

Dance on the 12th floor of the former GDR 'Haus des Reisens' (House of Travel). Lovers of house music between 20 and 40 hang out, with Alexanderplatz at their feet. Cool: the terrace on the 15th floor (summer only) with bar and view over the city. *Thurs, Fri&Sat from 11 pm | Admission: 12 euros | Mitte | Alexanderplatz 5 | www.week-end-berlin.de | U-/S-Bahn Alexanderplatz*

CABARET & VARIETY

BAR JEDER VERNUNFT ★ [120 C6]

The magnificent, mirrored Art Nouveau tent (the 'Spiegelzelt') puts on a sparkling programme, with stars of the chanson and comedy scene. Sophisticated eats round off the attraction. *Tickets: Mon–Sat noon–7 pm, Sun 3 pm–6 pm | Wilmersdorf | Schaperstrasse 24 | Tel. 883 15 82 | www.bar-jeder-vernunft.de | U 1, 9 | Spichernstrasse*

DIE STACHELSCHWEINE [121 E4–5]

West Berlin institution in the political cabaret arena: witty and spirited. *Tickets: Mon–Fri 11 am–8 pm, Sat 2 pm–9 pm | Charlottenburg | Tauentzienstrasse (Europa-Center) | Tel. 261 47 95 | www.stachelschweine-berlin.de | U 9, 15 | Kurfürstendamm*

DISTEL [122 C2]

Founded over 50 years ago, the troupe at 'The Thistle' were cautious, but highly accomplished critics of the GDR regime. Today, capitalism is more likely to come under fire. *Tickets: Mon–Fri noon–6 pm | Mitte | Friedrichstrasse 101 | Tel. 204 47 04 | U-/S-Bahn Friedrichstrasse*

TIPI, DAS ZELT [133 E3]

Big-name entertainers appear on the bill alongside a-capella ensembles or virtuoso drummers. Unpretentious atmosphere, next to the Kanzleramt. *Grosse Querallee | Tiergarten | Ticket hotline: 0180-327 93 58 | www.tipi-das-zelt.de | S 1, 2 | Brandenburger Tor*

Insider Tip **UFA-FABRIK** [147 D4]

Everything the fringe scene has to offer, located on the former UFA film studio site: children's circus (kids can join in, too), cabaret and variety theatre. *Tempelhof | Viktoriastrasse 13 | Tel. 75 50 30 | www.ufafabrik.de | U 6 | Ullsteinstrasse*

A town in miniature: UFA-Fabrik

CINEMAS

Around 300 cinema auditoria show an impressive range of films. Current programmes (plus cinema addresses) are to be found in Berlin's two listings magazines *Zitty* and *tip*. Look out for films marked *OmU*; this means the film is shown in the original language with German subtitles.

PUBS

DIENER – TATTERSALL [120 C4]

The walls speak volumes: many famous past and present regulars are immortalised here – photographically – including US director Billy Wilder. Still popular with actors and other bon viveurs who like to drop in for a beer and a bite. The likes of you and I are more than welcome, too! *Daily from 6 pm | Charlottenburg | Grolmanstrasse 47 | Tel. 881 53 29 | S-Bahn Savignyplatz*

LEMKE [123 E2]

Cosy brewery pub under the S-Bahn archway with several different beers on tap and tasty grub from the grill. Beer garden. *Daily from noon, Mon to Fri buffet noon–3 pm | Mitte | Dircksenstrasse 143 | Tel. 24 72 87 27 | S-Bahn Hackescher Markt*

RESTAURATION SOPHIEN 11 [123 E1]

Welcoming eatery with an idyllic courtyard where you can relax and enjoy beer and *Buletten* at reasonable prices. What's more, it's next to the Hackesche Höfe, too! *Mon–Fri from 5 pm, Sat&Sun from 3 pm | Mitte |*

Sophienstrasse 11 | Tel. 283 21 36 | www.sophien-elf.de | S-Bahn Hackescher Markt

ROCK'N'ROLL-HERBERGE ▶▶ [143 F1]
In the foyer of this trendy musicians' haunt you can enjoy a civilized glass of beer over a game of billiards or table football. Those who don't make it home can book one of the seven rooms for the night. *Sun–Thurs 9 am to 4 am, Fri&Sat 9 am–7 am | Kreuzberg | Muskauer Strasse 11 | Tel. 61 62 36 00 | www.rock-n-roll-herberge.de | U 1 | Görlitzer Bahnhof*

STÄNDIGE VERTRETUNG [134 A2]
This is where enterprising 'exiled' Bonn civil servants and politicians get together over a *Kölsch*. The place to celebrate carnival in true Rhineland style! *Daily 10.30 am–1 am | Mitte | Schiffbauerdamm 8 | Tel. 282 39 65 | U-/S-Bahn Friedrichstrasse*

YORKSCHLÖSSCHEN [143 D2]
Getting on a bit, but cosy. That's the view of the regulars who sip their beer listening to live concerts along jazz and blues lines. In summer, they relax in the pretty beer garden. One of the oldest and most popular jazz clubs in town. *Mon–Sat 5 pm–3 am, Sun from 10 am | Kreuzberg | Yorckstrasse 15 | Tel. 2 15 80 70 | www.yorckschloesschen.de | U 6, 7 | Mehringdamm*

Splendid backdrop for cabaret, music and variety: TIPI, das Zelt

CONCERTS

KONZERTHAUS AM GENDARMENMARKT [122 C4]
Built in 1818–21, Schinkel's Schauspielhaus now resounds mainly to the

music of the Berlin Symphony Orchestra. The acoustics can be disappointing, though, depending on where you sit. *Tickets: Mon to Sat noon–7 pm, Sun noon–4 pm | Mitte | Am Gendarmenmarkt | Tel. 203 09 21 01 | www.konzerthaus-berlin.de | U 2, 6 | Stadtmitte*

PHILHARMONIE ★ [133 E4]

Resident orchestra here is the Berlin Philharmonic under the baton of principal conductor Sir Simon Rattle. The acoustics in architect Hans Scharoun's building are judged to be superb. From September to June, Insider Tip free concerts on Tuesdays at 1 pm! *Tickets: Mon–Fri 3 pm–6 pm, Sat&-Sun 11 am–2 pm | Tiergarten | Matthäikirchstrasse 1 | Tel. 25 48 89 99 | www.philharmonie.de | U-/S-Bahn Potsdamer Platz*

MUSICAL, DANCE & OPERA

ADMIRALSPALAST [134 A2]

The former entertainment Mecca dating back to 1911 has been given a new lease of life: theatre, musicals and improvisation theatre enliven the stage next to Friedrichstrasse station. *Tickets: Mon–Sat noon–7 pm | Friedrichstrasse 101 | Mitte | Tel. 47 99 74 99 | U-/S-Bahn Friedrichstrasse*

DEUTSCHE OPER [120 A2]

Once the West Berlin counterpart of the Staatsoper in the Eastern sector, it now favours unconventional interpretations of classic works. *Tickets: Mon–Sat 11 am–7 pm, Sun 10 am to 2 pm | Charlottenburg | Bismarckstrasse 35 | Tel. 0700-6737237546 | www.deutscheoperberlin.de | U 2 | Deutsche Oper*

> BOOKS & FILMS

Berlin between zeitgeist and everyday life

> **Herr Lehmann (Berlin Blues)** – A tribute to West Berlin zeitgeist shortly before the fall of the Wall by Sven Regener.

> **Berlin Alexanderplatz** – Alfred Döblin's timeless classic of 1929 tells the story of a nobody, released from prison and trying to find his feet again in the big city.

> **The Spy who Came in From the Cold** – Ultimate spy novel, written in 1963 by John le Carré at the height of the Cold War. Subsequently filmed with Richard Burton.

> **Funeral in Berlin** – Another Cold-War classic from 1966, starring Michael Caine as a very un-Bond-like spy.

> **Berlin – The Architecture Guide** – The comprehensive account of the exciting architecture of the capital, written by Haubrich and Hoffmann is jam packed with photographs, maps and aerial images, plus numerous suggestions for tours of its highlights.

> **Good bye Lenin** – Prize-winning film (2003) by Wolfgang Becker taking an amusing, bittersweet look at the fall of the Berlin wall in an old GDR neighbourhood.

> **Lola rennt (Run, Lola, Run)** – Tom Tykwer's 1998 movie shows the people of Berlin as they really are: always in a hurry and short of a euro or two! (English subtitles)

Magnificent setting for great musical theatre: Staatsoper Unter den Linden

FRIEDRICHSTADTPALAST [122 C1]
Germany's only revue theatre and the largest in Europe. Plenty of glamour and high-kicking dancers. *Tickets: Sun&Mon 10 am–6 pm, Tues–Sat 10 am–7 pm | Mitte | Friedrichstrasse 107 | Tel. 23 26 23 26 | www.friedrichstadtpalast.de | U 6 | Oranienburger Tor*

HEBBEL AM UFER [142 A2]
Experimental concept with emphasis on dance theatre. Avant-garde productions and guest appearances on three stages.*Hau 1: Stresemannstrasse 29, Hau 2: Hallesches Ufer 32, Hau 3: Tempelhofer Ufer 10 | Kreuzberg | Tickets: daily noon–7 pm in Hau 2 | Tel. 25 90 04 27 | www.hebbel-am-ufer.de | U 1, 6 | Hallesches Tor*

KOMISCHE OPER [134 A3]
Modern productions and the children's programme make the opera a firm favourite. *Tickets: Mon–Sat 11 am–7 pm, Sun 1 pm–4 pm | Mitte | Behrenstrasse 55–57 | Tel. 47 99 74 00 | www.komische-oper-berlin.de | U 6 | Französische Strasse*

NEUKÖLLNER OPER [143 F6] Insider Tip
A relatively small theatre staging comic performances and putting an unusual slant on the art of lyrical drama. Genuine fringe opera. *Tickets: Tues–Fri 3 pm–7 pm | Sat&Sun on performance days only | Neukölln | Karl-Marx-Strasse 131 | Tel. 68 89 07 77 | www.neukoellneroper.de | U 7 | Karl-Marx-Strasse*

STAATSOPER UNTER DEN LINDEN ★ [123 D3]
The magnificent interior of Berlin's oldest opera house is showing its age and is getting a face-lift in 2010, during which it will be business as usual under General Musical Director Daniel Barenboim at the *Schillertheater (Charlottenburg | Bismarckstrasse 110). Tickets: Mon–Fri 11 am to 7 pm, Sat&Sun 2 pm–7 pm | Mitte | Unter den Linden 7 | Tel. 20 35 45 55 |*

www.staatsoper-berlin.de | U 6 | Französische Strasse

THEATER DES WESTENS [132 A5]
Musical theatre : The building dates back to the 19th century and has seen

Creative: theatre at the Sophiensäle

the likes of Josephine Baker and Hildegard Knef tread its boards. *Charlottenburg | Kantstrasse 12 | Ticket hotline: 01805-4444 | www.stage-entertainment.de | U-/S-Bahn Zoologischer Garten*

DANCE CLUBS

GRÜNER SALON [135 D1]
On Thursdays it's time to tango in the side wing of the Volksbühne, on Fridays you hear the sound of a swing orchestra. Tues: Salsa; Sat: concerts. *Mitte | Rosa-Luxemburg-Platz | Tel. 28 59 89 36 | www.gruener-salon.de | U 2 | Rosa-Luxemburg-Platz*

HAVANNA [141 D4]
Salsa, merengue, bachata and black music each have their own area; dancers can groove around, pausing only to grab an ice-cold drink on the way. *Wed (salsa only from 9 pm) and Fri&Sat (from 10 pm) | Schöneberg | Hauptstrasse 30 | Tel. 784 85 65 | www.havanna-berlin.de | U 7 | Kleistpark*

THEATRE

★ Berlin can rightly be proud of its theatres. Actors or directors who make it big here have truly reached the heights of the German theatre scene.

BERLINER ENSEMBLE [122 C2]
Once the domain of Bertolt Brecht, his dramas still play a major role here, although the ensemble has added other dramatists to its repertoire. Popular and therefore often sold out. *Tickets: Mon–Fri 8 am–6 pm, Sat&Sun 11 am–6 pm | Mitte | Bertolt-Brecht-Platz 1 | Tel. 28 40 81 55 | www.berliner-ensemble.de | U-/S-Bahn Friedrichstrasse*

DEUTSCHES THEATER [122 B1]
Under the great Max Reinhardt, 100 years ago, this became Germany's most famous theatre. Today it en-

deavours to pick up the threads of this glorious period. Dramas by Goethe, Schiller and Hauptmann are part of the repertoire. *Tickets: Mon–Sat 11 am–6.30 pm, Sun 3 pm–6.30 pm | Mitte | Schumannstrasse 13a | Tel. 28 44 12 25 | www.deutschestheater.de | U 6 | Oranienburger Tor*

MAXIM GORKI THEATER [123 D3]

From ambitious pieces by young playwrights to classics of the genre, the highly motivated ensemble doesn't restrict itself to Russian drama. *Tickets: Mon–Sat noon–6.30 pm, Sun 4 pm to 6.30 pm | Mitte | Am Festungsgraben 2 | Tel. 20 22 11 15 | www.gorki.de | S-Bahn Hackescher Markt*

SCHAUBÜHNE [139 D2]

The ensemble of the once legendary Schaubühne is currently competing with the Volksbühne when it comes to unconventional drama on contentious issues. Young theatre for an ever-young audience. *Tickets: Mon–Sat 11 am–6.30 pm, Sun 3 pm to 6.30 pm | Wilmersdorf | Kurfürstendamm 153 | Tel. 89 00 23 | www.schaubuehne.de | U 7 | Adenauerplatz*

SOPHIENSAELE [123 E1] Insider Tip

The décor and costumes may be somewhat rudimentary, but the creative spirit which permeates the theatre is all the richer. Its presentations of drama and dance are impressive. *Tickets: daily 9 am–5 pm | Mitte | Sophienstrasse 18 | Tel. 283 52 66 | www.sophiensaele.com | S-Bahn Hackescher Markt*

VOLKSBÜHNE [135 D1]

Cult directors like Frank Castorf and Christoph Schlingensief love to provoke with unconventional performances. *Tickets: daily noon–6 pm | Mitte | Rosa-Luxemburg-Platz | Tel. 24 06 57 77 | www.volksbuehne-berlin.de | U 2 | Rosa-Luxemburg-Platz*

> SPECTATOR SPORTS

Hertha, Union, Alba and the Eisbären ...

Football fans head for the Olympic stadium, the home of Bundesliga club Hertha BSC *(www.herthabsc.de)*. Tickets online or under *Tel. 01805/18 92 00*. The main office is at the Olympic stadium *(Hanns-Braun-Strasse | Friesenhaus II* [146 C3] *| Tel. 300 92 80)*. The second-largest football club, FC Union *(www.fc-union-berlin.de)*, plays two divisions below the Bundesliga at the stadium 'An der Alten Försterei' [147 E4] in Wuhlheide park in Köpenick. Tickets are available at advance booking offices and online. If you like basketball, then Bundesliga club Alba Berlin *(www.albaberlin.de)* is for you. Home games take place at the new O2-World arena *(Mühlenstrasse 12–30* [136 A–B4]*)* in Friedrichshain. Tickets: *Tel. 01805/57 00 11* and at the Max-Schmeling-Halle *(Mon–Fri 10 am–6 pm | Am Falkplatz* [128 C3] *| Tel. 300 90 50)*. Ice-hockey fans will enjoy watching the Eisbären (polar bears), German champions in 2009 *(www.eisbaeren.de)*. You can order tickets for DEL games under *Tel. 97 18 40 40* or online. Home venue is also the new O2-World arena at the Ostbahnhof (see above).

> GOOD NIGHT!

Hotels vie with each other in terms of luxury and service, but small guest houses are also booming

> If there's one branch in Berlin that's really booming, then it's tourism. The city has seldom welcomed as many visitors as in recent years, even in the days of the Wall. It's no wonder, then, that new hotels are mushrooming up all over the place.

Berlin can currently accommodate over 100,000 overnight guests! Architecturally speaking the hotels are also worth a closer look. Trendy designer hotels, such as the Q! or the Grand Hyatt on Potsdamer Platz, complete with wellness pool high above the roofs of the city, are setting new standards with regard to architecture and interior design.

One spectacular highlight is the Radisson Blu Hotel opposite the Berliner Dom. Here, there's a six-storey aquarium in the lobby with a lift built into the centre. The many small guest houses in the city have no need for such gimmicks. But they

Above: Hotel de Rome on Bebelplatz

ACCOMMODATION

have one advantage that money can't buy: their individual character. Knowing that the owner himself – or herself – stands in the kitchen and also serves the breakfast is worth more to many guests than any sumptuous buffet.

Thanks to the huge selection of hostels, private rooms and apartments, there's scarcely a cheaper place to stay than Berlin. Chains such as Motel One have a number of hotels in town, but small, privately run lodgings are also popular. So, even on a tight budget, you're sure of a good night's sleep.

Hotel information: *Tel. 25 00 25* | *www.visitberlin.de*.A list of hotels in the metropolis is available from *Berlin Tourismus Marketing* under the above telephone number or in writing from *Berlin Tourist Information (Am Karlsbad 11 | 10785 Berlin | www.visitberlin.de)*.

HOTELS €€€

BRISTOL HOTEL KEMPINSKI BERLIN [120 C4]

The classic hotel on Ku'damm. Comfortably furnished, it offers its guests a chance to relax. New: Berlin's biggest presidential suite over two floors. *302 rooms and suites | Charlottenburg | Kurfürstendamm 27 | Tel. 88 43 40 | Fax 883 60 75 | www.kempinski-berlin.de | U 1 | Uhlandstrasse*

ELLINGTON ★ [132 B6]

Laid-back, elegant, yet family-friendly luxury hotel around an idyllic summer garden in the inner courtyard. The first child under 12 sharing a room with two full-paying guests stays free of charge. Every other child pays 25 euros.*285 rooms and suites | Schöneberg | Nürnberger Strasse 50–55 | Tel. 68 31 50 | Fax 683 15 55 55 | www.ellington-hotel.com | U 1, 2, 3 | Wittenbergplatz*

Q! ★ [131 F6]

Opulent lounge design; even reception reminds you of the bar of a hip cocktail bar. Internationally acclaimed and much admired. *72 rooms | 4 studios | 1 penthouse | Charlottenburg | Knesebeckstrasse 67 | Tel. 810 06 60 | Fax 810 06 66 66 | www.loock-hotels.com/qhotel/ | U 1 | Uhlandstrasse*

RADISSON BLU ★ [123 E3]

The five-star hotel stands on the banks of the Spree, opposite the Berliner Dom. In the lobby you'll find the world's largest cylindrical aquarium with a capacity of one million litres of water. A lift takes you through the centre of this underwater world up to the 6th floor. *427 rooms Mitte | Karl-Liebknecht-Strasse 3 | Tel. 23 82 80 | Fax 238 28 10 | www.berlin.radissonblu.com | S-Bahn Hackescher Markt*

Futuristic lobby: Radisson Blu

HOTELS €€

ARTE LUISE KUNSTHOTEL ★ [122 B1]

Creative ambience: Each room in this art hotel has been designed by a different artist. What's more, comfort and homeliness have not been forgotten either. You don't have to be arty, though; the 'average' Berlin visitor stays here, too! *50 rooms | Mitte | Luisenstrasse 19 | Tel. 28 44 80 | Fax 28 44 84 48 | www.luise-berlin.com | U/S-Bahn Friedrichstrasse*

ARTEMISIA [139 E2]

All the rooms in this hotel are for female guests only. Tastefully decorated and with a roof terrace, ideal for relaxing after your city tour. *19 rooms Wilmersdorf | Brandenburgische Strasse 18 | Tel. 873 89 05 | Fax 861 86 53 | www.frauenhotel.info | U 7 | Konstanzer Strasse*

BOGOTA [120 B4]

Quiet hotel situated close to the Ku'damm which attracts many regular guests. Neat and tidy rooms, individual character, friendly service. *116 rooms Charlottenburg | Schlüterstrasse 45 | Tel. 881 50 01 | Fax 883 58 87 | www.hotel-bogota.de | U 7 | Adenauerplatz*

DORINT NOVOTEL AM TIERGARTEN [132 B4]

Modern hotel near the Tiergarten S-Bahn station. Unfussy, airy atmosphere. Attractive sauna area, plenty of non-smoking rooms and suitable for disabled guests. Up to two children sharing a room with their parents go free. *274 rooms | 11 suites | Tiergarten | Strasse des 17. Juni | Tel. 60 03 50 | Fax 60 03 56 66 | www.novotel.com | S 8, 9 & 75 | Tiergarten*

GATES BERLIN CITY WEST [120 C3]

Behind this pretty 'Gründerzeit' façade is a modern hotel with fast Internet access. Each room is equipped with a computer. There's also a bike rental service. *104 rooms | Charlottenburg | Knesebeckstrasse 8–9 | Tel. 31 10 60 | Fax 312 20 60 |*

MARCO POLO HIGHLIGHTS

★ Ellington
Modern, elegant atmosphere in historic office building (page 92)

★ Q!
Prize-winning design hotel with lounge character (page 92)

★ Radisson Blu
A huge aquarium towers up from the lobby to the 6th floor – wow! (page 92)

★ Arte Luise Kunsthotel
Creativity counts: Artists have given all 46 rooms their own imaginative look (page 92)

★ Hotel Concorde
Attractive designer rooms in star architect Jan Kleihues' new building (page 94)

★ Eastern Comfort
Guests are gently rocked to sleep on the hotel-boat (page 96)

★ Heart of Gold Hostel
Mitte's party hotspots close by, yet bright, quiet rooms for the medium to low budget (page 96)

★ Ackselhaus
Exotic: apartments with goldfish pond and Balinese garden (page 97)

HOTELS €€

www.hotel-gates.de | U 2 | Ernst-Reuter-Platz

Insider Tip **HOTEL FRIEDENAU** [120 C3]
Books line the walls of the breakfast room which is furnished with antiques and is also the venue for readings by well-known authors. Personal character. *18 rooms | Friedenau | Fregestrasse 68 | Tel. 859 09 60 | Fax 85 90 96 27 | www.hotel-friedenau.de | S 1, 25 | Friedenau*

IBIS BERLIN CITY OST [135 E5]
Centrally located on the banks of the Spree, this hotel offers good value for money. *242 rooms | Friedrichshain | An der Schillingbrücke 2 | Tel. 25 76 00 | Fax 25 76 03 33 | www.ibisberlin.de | S 8, 9, 75 | Ostbahnhof*

PARK INN BERLIN ALEXANDERPLATZ [123 F3]
Thirty-seven floors tower over Alexanderplatz. The rooms offer varying

> LUXURY HOTELS

Spend the night in style

ADLON KEMPINSKI [122 B3]
Superbly accomplished successor on the site of the original luxury hotel which was destroyed in the war. The service is not to be topped. *382 rooms and 78 suites | 224–12,500 euros | Mitte | Unter den Linden 77 | Tel. 226 10 | Fax 22 61 22 22 | www.hotel-adlon.de | S 1, 2, 25 | Brandenburger Tor*

HOTEL CONCORDE ★ [132 A5–6]
Purist, five-star designer hotel with generously proportioned rooms and suites close to the Gedächtniskirche. The Art-Deco-style, 17-storey building was designed by Jan Kleihues. *311 rooms and suites | 130–340 euros | Charlottenburg | Augsburger Strasse 41 | Tel. 800 99 90 | Fax 80 09 99 99 | www.concorde-hotels.com | U 3, 9 | Kurfürstendamm*

HOTEL DE ROME [134 B3]
New shrine to luxury next to the Staatsoper on Bebelplatz. The rooms and suites are furnished along modern lines, with elements reminiscent of the Schinkel tradition. Very attractive roof terrace with bar. *146 rooms and suites | 430–4,630 euros | Mitte | Behrenstrasse 37 | Tel. 46 06 09 20 00 | www.hotelderome.com | U 6 | Französische Strasse*

THE RITZ-CARLTON BERLIN [122 A4]
Top-class hotel in central location featuring classic design, large wellness area and pure luxury. *303 rooms and suites | 205–14,500 euros | Mitte | Potsdamer Platz 3 | Tel. 33 77 77 | Fax 337 77 55 55 | www.ritzcarlton.com/hotels/berlin | U-/S-Bahn | Potsdamer Platz*

SCHLOSSHOTEL IM GRUNEWALD [138 A5]
Elegant residence close to the Ku'damm with its own grounds, wellness area and gourmet restaurant. Karl Lagerfeld was responsible for the interior furnishings. The German national squad was based here during the World Cup in 2006. *53 rooms and suites | 239–3,000 euros | Wilmersdorf | Brahmsstrasse 10 | Tel. 89 58 40 | Fax 89 58 48 00 | www.schlosshotelberlin.com | S 7, 9 | Grunewald*

Schlosshotel im Grunewald: styling by Karl Lagerfeld

standards of comfort. Guests also get discount vouchers for the Galeria Kaufhof department store next door. There's a casino and a panorama terrace on the top floor. *1,012 rooms | Mitte | Alexanderplatz | Tel. 238 90 | Fax 23 89 43 05 | www.parkinn-berlin.de | U-/S-Bahn Alexanderplatz*

Insider Tip

HOTELS €

GASTEINER HOF [139 F4]
Small hotel in the west of the city. Reasonably priced double rooms with shared toilet facilities. *22 rooms | Wilmersdorf | Gasteiner Strasse 8 | Tel. 862 01 70 | www.gasteiner-hof.de | U 7 | Blissestrasse*

HOTEL DE FRANCE [147 D3]
Hotel formerly belonging to the Allied forces, now with discounts for schoolchildren and students. Pleasant rooms in 1960s building. *50 rooms | Wedding | Müllerstrasse 74 | Tel. 41 72 90 | www.hoteldefrance-berlin.de | U 6 | Rehberge*

INSEL RÜGEN [139 F2]
Charming guest house close to the Ku'damm with modest, but functional furnishings. Cosy dining room; lunch and/or evening meal can be booked for 8 euros each. *32 rooms | Wilmersdorf | Pariser Strasse 39–40 | Tel. 884 39 40 | www.insel-ruegen-hotel.de | U 1 | Uhlandstrasse*

MOTEL ONE [134 C2]
Designer hotel with reasonably priced rooms. Branches, for example, at Alexanderplatz (Mitte), on Moritzplatz (Kreuzberg) and near Schloss Bellevue (Tiergarten). *250 rooms | Charlottenburg | Kantstrasse 7–11a | Tel. 31 51 73 60 | www.motel-one.de | S 7, 9, 75 | Zoologischer Garten*

OSTEL [135 F4]
Pure (n)ostalgia! Typical 'Plattenbau' housing block, original GDR furniture and a portrait of Erich Honecker in the lobby. Located close to the Ostbahnhof, so good transport links.

43 rooms, 8 apartments | Friedrichshain | Wriezener Karree 5 | Tel. 25 76 86 60 | Fax 25 76 88 07 | www.ostel.eu | S 7, 8, 9 | Ostbahnhof

PETERS [120 C4]

Cosy non-smoking rooms – also for families – in a typical, old Berlin town house. Several decent restaurants nearby. *35 rooms | Charlottenburg | Kantstrasse 146 | Tel. 312 22 78 | Fax 312 35 19 | www.pension-petersberlin.de | S-Bahn Savignyplatz*

HOSTELS

A & O HOSTEL [136 C3]

Renovated brick-built hotel. Dormitory bed for 10 euros per night.

>LOW BUDGET

- The *WBM housing association* rents out ten pretty guest apartments at low rates in Mitte and Friedrichshain. *Scharnweber Strasse 23–27* [136 C3] | *Tel. 24 71 53 29 | www.wbm.de | U 5 | Samariterstrasse*
- A little off the beaten track, but idyllically placed on the banks of the Wannsee lake, the *Jugendherberge am Wannsee* also offers family rooms. Overnight stay from 15 euros per person. *Nikolassee | Badeweg 1* [0] | *Tel. 803 20 34 | www.jh-wannsee.de | S 1, 7 | Nikolassee*
- Stay the night in a hammock or a bed fit for a king – both are possible at the *Pension 11. Himmel*, located in a prefab concrete block in Marzahn. One night with breakfast: 22 euros. *5 rooms | Wittenberger Strasse 85 |* [147 E3] | *Tel. 93 77 20 52 | www.pension-11himmel.de | S 7 | Ahrensfelde*

International guests. *35 rooms | Friedrichshain | Boxhagener Strasse 73 | Tel. 297 78 10 | Fax 29 77 81 20 | www.aohostels.com | S 8, 9 | Ostkreuz*

EASTERN COMFORT ★ [136 A–B4]

Guests of the two small hotel-boats near the Oberbaumbrücke can experience sleeping on the Spree, but without the swell! *24 cabins | Mühlenstrasse 73–77 | Friedrichshain | Tel. 66 76 38 06 | Fax 66 76 38 05 | www.eastern-comfort.com | U-/S-Bahn Warschauer Strasse*

FABRIK [136 B5]

This is the ideal option for fans of Kreuzberg nightlife! Depending on room size, rates start at 18 euros. *45 rooms | Kreuzberg | Schlesische Strasse 18 | Tel. 611 82 54 | Fax 618 29 74 | www.diefabrik.com | U 1 | Schlesisches Tor*

GENERATOR [0]

Germany's biggest hostel, with over 900 beds, towers over the S-Bahn station Landsberger Allee. Overnight stay from 18.50 euros. *241 rooms | Prenzlauer Berg | Storkower Strasse 160 | Tel. 417 24 00 | Fax 41 72 40 80 | www.generatorhostels.com | S 41, 42 | Landsberger Allee*

HEART OF GOLD HOSTEL ★ [123 D1]

Close to the Oranienburger Strasse party zone, guests from all over the world find bright, quiet rooms in which an overnight stay costs from 15 euros. Stop over for more than six nights and get the seventh free. *140 rooms | Mitte | Johannisstrasse 11 | Tel. 29 00 33 00 | www.heartofgold-hostel.de | U 6 | Oranienburger Tor*

ACCOMODATION

Eastern Comfort: let the waves of the Spree rock you to sleep

APARTMENTS

ACKSELHAUS [129 D5]

Apartments with an Asian feel to them, a Balinese courtyard garden and goldfish pond. Rooms on the ground floor are accessed across stepping stones! To die for! *35 rooms | Prenzlauer Berg | Belforter Strasse 21 | Tel. 44 33 76 33 | Fax 441 61 16 | www.ackselhaus.de | U 2 | Senefelderplatz* | €€€

LUX ELEVEN [134 C2]

Ultra-modern apartment hotel: predominantly light colours and, in some cases, flat-screen TVs integrated into the walls. All apartments are equipped with a full-size kitchen (dishwasher, microwave oven). Ideal for a longer holiday. German-Mediterranean restaurant in the same building. *72 apartments | Mitte | Rosa-Luxemburg-Strasse 9–13 | Tel. 936 28 00 | Fax 93 62 80 80 | www.lux-eleven.com | U 8 | Weinmeisterstrasse* | €€€

PLATTE MITTE [134 C2] Insider Tip

The apartments on the 14th and 21st floor of the GDR prefabricated concrete high-rise, with a fine view of Alexanderplatz, the Fernsehturm and the Rotes Rathaus, are quite an experience. You can choose between rooms with furnishing styles of the 1960s, 1970s or the turn of the 20th century. *4 apartments | Mitte | Rochstrasse 9 | Tel. 0177/283 26 02 | www.plattemitte.de | U-/S-Bahn Alexanderplatz* | €

PRIVATE ROOMS

Private rooms and apartments can be booked on the Internet via *www.berlinzimmer.de*. The so-called 'Mitwohnagenturen', such as *Freiraum | Kreuzberg | Wiener Strasse 14 | Tel. 618 20 08 | Fax 618 20 06 | www.frei raum-berlin.com | U 1 | Görlitzer Bahnhof*, offer accommodation in temporarily empty apartments and rooms.

VOYAGE OF DISCOVERY

Kids love the city because there's a lot to discover and Berlin has plenty on that score. Enjoy yourself!

Insider Tip

BONBONMACHEREI [134 B2]

How are sweets actually made? In the demonstration workshop children can not only watch how the gooey candy is formed, but can also sample the still-warm sweets. Yummy! Of course you can also buy the finished products. *Wed–Sat noon–8 pm, closed Jul/Aug | Free admission | Mitte | Oranienburger Strasse 32 | Tel. 44 05 52 43| www.bonbonmacherei.de | S 1, 2, 25 | Oranienburger Strasse*

KINDERBAD MONBIJOU [134 B2]

Pretty paddling pool in the heart of Monbijoupark, reserved for children and accompanying adults. The pools are no deeper than 1.30 m. It's easy to get chatting to other parents at the poolside – ideal for practising your German! The over-15s are not allowed in the water, unless accompanying a child. *May–Sept: Mon–Fri 11 am–7 pm, Sat&Sun 10 am–7 pm | Admission: 4 euros | Mitte | Oranienburger Strasse 78 | Tel. 282 86 52| www.berlinerbaederbetriebe.de | S 1, 25 | Oranienburger Strasse*

KINDERINSEL [134 A1]

Would you like to do something without the children? Here, they are in good hands, either for an hour or more, or even overnight. Experienced teachers and a bright, friendly atmosphere make for plenty of fun for all involved. Children from 6 months to 14 years of age can be cared for. *Daily | Mitte | Eichendorffstrasse 17 | Tel. 41 71 69 28 | www.kinderinsel.de | 13 euros/hr; overnight: 69 euros; 50 per cent discount for brother/sister | U 6 | Naturkundemuseum*

KULTURPROJEKTE BERLIN

Almost all National Museums in Berlin put on regular children's tours and workshops about the art on display. At the Musical Instrument Museum, for example, children learn about the role of the different instruments in Sergej Prokofjew's 'Peter and the Wolf'. The museum staff has musical, art historical and pedagogical training and has no trouble getting the children interested. Up-to-the-minute

> TRAVELLING WITH KIDS

programme information on the Internet or from the Museums Educational Service. *Office: Mon–Fri 9 am–4 pm, Sat&Sun 9 am–1 pm | Mitte | Klosterstrasse 68 | Tel. 24 74 98 88 | www.kulturprojekte-berlin.de | U 2 | Klosterstrasse*

LOXX [135 D3]

One of the world's largest digitally-controlled model railways sets kids' hearts racing. ICEs, regional expresses, suburban S-Bahn trains and the like roll down four kilometres of track through a quaint Berlin landscape, complete with Brandenburger Tor, airport and a sea of houses. *Daily 10 am–8 pm | Admission: 9 euros, reduced: 4.50 euros | Mitte | Grunerstrasse 20 (in the Alexa shopping centre) | www.loxx-berlin.de | U-/S-Bahn Alexanderplatz*

MACH MIT! MUSEUM [129 E4]

The apse of this former church is now dominated by a huge, wooden climbing frame-cum-exhibition space. Printing press, 1920s soap shop, hall of mirrors – in the Children's Museum you'll come across the craziest things, and there's plenty to try out, too. Grown-ups are catered for in the family café. *Tues–Sun 10 am–6 pm | Admission: 4.50 euros, reduced: 3 euros | Prenzlauer Berg | Senefelderstrasse 5 | Tel. 74 77 82 00 | www.MachMitMuseum.de | S 41 | Prenzlauer Allee*

CITY TOURS FOR CHILDREN [127 D2] Insider Tip

On the trail of Emil and the Detectives or tracing the remains of the Wall: Stattreisen is a tour operator which gives children a good deal. Stories such as Erich Kästner's novel are linked in an entertaining way to the history of the city. The children become detectives, taking on the role of Emil or Pony-Hütchen, and discover that some places have changed considerably since the days before World War II when Emil was around. Office: *Mon–Fri 10 am–5 pm | Price: 5 euros | Wedding | Malplaquetstrasse 5 | Tel. 455 30 28 | www.stattreisen.de/berlin | U 6, 9 | Leopoldplatz*

> BETWEEN THE NEW MITTE AND THE OLD BORDER

On the trail of Berlin's history

The walks are marked in green on the map on the back cover and in the Street Atlas

1 WHERE THE WALL ONCE STOOD

Little visible evidence remains today to show that Berlin was once bisected by slabs of concrete and a mined border strip. In some places, however, it is still possible to sense the atmosphere of the divided city. A walk in Mitte between Checkpoint Charlie and Bahnhof Friedrichstrasse along the course of the Wall is particularly worthwhile. Duration: approx. 2 hours.

Above: Checkpoint Charlie on Friedrichstrasse

The walk begins at the former Checkpoint Charlie. All that is left of the border crossing point for visitors from the West is a small customs clearance hut and the oversized photographs of a Russian and an American soldier. The **Haus am Checkpoint Charlie** museum *(p.49)* gives an impressive documentary account of escape stories and living conditions in East and West. By sthe time it was brought down in 1989, 254 people

WALKING TOURS

had been killed by GDR border guards while trying to scale the Wall! With your back to the piled-up sand sacks, turn left into Zimmerstrasse; here, the Wall ran down the centre of the street, cutting off the view from one pavement to the other. The corner house is the oldest Baroque house in what was known as the Friedrichstadt district and was built in 1735, at first with one storey. On Zimmerstrasse you pass houses whose tenants could in effect enter the East by just reaching out of the window, since it was not the Wall which was the actual border, but an imaginary line which ran 2.5 m in front of it. Residents and passers-by were, strictly speaking, walking through East Berlin when they went down Zimmerstrasse. Cars were forbidden, and people had to carry their belongings up to 300 m, a fact which made things particularly difficult when moving house. This was a popular address, however, with tax exiles and criminals, since the police and other officials could not cross into East Berlin territory, and seizures of possessions were consequently impossible. The building with the brick façade on the other side of the border strip was the seat of the GDR foreign ministry, including a Stasi base and arms depot in the cellar.

We continue along Wilhelmstrasse towards the Martin-Gropius-Bau. Here stands one of the last sections of the 4-m-high Wall. The concrete slab is badly chipped and full of holes where souvenir hunters have broken out lumps to take home. The parts emblazoned with graffiti are particularly sought-after – the Wall was, after all, considered during the GDR regime to be the longest art gallery in the world, at least on the Western side. There's hardly a notable contemporary artist who didn't take the opportunity to decorate the Wall with some kind of image. The most famous Wall painters include Thierry Noir and Keith Haring.

On your left is the open-air exhibition **Topographie des Terrors** *(p.50)*. From here, at the former Gestapo and SS headquarters, the Nazis coordinated their reign of terror. Surely few other sites in the world have seen the planning and implementation of so many atrocities, acts of torture and murders.

The **Martin-Gropius-Bau** *(p.50)*, the former Arts and Crafts Museum, which was opened in 1881 and badly damaged in World War II, today stages changing exhibitions on historical, scientific and art historical themes. It was named after its architect, the great-uncle of the famous Bauhaus architect Walter Gropius. The Wall once blocked off the main entrance, so visitors to the museum had to use the back door. The building opposite, in the Italian High Renaissance style – then, too, on the Eastern side of the Wall – has been home since 1993 to the **Berliner Abgeordnetenhaus** (House of Representatives). It was inaugurated in 1892 as the seat of its Prussian forerunner. The severe war damage was repaired in a very make-shift fashion by the GDR authorities before it became part of the adjoining the **Haus der Ministerien** (House of Ministries). Look out for the squares of copper set into the ground which mark the course of the Wall. On Stresemannstrasse, **Potsdamer Platz** *(p.43)* comes into view on the right. Today, new buildings mask the original course of the Wall; it's left to a line of cobble stones along Stresemannstrasse to hark back to the divided city.

The area where the Sony and Daimler blocks today tower into the sky was once just a vast expanse of wasteland. In the days of the Wall, only two buildings stood on this 480,000-sq-m site, Weinhaus Huth and a small part of the once chic Hotel Esplanade. Until it was bombed out in World War II, this had been the busiest traffic intersection in Europe, a fact which necessitated the introduction of Berlin's first set of traffic lights in 1925. A tower at the entrance to the S-Bahn station commemorates this milestone in urban development.

Continue your walk along Ebertstrasse towards **Pariser Platz**. On the

Favourite venue for mega events: street party at the Brandenburger Tor

right are the so-called **Ministergärten**, around a grouping of federal state offices. Alongside is the **Denkmal für die ermordeten Juden Europas** *(p.41)*, designed by New York architect Peter Eisenman.

Arriving at the **Brandenburger Tor** *(p. 40)*, we recommend you stop for a break and visit the 'Raum der Stille' (quiet room) which is located in the northernmost column. Here, you can give your tired feet a well-earned rest!

It's hard to imagine that only 22 years ago no one was allowed to pass through the Brandenburg Gate since it stood in no-man's land between East and West. The first joint New Year's Eve celebrations in 1989–90 saw over 2 million revellers milling around the Gate. The buildings to the north are new, even if they don't look it. If you fancy a coffee or a bite to eat, you should pop into the **Theodor Tucher** café *(p.63)* where you'll find a gallery full of tempting books to browse through and comfortable armchairs to sink into. Suitably revitalised, head for the **Reichstag** *(p.44)*, now the seat of the Federal Government, the Bundestag. From the cupola visitors have a sensational view across the city centre. The Wall once ran behind the parliament building on the Spree side. Opposite the Reichstag, behind the Marie-Elisabeth-Lüders-Haus, stands the memorial entitled 'Parliament of Trees against War and Violence', conceived in 1990 by Berlin eco-artist Ben Wargin. It consists of sections of Wall and trees planted in a square formation. From the riverside path you now continue past the Berlin studios of the ARD television company towards the station at Friedrichstrasse and the end of this walk.

2 A STROLL THROUGH BERLIN'S HISTORY: THE SPANDAUER VORSTADT

The name says it all: the 'Spandau suburb' was established as a new development area and so named in the 18th century because of its location beyond the city gate leading to Spandau. Today it is home to numerous media companies and trendy boutiques and bars. Duration: approx. 1 hour

The Scheunenviertel (barn district), which is today considered part of the Spandauer Vorstadt, lies to the north of the S-Bahn station Hackescher Markt. In the 18th century a string of barns stood outside the city gates. It was hoped that by locating them outside the city boundary, the danger of major fires within the city could be averted. Originally, activities centred on agriculture and trade, but the suburb became increasingly urbanised over the years. The 'golden' era of the 1920s saw a blossoming in terms of culture and craftsmanship. Religious tolerance was the norm, and many Jews, principally from Eastern Europe, lived in the Scheunenviertel to the east. At present, the district is picking up the threads of this tradition with its many theatres, craft industries, shops and cafés.

The **S-Bahn station Hackescher Markt**, where our walk begins, stands almost exactly on the old city boundary; the S-Bahn tracks and the main-line rail services between the Jannowitzbrücke and Friedrichstrasse run along the foundations of the original city wall. The station takes it name from the then military governor of the city, von Hacke, who had this marshy land drained in the middle of the 18th century. He also gave his name to the **Hackesche Höfe** *(p. 32)* which are located opposite the station concourse. Europe's largest courtyard complex, made up of eight interlinked courtyards arranged in series, has lots of culture and crafts on offer. If you cross all eight courtyards you will reach Sophienstrasse, on the other side, a prettily renovated street which was given a make-over in the 1980s on the orders of the East Berlin authorities to mark the city's 750th birthday celebrations. At the same time, however, the Spandauer Vorstadt just round the corner was left to sink into decay. Turning left, after some 50 m, you pass the churchyard of the **Sophienkirche** which boasts the oldest Baroque church tower in the city. On the right stands the **Handwerksvereinshaus** (trade corporation building): built in 1844, it was home to Berlin's first independent labour organisation. Up to 3,000 people could meet and debate in its halls. In the 1920s, in particular, it was the location for Communist, Social Democrat and National Socialist party conferences.

Just a few metres on, our route takes you through an archway into the **Sophie-Gips-Höfe**. Media agencies, galleries and gastronomic outlets have set up shop here. The concept of living, working and playing under one roof, as widely practised in Berlin in the past, is very much alive and kicking here. The rear exit of the courtyard ensemble leads into **Gipsstrasse**. This is one of the oldest streets in the Spandauer Vorstadt. It used to be the site of a plaster works (Gips = plaster), which gave it its current name. Following the street to the left, you pass a number of *Gründerzeit* residences which have now been renovated. Don't forget to take a look into the rear courtyards which often feature single-storey outbuildings.

Turn into Auguststrasse and then, after around 50 m, left into the **Grosse Hamburger Strasse**. In the 1920s it was famous for its harmonious residential mix of Jews, Protestants and Catholics. On the right-hand side, the attractive brick façade of the **St.-Hedwig-Krankenhaus** (hospital) comes into view. It was built in 1888 to care for the elderly and infirm and was dedicated to St. Hedwig, who was renowned for her work with the poor and sick during the Christianisation of Silesia in the 12th century. At No. 27 the Jewish Community runs a school. Next to the school there was originally a Jewish cemetery which was converted in 1827 into a park serving the former Jewish home for the aged, which today no longer exists. It was from the home that the SS organised a large proportion of the deportations to the concentration camps. A commemorative plaque and a sculpture pay tribute to the 56,000 Berlin Jews who were sent to the death camps. Opposite the former cemetery, **house No. 19a** rates as the oldest house in the Spandauer Vorstadt. At the end of the Grosse Hamburger Strasse you turn left into Oranienburger Strasse. After about 100 m you will see the Hackescher Markt again, the end of this tour.

An intimate corner: Sophie-Gips-Höfe in the Spandauer Vorstadt

A DAY IN BERLIN

Non-stop action and one-off experiences. On tour with our scene scout

INTO THE BLUE BY MOTOR BOAT

9:00

Racing across a smooth, glassy lake in a motor boat, the wind in your hair: a dream which can come true in Berlin, even without a licence. Anyone can go for a spin on the romantic Müggelsee lake. Don't forget your bikini, swimming trunks and a picnic! **WHERE?** *Rent a boat at Bootsverleih Spreepoint | Müggelseedamm 70 | S-Bahn Friedrichshagen | Tel. 641 12 91 | From approx. 17 euros per hour | www.bootsverleih-spreepoint.de*

12:30

HELIUM HIGH FLYER

Noiselessly, the basket rises 150 m into the Berlin sky, suspended from one of the biggest helium balloons in the world. A steel cable keeps you in touch with mother Earth. Sensational views! **WHERE?** *At Checkpoint Charlie | Wilhelmstrasse/ Zimmerstrasse | Apr–Oct daily 10 am–10 pm, Nov–Mar 11 am–6 pm | Wind hotline: 226 67 88 11 | 19 euros | www.air-service-berlin.de*

LUNCH WITH THE IN-CROWD

13:00

Down to earth and off to hip Kastanienallee, not without reason dubbed 'casting alley': it's time for a break! Ideally over lunch at 103, the 24-hr chilling zone for anybody who's anybody. **WHERE?** *Café Bar 103 | Kastanienallee 49 | www.agentur103.de*

SHOPPING STOP

15:00

In between times it's worth stopping off at Berlin's coolest concept store, The Corner. You'll find designer fashion, coffee table books and music. If you fancy a drink, just head for the bar. **WHERE?** *Französische Strasse 40 | www.thecornerberlin.de*

16:00

DARK DEPTHS

A green door is the entrance to Berlin's underworld. Without a torch, you're done for: labyrinthine passageways, dingy bunkers, dark shafts and abandoned stations feature on your route. **WHERE?** *Berliner Unterwelten | Meeting point: Brunnenstrasse 105 | www.berliner-unterwelten.de*

24h

HIT THE JACK

18:00

On the Paul-Lincke-Ufer in Kreuzberg it's time to get out those boules! Fans get together here every day, whatever the weather. Beginners and professionals alike (including the German Champion) endeavour to get as close as possible to the jack. Tip: Every Friday at 6.30 pm in spring and summer, ad hoc teams battle it out. **WHERE?** *Between Forster Strasse and Liegnitzer Strasse*

20:00

GERMAN TAPAS

Is your stomach rumbling? You can't beat German tapas! The typical Spanish titbits are translated into 18 German variations at the *Schnitzelei* – from Königsberger Klopsen (meatballs) and Wirsingrouladen (beef olives in savoy cabbage) to plums wrapped in bacon. **WHERE?** *Röntgenstrasse 7 | www.schnitzelei.de*

SING-IN

21:30

Have you oiled your vocal chords? Then grab the mike! At *Monster Ronson's Ichiban Karaoke* there's no need to be shy. Hire a private booth and warble away without an audience. **WHERE?** *Warschauer Strasse 34 | www.karaoke monster.com*

23:00

GOOD VIBES

Spacy! A glass-sided lift glides up the façade to the 17th floor. Here, probably the finest lounge in Berlin awaits you – das Solar, where the DJ serves up smooth sounds. Still not had enough? Then get down to the Klub der Republik, the cult party venue with GDR ambience! **WHERE?** *Solar | Stresemannstrasse 76 | www. solarberlin.com | Klub der Republik | Pappelallee 81 | Tues–Sun from 8 pm | www.myspace.com/klubderrepublik*

> PRUSSIAN GLORY

The countryside around Berlin is not only characterised by forest and water, but also palatial residences

The outings are marked in green on the map on the back cover and in the Street Atlas

1 KÖPENICK

[147 E4] **Characterised by its waterside location, the district of Köpenick in Berlin's southeast is best known thanks to the story of the phony captain who confiscated the town's treasury in 1906. Köpenick has been part of Berlin since 1920 and has retained its own particular charm. Apart from the picturesque old town with its castle, the Müggelsee lake is a multi-faceted choice for a day trip.**

Ideally, you should arrive in Köpenick by water. Boats run by the Stern- und Kreisschifffahrt *(www.sternundkreis.de)* operate every hour in summer from the Treptower Hafen. In precisely 60 minutes, the pleasure boats cruise up the Spree, past industrial plants from GDR times, the Plänterwald forest and idyllic riverside properties. Visitors to Köpenick

Above: Palace Gardens at Babelsberg

OUTINGS

disembark at the centrally located Luisenhain landing stage. Directly opposite is the famous red-brick **Rathaus** (Town Hall). In 1906, one year after its inauguration, unemployed shoemaker Wilhelm Voigt was tempted to enter the building clad in captain's uniform, arrest the mayor and steal the town's coffers. An exhibition in the Rathaus *(daily 10 am–5.30 pm | Free admission)* documents the tale, which was the inspiration behind Carl Zuckmayer's folk play The Captain of Köpenick. The story is re-enacted every Wednesday and Saturday at 11 am in front of the Rathaus.

Some 200 m to the south is the magnificent, renovated **Köpenicker Schloss**, a 17th-century moated castle, once erected for the subsequent King of Prussia, Frederick I. A branch of Berlin's *Kunstgewerbemuseum (Tues–Sun 10 am–6 pmAdmission: 4* *euros)* is now housed here, showcasing historical arts and crafts. The **Schlosspark** with its pretty café is ideal for taking a break and enjoying the view of the **Frauentog**, a bay in the River Dahme. At the **Solar Boat Pavilion** *(Mar–Oct: 10 am–7 pm | www.solarwaterworld.de)* you can rent a solar-powered boat, for as little as 10 euros per hour, and silently cruise Spree and Dahme. From the water you can see the **Fischerkiez**, a pretty neighbourhood on the eastern bank of the Frauentog, with historic fishermen's cottages and the lido, **Flussbadeanstalt Krokodil** *(May–Sept: daily 10 am–6 pm | Admission: 3 euros).*

Pleasure boats leave Luisenhain for the **Müggelsee**. You can also get to Berlin's largest lake in 20 minutes by taking tram 60 or 61 in the direction of the Altes Wasserwerk. Get off at the Bölschestrasse/Am Wasserwerk stop and walk the 300 m to the lake and its beer garden, beach bar and small but excellent French restaurant, *Domaines (www.domaines-berlin.de | €€)*. Go through the Spreetunnel to get to the western shore of the lake, where you'll find a number of bathing areas. A stroll along the lakeside will take you to the *Rübezahl tourist café*. From here, passenger boats travel back to Friedrichshagen every hour during the summer season. The quickest way back to Berlin's inner city is with the S-Bahn from the station at Friedrichshagen.

Köpenick Tourist Information | Mon–Fri 9 am–6.30 pm, Sat 10 am to 1 pm; summer also Sun 10 am to 1 pm | Alt-Köpenick 31–33 (Am Schlossplatz) | Tel. 65 57 55 01 | www.berlin-tourismus-online.de

2 POTSDAM

[146 B4–5] The capital of the state of Brandenburg owes its charm to chic villas, beautiful palaces and Prussian military history. Potsdam is situated to the southwest of Berlin on the opposite bank of the River Havel and can be reached by S-Bahn (S 1, every 10 minutes).

Once seat of the Prussian kings, the town can boast a unique cultural and garden landscape. Since 1990 large parts of Potsdam have been declared part of the World Heritage by UNESCO, including the landscaped gardens at Sanssouci, the Neuer Garten, Babelsberg palace and, on the Berlin side of the Havel, Glienicke palace and hunting lodge. The park at ★ *Schloss Sanssouci* is held to be a superb example of French- and Italian-style landscape gardening. This is where our tour begins. The express bus service X15 (Apr–Oct) connects the railway station Potsdam Stadt (also the terminus for the S-Bahn from Berlin) and the park; stop: Schloss Sanssouci (in winter: bus route 695).

The palace – a summer residence for Frederick II (the Great) – was completed in only two years (1745 to 47). For the young king, the relatively small Schloss Sanssouci (Eng: 'without cares') was to serve as a place of relaxation. It was here that he passed the summer with philosophy, music and literature and received his guests.

In addition to Schloss Sanssouci Frederick II commissioned other buildings, including **Neues Palais** and the **Chinesische Teehaus**. The Palais was the last and also largest 18th-century addition to the park. It was constructed between 1763 and 1769; Frederick the Great's intention here was to demonstrate that the Silesian wars had not lessened his power. A walk through the park takes you past the **Orangerie** and numerous themed gardens.

A signposted, 15-minute walk takes you from the eastern park entrance into the town centre. The Holländisches Viertel begins at the Nauener Tor. The Dutch quarter was built in 1732–42 for Dutch immigrant workers brought to Potsdam by the 'Soldier King' Frederick William I. He badly needed skilled craftsmen to help extend his garrison town. Today the district is especially popular due to its colourful mixture of small shops and pubs.

Take bus route 692 from Nauener Tor to **Schloss Cecilienhof**, where the 1945 Potsdam Conference of the four victorious allies took place. Alongside an exhibition about the conference, the palace also houses a hotel with a good restaurant *(daily noon–9.30 pm | Tel. 0331/370 50 | €€)*. Modelled on the Tudor-style English country houses, Cecilienhof was constructed in 1914–17 for Crown Prince William and his wife Cecilie, and was the last palace to be commissioned by the Hohenzollern dynasty.

Typical bell gables in the Holländisches Viertel in Potsdam

Insider Tip

Potsdam Tourist Information | Apr to Oct: Mon–Fri 9.30 am–6 pm, Sat& Sun 9.30 am–4 pm; Nov–Mar: Mon to Fri 10 am–6 pm, Sat&Sun 10 am to 2 pm | Brandenburger Strasse 3 | Tel. 0331/27 55 80 | www.potsdam.de

> FROM BANKS TO TIMEZONES

Holiday from start to finish: useful addresses and information for your trip to Berlin

BANKS

A number of banks are now also open on Saturdays until 2 pm. Banking hours in most branches are generally *Mon–-Fri 10 am–5 pm.* Cash is available as usual around the clock from cash dispensers.

EMERGENCY TELEPHONE NUMBERS IN CASE OF EC OR CREDIT CARD LOSS

– *Amex, EC, Eurocard: Tel. 11 61 16*
– *Diners Club: Tel. 01805-07 07 04*
– *Visa card: Tel. 0800-811 84 40*

BICYCLE & VELOTAXI

The ideal way to discover the city under your own steam is by bike. Bicycles can be hired at most inner-city dealers. 'Call a Bike', a practical service offered by the German railway company, Deutsche Bahn, has eye-catching, metallic-painted DB bikes stationed around the city. Just pick a bike, take your mobile phone, dial *07000/522 55 22* or register online at *www.callabike.de* and state your credit card number. A radio signal releases the bike lock, and you're off! Five euros are deducted immediately to get you going. The basic rate is then 8 cents per minute, (max. 15 euros per day (24 hrs)), based on the time between the booking and return calls. When you've had enough, just park the bike – it's a simple as that.

If you would prefer not to peddle yourself, you could just hire a *Biketaxi* (bicycle rickshaw). They operate between March and October on two routes: in Charlottenburg from Ku'damm towards Schöneberg and in the east from Potsdamer Platz via Brandenburger Tor to Alexanderplatz. A half-hour, individual tour costs 18 euros. Book in advance under *Tel. 89 23 55 00 77 (www.biketaxi.de)*. Or just stop an unoccupied rickshaw on the street and hop in! The first kilometre costs 5 euros, thereafter there's an hourly rate.

BREAKDOWN SERVICES

ALLGEMEINER DEUTSCHER AUTOMOBILCLUB (ADAC)

– *ADAC info service: Tel. 0180-5101112 (0.12 euros/min.)*
– *ADAC breakdown service: Tel. 0180-222 22 22*

CUSTOMS

Travellers from within the EU are no longer subject to customs checks. Visitors from other countries must observe the following limits, except for items for personal use. Duty free are: max. 50 g perfume, 200 cigarettes, 50 cigars, 250 g tobacco, 1 l of spirits (over 22% vol.), 2 l of spirits (under 22% vol.), 2 l of any wine. Gifts to the value of up to 175 euros may be brought into Germany.

DRIVING

Drivers require a valid driving licence and vehicle documentation. It is advisable to carry an international green insurance card. The statutory speed limits are as follows: highways: 130 km/h (80 mph) (recommended); overland: 80/100 km/h (50 mph/62 mph); built-up areas: 50 km/h (30 mph). The maximum level of alcohol in the blood is 0.5 mg/l. The wearing of seatbelts is compulsory for all drivers and passengers.

EMBASSIES

UK

Mitte | Wilhelmstrasse 70–71 | 10117 Berlin | Tel. 20 45 70 | S-Bahn Unter den Linden | Bus 100 | Unter den Linden S-Bahn

USA

Mitte | Neustädtische Kirchstrasse 4–5 | 10117 Berlin | Tel. 830 50 | S-Bahn Unter den Linden | Bus 100 | Unter den Linden Glinkastrasse

CANADA

Mitte | Leipziger Platz 17 | 10117 Berlin | Tel. 20 31 20 | U-/S-Bahn Potsdamer Platz

EMERGENCIES

24-hr emergency doctor:
Tel. 31 00 31
Fire brigade: Tel. 112
Poisons hotline: Tel. 192 40
Police: Tel. 110
Wheelchair breakdown service:
Tel. 0177-833 57 73
Spiritual guidance: 0800-111 01 11
Emergency dental service:
Tel. 89 00 43 33

EURO

Legal tender in Germany is the euro. One euro = 100 cents. Bank notes to the value of 5, 10, 20, 50, 100, 200 and 500 euros and coins to the value of 1, 2, 5, 10, 20, 50 cents and 1 and 2 euros are in circulation.

WHAT DOES IT COST?

COFFEE	2–3 EUROS	a cup in a café
ICE-CREAM	2 EUROS	two scoops of ice-cream
WINE	3–7 EUROS	a glass of wine
DONER	2.50–3 EUROS	a doner-kebab
MUSEUM	4–8 EUROS	admission to state-owned museums
BUS RIDE	2.10 EURO	a single bus ticket

GETTING TO BERLIN

BY CAR

The highways serving Berlin have been brought up to a good standard: the A2 from Hanover to the west is even six-lane. Traffic jams are, however, a big problem on the orbital highway. The city centre, within the inner S-Bahn ring, is now a so-called 'Umweltzone' (environmental zone). With effect from 1 January 2010, only cars bearing a green sticker can drive in this area. For further information, visit *www.umwelt-plakette.de*.

BY RAIL

The most comfortable way to arrive overland. Express trains (ICE and IC) from all over Europe arrive every hour at the following stations: Berlin-Spandau, Hauptbahnhof and Ostbahnhof. There is an overnight link from London, via Brussels. The new main railway station is Europe's largest and was opened in 2006. Travel information: *Tel. 0800-1507090 | www.bahn.de*

BY BUS

Coaches are often a cheap alternative to train travel, and there are frequent links from major cities and towns in Germany and several weekly connections with the rest of Europe, including a Eurolines overnight service from London, via Brussels and Hanover. Berlin's *main bus station (ZOB)* is in Charlottenburg, opposite the exhibition grounds at the Funkturm [130 B5]. *Information: Tel. 86 09 62 11 | www.berlinlinienbus.de*

BY AIR

Following the closure of Tempelhof, tourists can reach Berlin via two airports. Most flights currently land at and take off from *Tegel* [124 C1] in the northwest of the city. From here it is just a roughly 15-minute ride with the express bus to the Kurfürstendamm. *Schönefeld* [147 E5] handles largely charter flights and connections to and from Eastern Europe. When Schönefeld is extended as planned by 2011, to become the new Berlin Brandenburg International Airport, Tegel will be closed, since it lies too close to residential areas. Direct flights from the USA depart from New York. Visitors from Canada fly, say, via London or Frankfurt. Check with your local travel agent for details. *Flight information: 0180/ 500 01 86 (0.14 euros/min.) | www.berlin-airport.de*

INFORMATION

BERLIN TOURISMUS MARKETING GMBH

Karlsbad 11 | 10785 Berlin | Tel. 25 00 25 | www.visitberlin.de

Branches at: Mitte | Pariser Platz (Brandenburg Gate, south wing) | daily 10 am–6 pm | Mitte | Grunerstrasse 20 (in the Alexa Shopping-center) | Mon–Sat 10 am–10 pm | Mitte | Hauptbahnhof | Europaplatz 1 | daily 8 am to 10 pm | Charlottenburg | Kranzler-Eck | Passage Kurfürstendamm 21 | daily 10 am–6 pm

Berlin Tourist Information call centre: Mon–Fri 9 am–7 pm, Sat 10 am to 6 pm | Tel. 030-25 00 25 | Fax 25 00 24 24

INTERNET

www.berlin.de – Information on sights, museums and events. Tickets, weather and traffic information also available.

www.zitty.de – Internet version of the listings magazine of the same name (German only).

www.berlin-tourist-information.de – Comprehensive service, including information on opening times, emergency pharmacies, theatre and concert programmes and much more.

www.smb.spk-berlin.de – Website of the National Museums of Berlin.

www.reiseland-brandenburg.de – Site by the tourist information authorities in Berlin's neighbouring federal state, Brandenburg.

INTERNETCAFÉS

There is a raft of cafés and pubs with Wi-Fi connectivity.

AL HAMRA [129 D3]

Surf and smoke shisha or drink cocktails at the same time: 2 euros/hr, use of Wi-Fi hot spots free. *Daily from 9 am | Raumerstrasse 16 | Prenzlauer Berg | Tel. 42 85 00 95www.alhamra.de | S-Bahn Prenzlauer Allee*

LOG-IN-CAFÉ [131 F5]

Fifteen computers at which you can not only surf, but also scan, burn disks and try out new PC games for 3 euros/hr. *Open 24 hrs | Charlottenburg | Knesebeckstrasse 38–49 | Tel. 883 39 12 | www.log-in-cafe.de | S-Bahn Savignyplatz*

SURF & SUSHI [132 A5]

While you're chatting for free at one of the terminals, the friendly staff serve caffè latte or sushi. *Daily noon–1 am | Mitte | Oranienburger Strasse 17 | Tel. 28 38 48 98 | S 1, 2 & 25 | Oranien-burger Strasse*

LOST PROPERTY

POLICE [142 A5]

Tempelhof | Platz der Luftbrücke 6 | Tel. 902 77 31 01 | U 6 | Platz der Luftbrücke

DEUTSCHE BAHN/S-BAHN

Döppersberg 37| 42103 Wuppertal | Service hotline: 0900-199 05 99 (0.59 euros/min. from German fixed-line network)

BERLIN TRANSPORT AUTHORITY BVG [141 D3]

Schöneberg | Potsdamer Strasse 180 | Tel. 25 62 30 40 | U 7 | Kleistpark

MEDICAL SERVICES

British nationals can claim any health service costs incurred in Germany on returning home. Be sure to apply for the EHIC (European Health Insurance Card), which replaced the old E111 form in 2005, before leaving Britain. US and Canadian nationals should check with their health Insurance company to see whether they are covered for trips abroad and, if so, should be sure to carry proof of cover with them.

PASSPORT & VISA

Visas are not required for EU citizens; citizens of the USA or Canada require a visa only if staying for longer than three months. A valid identity card or passport is sufficient to allow entry into Germany.

POST & TELEPHONE

The international dialling code for Germany is *010 49* (from Great Britain) and *001 49* (from the USA and Canada). Within Germany the area code for Berlin is *030*. From Berlin, dial *0044* for Great Britain and *001* for the USA and Canada.

Most post offices in Berlin are open as follows: *Mon–Fri 9 am to 6 pm, Sat until 1 pm.* Outside these times, the following have extended opening times:

POSTAMT HAUPTBAHNHOF [133 E2]
Mon–Fri 7 am–10 pm, Sat&Sun 8 am–10 pm | Tiergarten | Europaplatz 1 | S-Bahn Hauptbahnhof

POSTAMT MITTE [122 C2]
Mon–Fri 6 am–10 pm, Sat&Sun 8 am to 10 pm | Mitte | Georgenstrasse 12 | U-/S-Bahn Friedrichstrasse

PUBLIC TRANSPORT

On Fridays and Saturdays almost all U-Bahn services operate around the clock. Beyond the U-Bahn network, night buses are in operation to ferry guests back to their hotel beds! S-Bahn trains usually run until 1 am.

Berlin's public transport network is divided into three tariff zones. A and B cover the whole city and C covers the outskirts, including Potsdam. A single ticket currently costs (A) 2.10 euros, (reduced fare: 1.40 euros); a day ticket costs 6.10 euros. Tariffs have changed frequently in recent years, so it's a good idea to check in advance: *Berlin Transport Authority (BVG)*: *Tel. 194 49 | www.bvg.de*

An ideal alternative for families is the Berlin Tourismus Marketing GmbH's *Welcome Card.* Valid for 3 days, at a price of 25 euros, the card entitles you to free travel in Berlin and Potsdam on buses and trains within the Berlin-Brandenburg transport authority and vouchers give you free or reduced admission to many sights and attractions. Adults with a valid Welcome Card can take up to three children under 14 with them. Adults only pay 22 euros. The Welcome Card is available online from *www.visitberlin.de*, and at S-Bahn, BVG, DB Regio AG ticket offices and at tourist information centres run by the Berlin Tourismus Marketing GmbH and from many Berlin hotels.

SIGHTSEEING TOURS

The best way to get an impression of the city is to take the bus. A cheap alternative is a journey on route 100 from Bahnhof Zoo to Alexanderplatz.

WEATHER IN BERLIN

	Jan	Feb	Mar	Apr	May	June	July	Aug	Sept	Oct	Nov	Dec
Daytime temperatures in °C/F	2/36	3/37	8/46	13/55	19/66	22/72	24/73	23/73	19/66	13/55	7/45	3/37
Night-time temperatures in °C/F	-3/27	-3/27	0/32	4/40	8/46	12/54	14/57	13/55	10/50	6/43	2/36	-1/30
Sunshine: hours per day	2	2	5	6	8	8	8	7	6	4	2	1
Rainfall: days per month	11	9	8	9	9	9	11	9	8	9	10	9

It takes you past the most important sights in the city centre.
Guided tours:

BEROLINA SIGHTSEEING
City-Circle-Tour with 16 stopping points, at which you can join or leave the tour. Buses run in summer every 15 minutes between 10 am and 4 pm. Day ticket: 20 euros, half-day ticket: 15 euros; Start: Kurfürstendamm/ Meinekestrasse. *Information: Tel. 88 56 80 30 | U 9, 15 | Kurfürstendamm | www.berolina-berlin.com*

LÜGENTOUR
'Lügen' are lies, and guide Christa Saffrahn does slip in the occasional untruth among the facts on her tours through Kreuzberg, Mitte or round Potsdamer Platz. Participants have to guess what's true and what isn't. Good fun, and you learn a lot in the process. *10 euros/person | Tel. 0179/ 920 44 59 | www.luegentour.de*

PANORAMA-BAHN
A real gem of a tour is a moderated round trip with the *Panorama-Bahn* (Sat&Sun). Tickets are available online under *www.s-bahn-berlin.de* and from S-Bahn customer service centres at Alexanderplatz and Ostbahnhof *(Tel. 29 74 36 86). Fare: 16 euros, children: 9.50 euros*

Insider Tip
PLATTENBAU-TOUR
This tour of Marzahn (2 hrs) gives you an insight into life in a typical, GDR pre-fab block of flats. You can take a look at an apartment, furnished in 1970s style, too. *15 euros/person | Tel. 28 09 76 55 | www.pionier-berlin.de*

TAXI-WALL-FAHRTEN
Insider Tip
Thomas Lehman takes his passengers on a two-hour taxi 'pilgrimage' on the trail of the Berlin Wall. The highly personal tour, including interesting commentaries on the history of the city, features stops at historically important sites. Price: 60 euros/passenger; each additional passenger: 10 euros. *Tel. 0160/95 32 80 52 | www.taxi-wall-fahrten.de*

TAXIS

The basic tariff is 3.20 euros; the normal rate for the first 7 km is 1.65 euros/ km, then 1.28 euros for every further km. Short trips of less than 2 km, lasting no longer than 10 minutes, cost 4 euros per trip. Note: these tariffs are only valid for taxis flagged down on the street.

THEATRE & CONCERT TICKETS

Last-minute theatre- and concert-goers can find tickets at half-price, even shortly before the performance begins, at *HEKticket.* Cheaper tickets for museums, too, (e.g. for Madame Tussauds) are also to be had. There's a branch at Bahnhof Zoo *(Hardenbergstrasse 29d | Tel. 230 99 30 | www.hekticket.de).* Insider Tip

All branches of Karstadt, Hertie and Wertheim department stores and KaDeWe sell *Showtime-Konzert- und Theaterkassen* tickets for all cultural events in Berlin, *Tel. 80 60 29 29 | www.showtimetickets.de*

TIME ZONES

Germany is six hours ahead of US Eastern Standard Time and one hour ahead of Greenwich Mean Time.

Bundeskanzleramt

> ON THE ROAD IN BERLIN

Please refer to the back cover
for an overview of this Street Atlas

STREET ATLAS

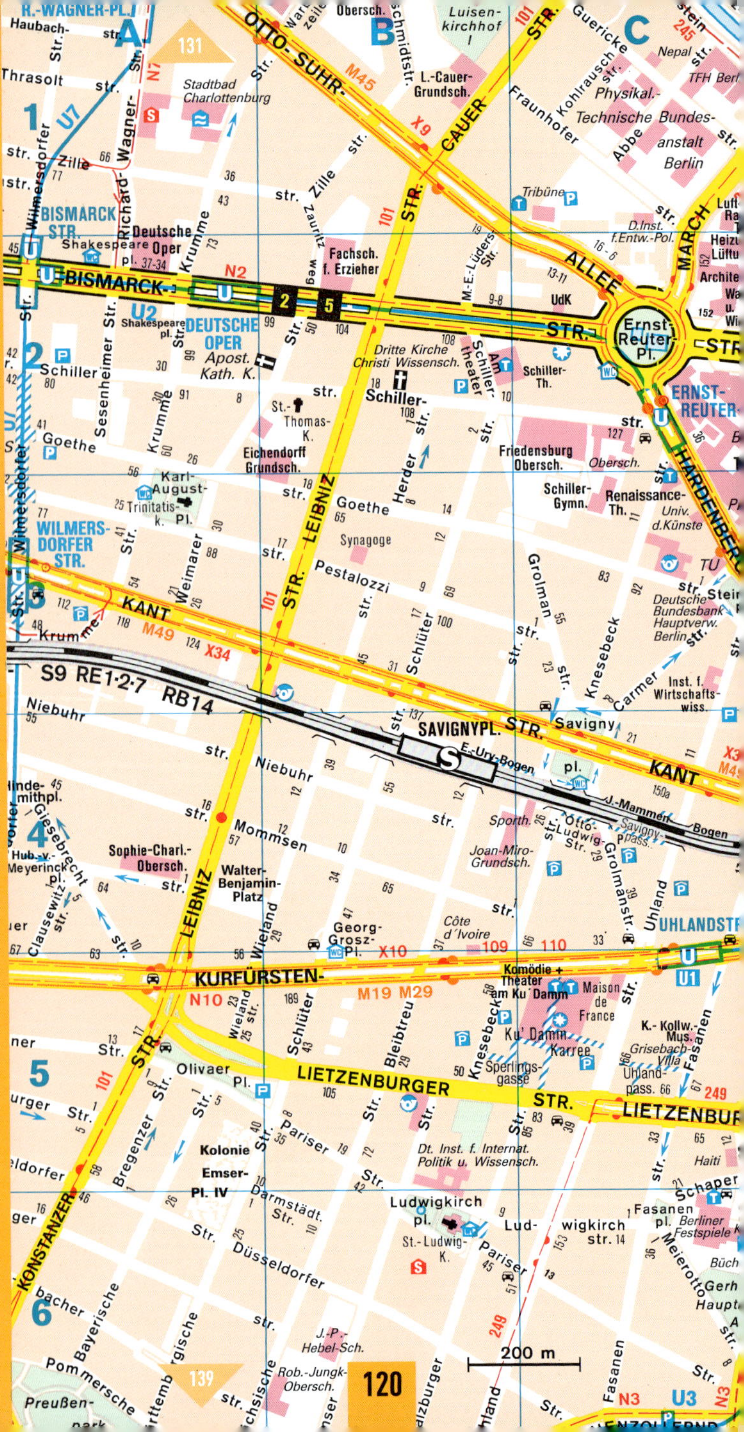

A
B
C
1
2
3
4
5
6
131
139
R.-WAGNER-PL.
Haubach-str.
Thrasolt str.
Stadtbad Charlottenburg
OTTO-SUHR-
Luisen-kirchhof I
L.-Cauer-Grundsch.
CAUER STR.
Guericke str.
Kohlrausch str.
Physikal.-Technische Bundes-anstalt Berlin
Nepal
TFH Berlin
Fraunhofer
Abbe
Tribüne
D.Inst. f.Entw.-Pol.
ALLEE
MARCH
Zille
Wilmersdorfer
Richard-Wagner-Str.
BISMARCK STR.
Deutsche Oper
Shakespeare pl.
Krumme
Zauritz weg
Fachsch. f. Erzieher
M.-E.-Lüders-Str.
UdK
Ernst-Reuter-Pl.
ERNST-REUTER-
BISMARCK-
STR.
U2
DEUTSCHE OPER
Apost. Kath. K.
Dritte Kirche Christi Wissensch.
Schiller-theater
Am
Schiller-Th.
Schiller str.
Schiller-
St.-Thomas-K.
Eichendorff Grundsch.
Herder str.
Friedensburg Obersch.
Obersch.
Goethe str.
Sesenheimer Str.
Karl-August-Pl.
Trinitatis-k.
Goethe
Schiller-Gymn.
Renaissance-Th.
Univ. d.Künste
HARDENBERG
WILMERS-DORFER STR.
Weimarer
LEIBNIZ STR.
Synagoge
Pestalozzi str.
Grolman str.
Knesebeck
TU
Deutsche Bundesbank Hauptverw. Berlin
KANT
M49
X34
Schlüter
Carmer
Steinpl.
Inst. f. Wirtschafts-wiss.
S9 RE1·2·7 RB14
Niebuhr str.
SAVIGNYPL.
Savigny pl.
KANT STR.
E.-Ury-Bogen
J.-Mammen-Bogen
Savigny-pass.
Hinde-mithpl.
Giesebrecht
Hub.-v.-Meyerinck-pl.
Sophie-Charl.-Obersch.
Mommsen str.
Walter-Benjamin-Platz
Sporth.
Otto-Ludwig-Str.
Joan-Miro-Grundsch.
Grolmanstr.
Uhland
UHLANDSTR.
Clausewitz str.
Wieland
Georg-Grosz-Pl.
Côte d'Ivoire
X10
109
110
KURFÜRSTEN-
N10
M19 M29
Komödie + Theater am Ku' Damm
Maison de France
U1
Bleibtreu
Ku' Damm Karree
K.-Kollw.-Mus.
Grisebach-Villa
Fasanen
Uhland-pass.
Sperlings-gasse
Olivaer Pl.
LIETZENBURGER STR.
LIETZENBURGER
249
Bregenzer Str.
Konstanzer
Kolonie Emser-Pl. IV
Pariser Str.
Dt. Inst. f. Internat. Politik u. Wissensch.
Haiti
Schaper
Fasanen pl.
Berliner Festspiele
Darmstädt. Str.
Ludwigkirch pl.
St.-Ludwig-K.
Ludwigkirch str.
Meierotto
Düsseldorfer Str.
Bayerische
Pommersche
Preußen-park
J.-P.-Hebel-Sch.
Rob.-Jungk-Obersch.
200 m
N3
U3

Hansaviertel
Spree
Landwehrkanal
Hansa-Ufer
Wullenweber-steg
Schleswiger Ufer
Flotowstr.
Altonaer Str.
Lessingstr.
Händelallee
Klopstockstr.
Grips-Theater
Hansapl.
Kaiser-Friedr.-Gedächtnis-K.
Straße des 17. Juni
Tiergarten
Ernst-Reuter-Pl.
Charlottenbg. Tor
Deutsch. Städtetag
Englische Str.
Wegelystr.
Königl. Porzellanmanufaktur KPM
Herbert-Lewin-Pl.
Hochspannungstechnik
Univers. der Künste
Techn. Chemie
Chemie
Universität
Müller-Breslau-Str.
Versuchsanst. f. Wasser- u. Schiffbau
Gaslaternen Freilichtmus.
Großer Weg
Neuer See
Bremer Weg
Untere Freiarchenbr.
Tiergartenschleuse
Zoowirtschaftshof
Hertzallee
TU Berlin
Oberfinanzdir.
Gartenufer
Tiergartenufer
Hopfengrabenbr.
Lichtensteinbr.
Lichtensteinallee
Thomas-Dehler-Str.
Drakestr.
Katharina-Heinroth-Ufer
Corneliusstr.
Eingang Löwentor
Berlin Zoolog. Gtn.
Zoologischer Garten
Vierwaldstätter See
Waldschänkenteich
Grottenteich
Neptunteich
Eingang Elefantentor
Aquarium
Olof-Palme-Pl.
Hardenbergpl.
Jebensstr.
Amerika hs
Börse Ind. u. Handelskammer
Budapester Str.
Kurfürstendamm
Kurfürstenstr.
Tauentzienstr.
Kaiser-Wilhelm-Gedächtnis-K.
Breitscheidpl.
Europa-Center
Spielbank
Tourist. Info.
Stachelschweine
Joachimstaler Str.
Augsburger Str.
Los-Angeles-Pl.
Marburger Str.
Rankestr.
Eislebener Str.
Nürnberger Str.
Passauer Str.
Ansbacher Str.
Bayreuther Str.
Keithstr.
Wittenbergpl.
Kleiststr.
An der Urania
Urania
Martin-Luther-Str.
Fuggerstr.
Geisbergstr.
Ettaler Str.
Spichernstr.
Regensburger Str.
Franzisk.-Krkhs.
Burggrafenstr.
Wichmannstr.
Landgrafenstr.
Klinik Hygiea
Finow-Grundsch.
Sport-halle
Kalckreuthstr.
Courbièrestr.
Bundeshaus
132
140

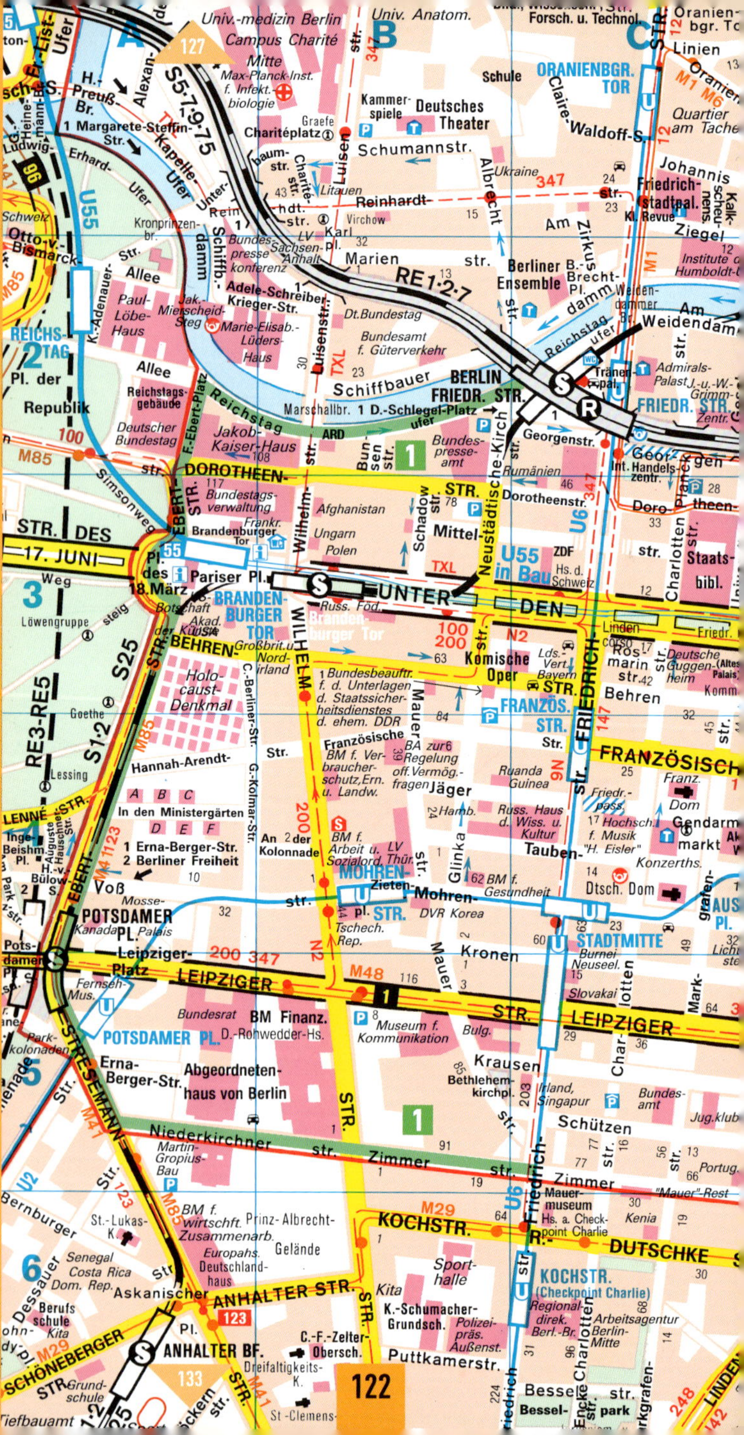

Univ.-medizin Berlin Campus Charité Mitte
Univ. Anatom.
Forsch. u. Technol.
Oranienbgr. Tor
Linien
127
Max-Planck-Inst. f. Infekt.-biologie
Kammerspiele
Deutsches Theater
Schule
ORANIENBGR. TOR
Claire-Waldoff-Str.
Quartier am Tacheles
H.-Preuß-Br.
1 Margarete-Steffin-Str.
Kapelle-Ufer
Alexanderufer
S5·7·9·75
Charitéplatz
Graefe
Schumannstr.
Erhard-Ufer
Ukraine
Johannisstr.
Kalkscheunenstr.
Friedrichstadtpal.
Kl. Revue
Reinhardtstr.
Albrechtstr.
U55
Kronprinzenbr.
Virchow
Luisenstr.
Litauen
Karl pl.
Marienstr.
Am Zirkus
Ziegelstr.
Otto-v.-Bismarck-Allee
Schiffbauerdamm
Unterbaumstr.
Bundespressekonferenz
Sachsen-Anhalt
RE1·2·7
Berliner Ensemble
B.-Brecht-Pl.
Weidendammer Br.
Am Weidendamm
Institute d. Humboldt-Univ.
Paul-Löbe-Haus
K.-Adenauer-Str.
Jak.-Mierscheid-Steg
Adele-Schreiber-Krieger-Str.
Marie-Elisab.-Lüders-Haus
Dt. Bundestag
Bundesamt f. Güterverkehr
Reichstagufer
Tränenpal.
Admirals-Palast
J.-u.-W.-Grimm-Zentr.
REICHSTAG
Pl. der Republik
Reichstagsgebäude
Deutscher Bundestag
F.-Ebert-Platz
Jakob-Kaiser-Haus
Schiffbauerdamm
BERLIN FRIEDR. STR.
Marschallbr.
1 D.-Schlegel-Platz
ARD
Bunsenstr.
Bundespresseamt
Neustädtische Kirchstr.
Georgenstr.
FRIEDR. STR.
Int. Handelszentr.
M85
100
Simsonweg
DOROTHEENSTR.
Bundestagsverwaltung
Afghanistan
Ungarn
Polen
Schadowstr.
Mittelstr.
Dorotheenstr.
Rumänien
U6
Dorotheenstr.
Planckstr.
Charlottenstr.
Staatsbibl.
STR. DES 17. JUNI
Ebertstr.
Brandenburger Tor
Frankr.
Wilhelmstr.
U55 in Bau
ZDF
Hs. d. Schweiz
Pl. des 18. März
Pariser Pl.
BRANDENBURGER TOR
Russ. Föd.
Brandenburger Tor
UNTER DEN LINDEN
TXL
Lindencorso
Weg
Löwengruppe
Botschaft
Akad. d. Künste
Großbrit. u. Nordirland
Behrenstr.
Komische Oper
N2
Lds.-Vert. Bayern
Rosmarinstr.
Deutsche Guggenheim
Altes Palais
Kommode
S25
RE3-RE5
S1·2
Goethe
Holocaust-Denkmal
C.-Berliner-Str.
1 Bundesbeauftr. f. d. Unterlagen d. Staatssicherheitsdienstes d. ehem. DDR
Mauerstr.
FRANZÖS. STR.
FRIEDRICHSTR.
Französische Str.
Lessing
Hannah-Arendt-Str.
BM f. Verbraucherschutz, Ern. u. Landw.
BA zur Regelung offener Vermögensfragen
Jägerstr.
Ruanda
Guinea
Friedr.-pass.
Franz. Dom
Gendarmenmarkt
In den Ministergärten
A B C D E F
1 Erna-Berger-Str.
2 Berliner Freiheit
G.-Kolmar-Str.
An der Kolonnade
BM f. Arbeit u. Soziales
LV Sozialord. Thür.
Hamb.
Russ. Haus d. Wiss. u. Kultur
Glinkastr.
17 Hochsch. f. Musik "H. Eisler"
Taubenstr.
Konzerths.
LENNÉSTR.
Inge-Beisheim-Pl.
H.-v.-Karajan-Str.
Auguste-Hauschner-Str.
Bülowstr.
Voßstr.
Mossestr.
MOHRENSTR.
62 BM f. Gesundheit
Zietenpl.
Mohrenstr.
Dtsch. Dom
Markgrafenstr.
POTSDAMER PL.
Kanada
Palais
DVR Korea
Tschech. Rep.
STADTMITTE
Potsdamer Platz
Leipziger Platz
200 347
Kronenstr.
Burnei
Neuseel.
Fernseh-Mus.
LEIPZIGER STR.
M48
Slovakai
Bundesrat
BM Finanz.
D.-Rohwedder-Hs.
Museum f. Kommunikation
Bulg.
POTSDAMER PL.
Park-kolonaden
Erna-Berger-Str.
Abgeordnetenhaus von Berlin
Krausenstr.
Bethlehemkirchpl.
Irland, Singapur
Bundesamt
Jug.klub
STRESEMANNSTR.
Schützenstr.
M41
Niederkirchnerstr.
Martin-Gropius-Bau
Zimmerstr.
Mauermuseum Hs. a. Checkpoint Charlie
"Mauer"-Rest
Portug.
Kenia
Bernburger Str.
St.-Lukas-K.
BM f. wirtschft. Zusammenarb.
Prinz-Albrecht-Gelände
Europahs. Deutschlandhaus
KOCHSTR.
M29
R.-DUTSCHKE-STR.
Senegal
Costa Rica
Dom. Rep.
Askanischer Pl.
Sporthalle
KOCHSTR. (Checkpoint Charlie)
Dessauer Str.
Berufsschule
Kita
ANHALTER STR.
123
Kita
K.-Schumacher-Grundsch.
Polizeipräs. Außenst.
Regionaldirek. Berl.-Br.
Arbeitsagentur Berlin-Mitte
SCHÖNEBERGER STR.
ANHALTER BF.
C.-F.-Zelter-Obersch.
Dreifaltigkeits-K.
Puttkamerstr.
Grundschule
133
Tiefbauamt
St.-Clemens
Besselstr.
Besselpark
Charlottenstr.
Friedrichstr.
Markgrafenstr.
248
LINDENSTR.

D
E
F
129
135
ORANIENBGR. STR.
Synagoge Centr. Judaicum
Krausnick str.
Krausnick park
Deutsche Telekom AG
Zentrum f. Experim. Med.
Monbijoustr.
Monbijou-park
Monbijou br.
Kinderbad
Bode-mus.
St.-Hedwig-Krkhs.
August str.
Gips str.
Hamburger Str.
Kastanienbaum-Grundsch.
Sophien-str.
Sophienk.
Sophien-Kirchhof I
Jüd. Friedhof
Mus. Blinden-werkstatt
Große Präsid. str.
Hackescher Markt
N. Prom.
A. Zwirngr.
Dircksen
ROSENTHALER STR.
Sporth.
Sport-halle
Standes-amt I
Mulack
Rücker
Kita
LUXEMBURG PL.
Freie Waldorfsch.
Schönhauser
WEIN-MEISTER STR.
Schüler-freizeit-zent.
Alte
Max-Beer-
Almstadt
Hirten
Neue Schönhsr. Str.
Goethe-Inst.
MÜNZSTR.
MEM-HARD S.
Luxemburg
James-Simon-Park
HACKESCHER MARKT
Museums-
Alte National-galerie
Pergamon-mus.
ehem. Neues Mus. (R.)
Friedrichs br.
insel
Garn. Kirch-pl.
Anna-Louisa-Karsch-
SPANDAU
Heilig-Geist-Kap.
Rosenstr
Heidereuter G.
Hs. d. Ungar. Kultur
Heiliggeistpl.
Berlin-Carré
LIEBKNECHT
ALEXANDER PL.
St.-Marien-K
Luther
Panorama str.
Ausstellungs-zentrum a. Fernsehturm
Neptun-br.
Alexander-pl.
Gontard
AquaDom Sea Life Center
St.-Wolfgang-Str.
Bode
Altes Museum
Berliner Dom
Lust-garten
Liebknecht br.
Eiserne Br.
Gorki-Th.
Studio-bühne
Palais
Gießhs.
Am Zeughs
Zeughs.
H. d. Dtsch. Hist. Mus.
Mahnmal (N. Wache)
LINDEN (Zeughs.)
Schloßbr.
KARL
Marx-Engels-
Forum
SPANDAUER STR.
Rathaus
Rathaus von Berlin
Jüdens.
Staats-oper
St.-Hedwigs-Kath.-Kirche
Friedr.-Werder.-K.
Schinkel-mus.
Schloss-
Kellergewölbe d.ehem.Schlosses
pl.
3 A.d.Kommandantur
4 Prinzengasse
5 Werdersche Rosenstr.
6 Falkoniergasse
Rathaus br.
Rathausstr.
Spree
Propststr.
Nikolai-kirche
Nikolai-
H.-Zille-Mus.
Hanf-Mus.
Ephraim-pal.
Ufer
(Marstall)
Berliner Stadtbibl.
Molken markt
Am Krögel
Mühlendamm
Mühlendamm-schleuse
Mühlen-dammbr.
Niederl. ufer
Neue Jüdenstr.
Roland-
Klosterk.
Neues Stadths.
Parochial-K.
Sen. f. Inneres
Sen. f. Finanzen
KLOSTER-STR.
GRUNER STR.
STRALAUERSTR.
Waisenstr.
Littenstr.
WERDER-SCHER MARKT
SCHLOSSPL.
BREITE
Schleusen-br.
BND Verb.-Büro
BM
Aus-wärtiges Amt
Unterwasserstr.
Oberwasserstr.
Jungfern-br.
Sperlingsg.
Brüderstr.
Neumannsg.
Landesvertr. Sachsen
Scharrenstr.
Petri-pl.
GERTRAUDEN
FISCHER INSEL
Fischer-insel
Schw. Fischerinsel
1 Kl. Gertrauden-str.
Gertrauden-br.
Roßstr.-br.
Grünstr.-br.
Schiffs-Museum
Inselbr.
Otto-Nagel-Hs.
Ermeler Hs.
Märkisches Ufer
Märkisches Museum
MÄRK. MUSEUM
Australien
Inselstr.
Runge-
Köpenicker
Köllnischer Park
Wallstr.
Oberwall
Caroline-von-Humboldt-Weg
Kur
Slowenien
Hausvogtei pl.
Niederwall
Marokko
Kl. Jägerstr.
Alte Leipziger Str.
Kreuz-str.
Bischöfl. Ordinariat
Kita
Jerusalem-Str.
Spindlerbr.
Spittel-markt
SPITTELMARKT
Sen. f. Schule Jug.u.Sport
Seydel-
Beuthstr.
Simbabwe
Dt. Rentenvers.
Ev. Kirche
Elisabeth-Mara-Str.
Zypern
Schul-mus.
Schulen
Schulze-Delitzsch-Pl.
Fin.-Amt
Neue Jakobstr.
NEUE ROSS-STR.
H.-HEINE-STR.
Schule
ANNEN-STR.
Annenstr.
Altluth. K
Uganda
Sambia
Aserbaidschan
Mauret.
Kommandanten
Axel-Springer-
Jugend-zentr.
Bundes-druckerei
Neue str.
Alte Jakob
Stallschreiber
Otto-Suhr-Siedl.
Sebastian
200m
ORANIEN STR.
Landesamt für Gesundheit u. Soziales
Waldeck-park
Alexandrin
TORSTR.

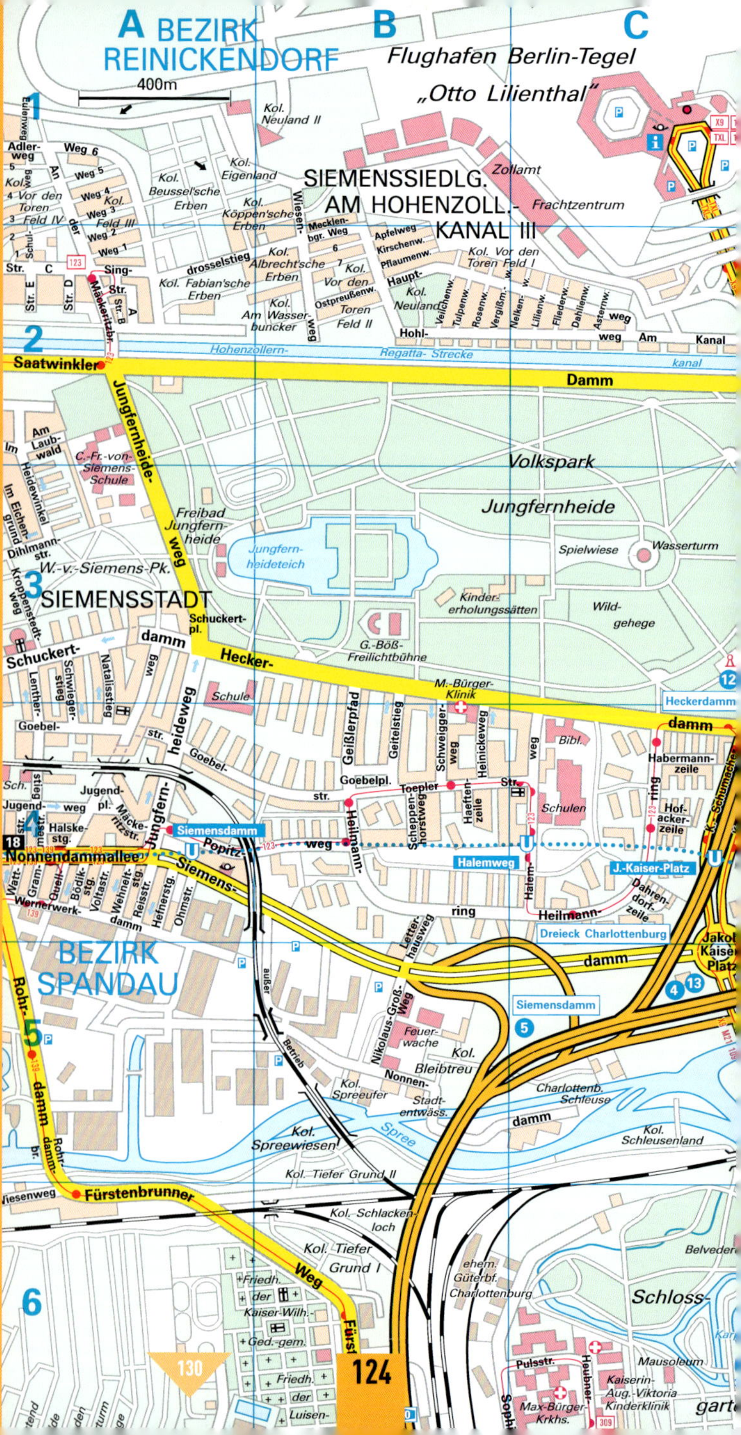
A
B
C
BEZIRK REINICKENDORF
400m
Flughafen Berlin-Tegel
„Otto Lilienthal"
Kol. Neuland II
Kol. Eigenland
Kol. Beussel'sche Erben
Kol. Köppen'sche Erben
SIEMENSSIEDLG. AM HOHENZOLL.-KANAL III
Zollamt
Frachtzentrum
Adler-weg
Weg 6
Weg 5
Weg 4
Weg 3
Weg 2
Weg 1
Kol. Vor den Toren
Feld IV
Kol. Feld III
Str. C
Sing-
drosselstieg
Kol. Fabian'sche Erben
Kol. Albrecht'sche Erben
Kol. Am Wasser-buncker
Wiesen-weg
Mecklenbgr. Weg
Kol. Vor den Toren Feld II
Ostpreußenw.
Apfelweg
Kirschenw.
Pflaumenw.
Haupt-
Kol. Neuland
Kol. Vor den Toren Feld I
Veilchenw.
Tulpenw.
Rosenw.
Vergißm.-w.
Nelken-w.
Lilienw.
Fliederw.
Dahlienw.
Asternw.
Hohl-weg
Am Kanal
Hohenzollern-
Regatta-Strecke
kanal
Saatwinkler Damm
Jungfernheide-weg
Am Laub-wald
C.-Fr.-von-Siemens-Schule
Heidewinkel
Im Eichengrund
Dihlmann-str.
W.-v.-Siemens-Pk.
Freibad Jungfern-heide
Jungfern-heideteich
Volkspark
Jungfernheide
Spielwiese
Wasserturm
Kinder-erholungssätten
Wild-gehege
G.-Böß-Freilichtbühne
SIEMENSSTADT
Schuckert-pl.
Schuckert-damm
Hecker-damm
Kroppenstedt-weg
Schwieger-stieg
Natalisstieg
Lenther-
Goebel-str.
Schule
M.-Bürger-Klinik
Heckerdamm
Geißlerpfad
Geitelsteig
Schweigger-weg
Heinickeweg
Bibl.
Habermann-zeile
Hofacker-zeile
Goebelpl.
Toepler-str.
Heilmann-ring
Scheppen-horstweg
Haeften-zeile
Schulen
K.-Schumacher-
Jugend-weg
Jugend-pl.
Halske-stg.
Mäcke-ritzstr.
Jungfern-heideweg
Siemensdamm
Popitz-weg
Halemweg
J.-Kaiser-Platz
Nonnendammallee
Siemens-damm
Wernerwerk-damm
Watt-str.
Gram-mestr.
Quell-weg
Bödik-stg.
Voltastr.
Wehnelt-steig
Reisstr.
Hefnerstg.
Ohmstr.
Halem-weg
Dahren-dorf-zeile
Dreieck Charlottenburg
Jakob-Kaiser-Platz
BEZIRK SPANDAU
Letter-hausweg
Nikolaus-Groß-Weg
Feuer-wache
Kol. Bleibtreu
Kol. Spreeufer
Nonnen-damm
Stadt-entwäss.
Charlottenb. Schleuse
Kol. Schleusenland
Kol. Spreewiesen
Spree
Kol. Tiefer Grund II
Rohr-damm
Rohrdamm-br.
Wiesenweg
Fürstenbrunner Weg
Kol. Schlacken-loch
Kol. Tiefer Grund I
Friedh. der Kaiser-Wilh.-Ged.-gem.
Friedh. der Luisen-
ehem. Güterbf. Charlottenburg
Belvedere
Schloss-garten
Mausoleum
Pulsstr.
Heubner-
Kaiserin-Aug.-Viktoria Kinderklinik
Max-Bürger-Krkhs.
Sophie-
Fürst-
1
2
3
4
5
6

130

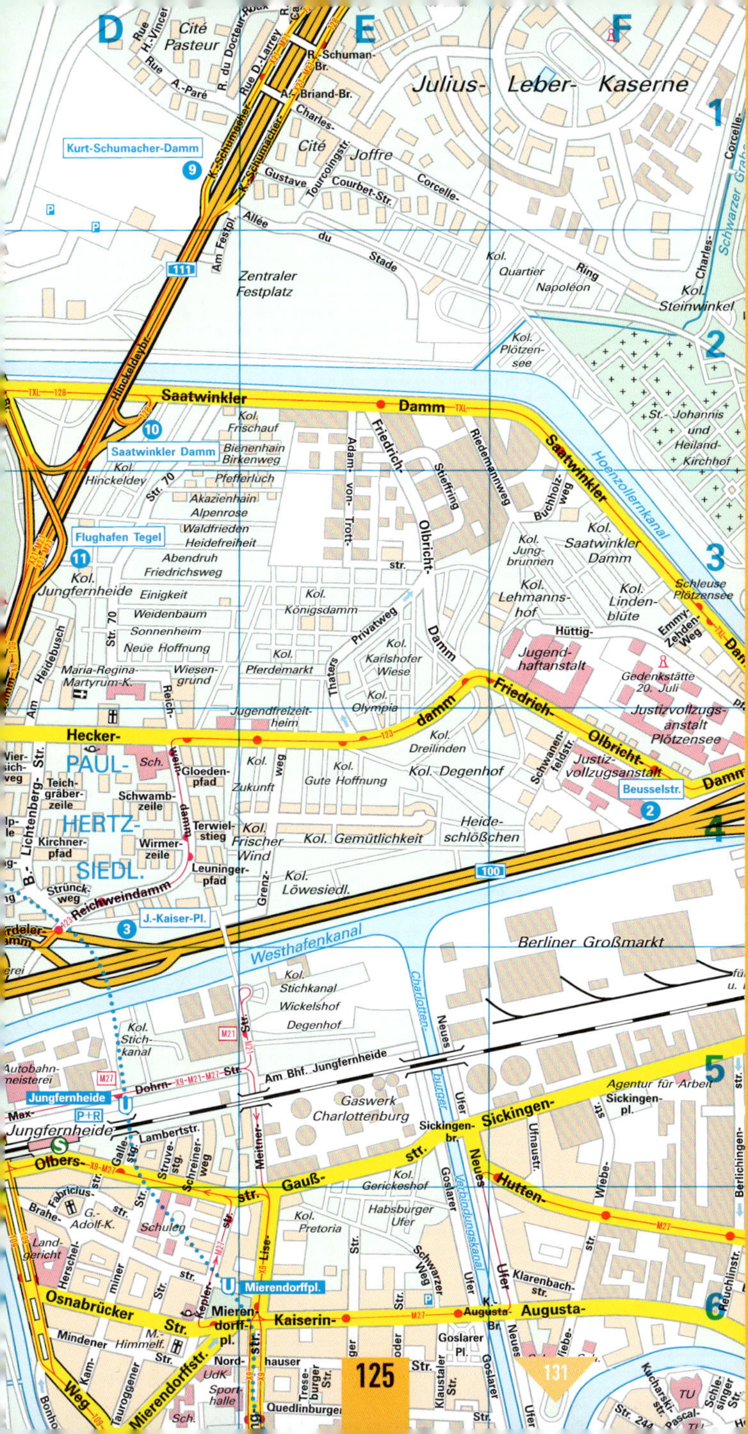
D
E
F
1
2
3
4
5
6
Cité Pasteur
Rue H.-Vincent
Rue A.-Paré
R. du Docteur-Roux
Rue D.-Larrey
R.-Schuman-Br.
A.-Briand-Br.
Julius- Leber- Kaserne
Kurt-Schumacher-Damm
K.-Schumacher-
Charles-
Cité Joffre
Gustave
Tourcoingstr.
Courbet-Str.
Corcelle-
Allée du Stade
Am Festpl.
111
Zentraler Festplatz
Kol. Quartier Napoléon
Ring
Kol. Steinwinkel
Charles-
Corcelle-
Schwarzer Graben
Kol. Plötzensee
St.- Johannis und Heiland- Kirchhof
Hinckeldeybr.
Saatwinkler Damm
TXL
128
10
Saatwinkler Damm
Kol. Frischauf
Bienenhain Birkenweg
Kol. Hinckeldey
Str. 70
Pfefferluch
Akazienhain
Alpenrose
Waldfrieden
Heidefreiheit
Abendruh
Friedrichsweg
Flughafen Tegel
11
Kol. Jungfernheide
Einigkeit
Weidenbaum
Sonnenheim
Neue Hoffnung
Adam- von- Trott-
Friedrich- Olbricht-
Stieffring
Riedemannweg
Buchholzweg
Saatwinkler
Hoenzollernkanal
Kol. Saatwinkler Damm
Kol. Jungbrunnen
Kol. Lehmannshof
Kol. Lindenblüte
Schleuse Plötzensee
Emmy-Zehden-Weg
Kol. Königsdamm
Privatweg
Kol. Karlshofer Wiese
Damm
Hüttig-
Jugendhaftanstalt
Gedenkstätte 20. Juli
Justizvollzugsanstalt Plötzensee
Am Heidebusch
Maria-Regina-Martyrum-K.
Wiesengrund
Kol. Pferdemarkt
Thaters
Kol. Olympia
Reich-
Jugendfreizeitheim
Friedrich-Olbricht-Damm
123
Kol. Dreilinden
Hecker-
Paul-Hertz-Siedl.
Sch.
Lichtenberg-Str.
Teichgräberzeile
Schwambzeile
Gloedenpfad
Kol. Zukunft
weg
Kol. Gute Hoffnung
Kol. Degenhof
Schwanenfeldstr.
Justizvollzugsanstalt
Beusselstr.
2
Kirchnerpfad
Wirmerzeile
Terwielstieg
Kol. Frischer Wind
Kol. Gemütlichkeit
Heideschlößchen
Leuningerpfad
Grenz-
Kol. Löwesiedl.
100
B.
Strünckweg
Reichweindamm
J.-Kaiser-Pl.
3
Westhafenkanal
Berliner Großmarkt
Kol. Stichkanal
Wickelshof
Degenhof
Kol. Stichkanal
Charlottenburger
Neues Ufer
M21
Autobahnmeisterei
M27
Dohrn-Str.
X9-M21-M27
Am Bhf. Jungfernheide
Gaswerk Charlottenburg
Agentur für Arbeit
Sickingenpl.
Jungfernheide
P+R
Max-
Lambertstr.
Sickingenbr.
Sickingen-
Olbers-
Galle-stg.
Struvestg.
Schreinerweg
Meitner-
Gauß-str.
Kol. Gerickeshof
Goslarer
Hutten-
Uhnaustr.
Wiebestr.
Berlichingenstr.
Fabricius-
Brahe-
G.-Adolf-K.
Schulen
Kol. Pretoria
Habsburger Ufer
Verbindungskanal
Landgericht
Herschel-
miner
Kepler-
Lise-
Schwarzer Weg
Ufer
Klarenbachstr.
Reuchlinstr.
Mierendorffpl.
Osnabrücker Str.
Mierendorffpl.
Kaiserin-
Augusta-
Mindener
M.-Himmelf.
Nord-hauser
Tresebürger Str.
Goslarer Pl.
Kamweg
Tauroggener
Mierendorffstr.
UdK Sporthalle
Quedlinburger
Klaustaler Str.
Kucharski-str.
TU
Schlesinger Str.
Str. 244
Pascal-
131

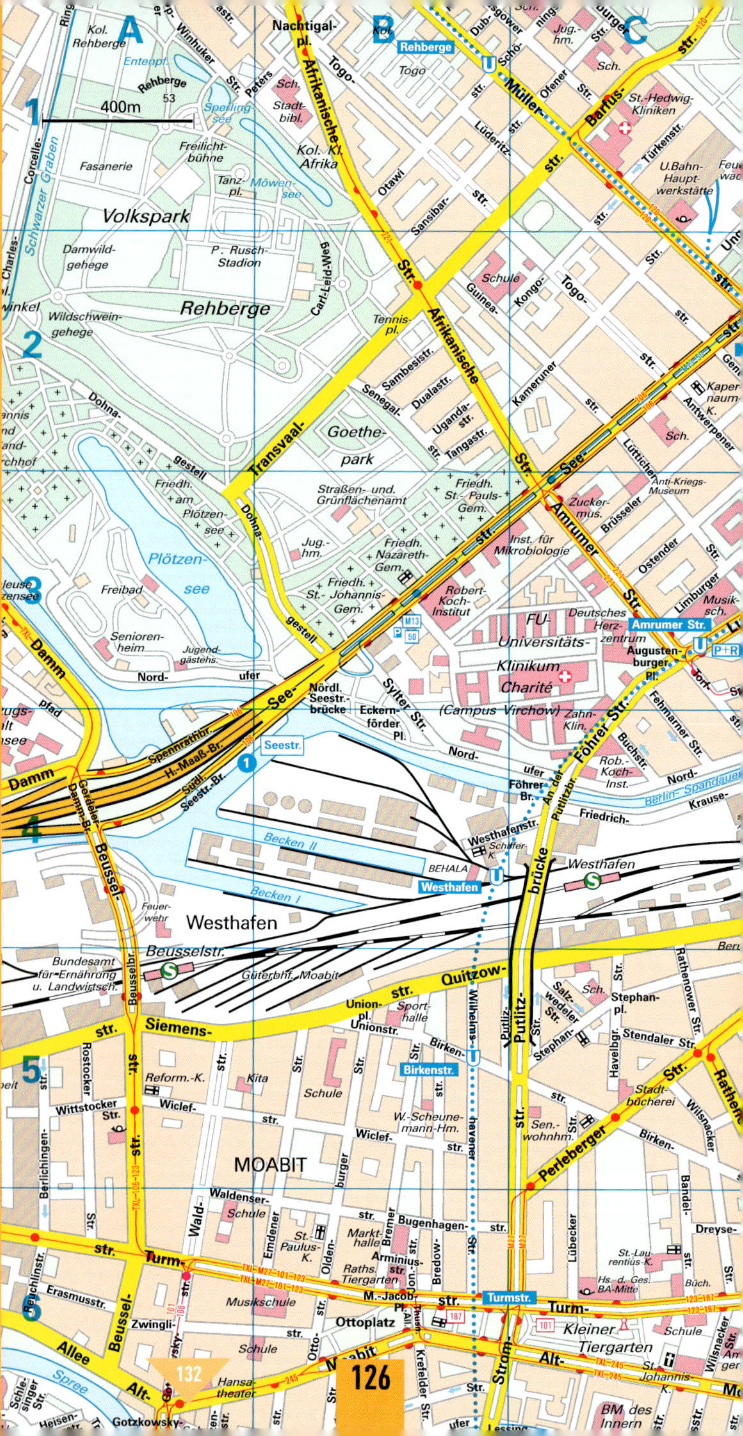
A
B
C
1
2
3
4
5
6
400m
Kol. Rehberge
Entenpf.
Rehberge
Sperlingsee
Möwensee
Freilichtbühne
Tanzpl.
Fasanerie
Volkspark
Rehberge
Damwildgehege
Wildschweingehege
P. Rusch-Stadion
Carl-Leid-Weg
Corcelle-
Schwarzer Graben
Charles-
Winhuker
Peters
Nachtigalpl.
Afrikanische
Kol. Kl. Afrika
Stadtbibl.
Sch.
Togo-
Togo
Kol. Rehberge
Rehberge
Otawi
Sansibar-
Lüderitz-
Müller-
Ofener
Barfus-
Dubliner
Sch.
Jug.-hm.
St.-Hedwig-Kliniken
Türkenstr.
U.Bahn-Hauptwerkstätte
Schule
Guinea-
Kongo-
Togo-
Tennispl.
Sambesistr.
Dualastr.
Senegal-
Ugandastr.
Tangastr.
Kameruner
Goethepark
Transvaal-
Dohna-
Dohnagestell
Straßen- und Grünflächenamt
Friedh. St.-Pauls-Gem.
Friedh. Nazareth-Gem.
Friedh. St.-Johannis-Gem.
Friedh. am Plötzensee
Jug.-hm.
Kapernaum-K.
Antwerpener
Sch.
Lütticher
Anti-Kriegs-Museum
Zuckermus.
Brüsseler
Amrumer
Inst. für Mikrobiologie
Robert-Koch-Institut
Ostender
Limburger
Musiksch.
Deutsches Herzzentrum
Amrumer Str.
Augustenburger Pl.
P+R
FU-Universitäts-Klinikum Charité (Campus Virchow)
Zahn-Klin.
Plötzensee
Freibad
Seniorenheim
Jugendgästehs.
Nordufer
See-
Nördl. Seestr.-brücke
Eckernförder Pl.
Sylter Str.
Fehmarner Str.
Föhrer Str.
Buchstr.
Rob.-Koch-Inst.
Föhrer Br.
Nordufer
Berlin-Spandauer
Krause-
Friedrich-
Damm
Spennrathbr.
H.-Maaß-Br.
Südl. Seestr.-Br.
Seestr.
Gordeler-Damm-Br.
Beussel-
Becken II
Becken I
Westhafenstr.
Schiffer-K.
BEHALA
Westhafen
Putlitzbr.
Westhafen
Feuerwehr
Westhafen
Beusselstr.
Bundesamt für Ernährung u. Landwirtsch.
Güterbhf. Moabit
Quitzow-
Siemens-
Union-pl.
Unionstr.
Sporthalle
Birken-
Birkenstr.
Wilhelmshavener
Putlitz-
Salzwedeler Str.
Sch.
Stephanpl.
Stephan-
Havelbgr.
Stendaler Str.
Rathenower Str.
Perleberger
Stadtbücherei
Wilsnacker
Birken-
Sen.-wohnhm.
Rostocker
Reform.-K.
Kita
Schule
Wittstocker Str.
Wiclef-
W.-Scheunemann-Hm.
MOABIT
Berlichingen-
Waldenser-
Schule
Wald-
Emdener
St.-Paulus-K.
Oldenburger
Markthalle
Bremer
Bugenhagen-
Arminius-
Raths. Tiergarten
Bredow-
Lübecker
Bandel-
Dreyse-
St.-Laurentius-K.
Hs. d. Ges. BA-Mitte
Turm-
Turmstr.
M.-Jacob-Pl.
Ottoplatz
Musikschule
Erasmusstr.
Reuchlinstr.
Zwingli-
Kleiner Tiergarten
Schule
St. Johannis-K.
Alt-Moabit
Allee
Spree
Schlesinger Str.
Heisen-
Gotzkowsky-
Hansatheater
Schule
Krefelder Str.
Strom-
Lessing
BM des Innern
Ufer

132

WEDDING
BEZIRK MITTE
Osloer Str.
Leopoldplatz
Nauener Platz
Wedding
Reinickendorfer Str.
Schwartzkopffstr.
Humboldthain
Müller-Str.
Schul-str.
Reinickendorfer Str.
Chaussee-str.
Pank-str.
Hussiten-str.
Fenn-str.
Seller-str.
Heide-str.
Invaliden-str.
Lehrter Str.
Brunnenplatz
Nettelbeckpl.
Rathaus
Urnenfriedh.
Garnisonfriedh.
Städt. Urnen-Friedhof
Plötzensee-Kanal
Schiffahrtskanal
Nordhafen
Erika-Hess-Eisstadion
Bundeswehr-Krkhs.
Invaliden-Friedhof
Golfzentrum
Museum für Naturkunde
Bundesamt für Geologie
BM für Verkehr, Bau- und Wohnungswesen
BM für Wirtschaft und Arbeit
Invaliden-park
Museum für Gegenwart
Bündnis 90 Die Grünen
Charité-Hochhaus
Charité Universitätsmedizin
Humboldt-Universität
Anatomisches Theater
Humboldthafen
Berlin Hbf. (Lehrter Bf.)
Geschichtspark
Poststadion
Amtsgericht Tiergarten
JVA
Fritz-Schloß-Park
Seydlitzplatz
Seniorenheim
Stadtbad Wedding
Dankeskirche
Weddingpl.
Dorotheenstadt II
Friedh. St. Hedwig u. Franz. Dom
Climbing Center
Heimatmus.
Osloer Str.
Louise-Schröder-Pl.
Hallen- u. Sommerbad
Hosp. zum Hl. Geist u. St. Georg
DRK-Kliniken Mark-Brandenburg
Exerzier-str.
Iranische Str.
Liebenwalder Str.
Gerichtstr.
Ravenéstr.
Schönwalder Str.
Wiesenstr.
Kolberger Str.
Scharnhorststr.
Habersaathstr.
Schwarzer Weg
Minna-Cauer-Str.
Alt-Moabit
127
133

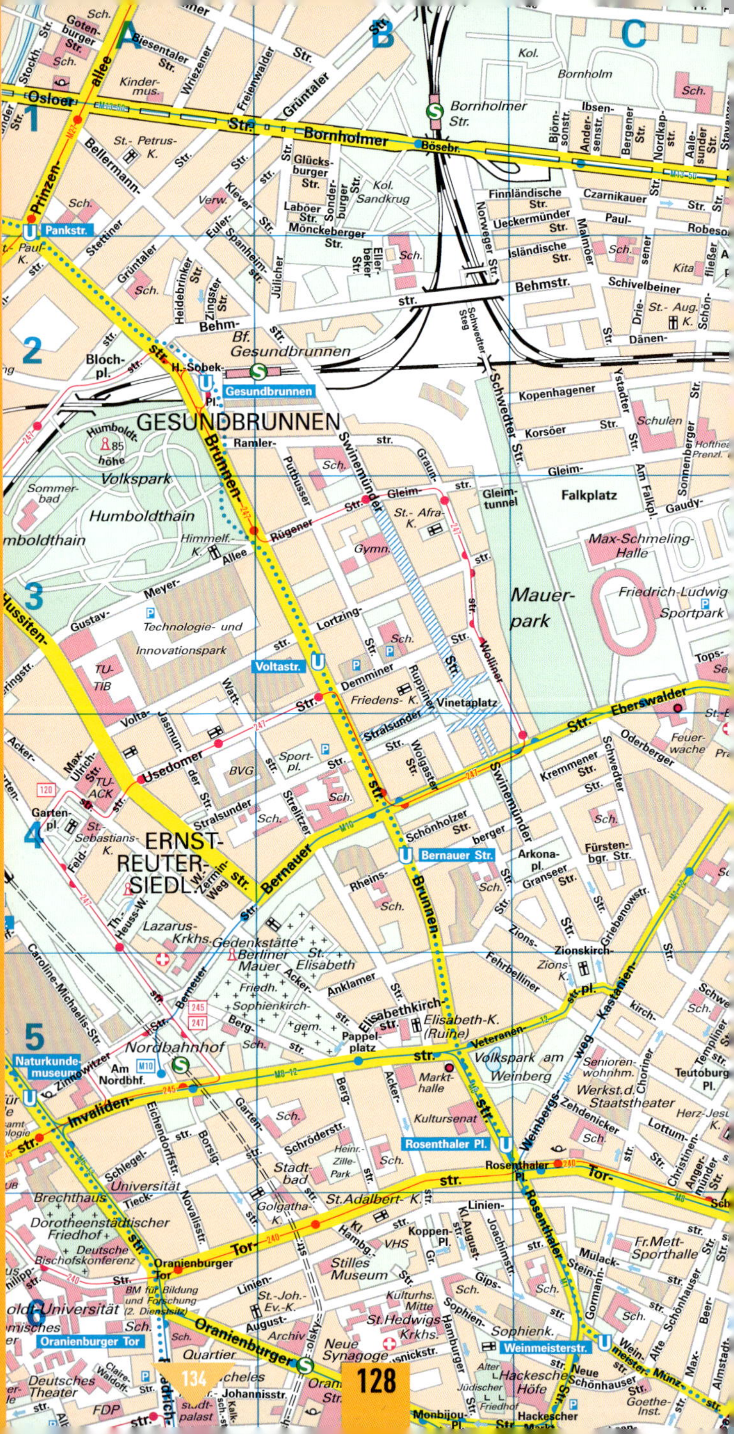
A
B
C
1
2
3
4
5
6
GESUNDBRUNNEN
ERNST-REUTER-SIEDL.
Osloer Str.
Bornholmer Str.
Bösebr.
Bornholm
Prinzenallee
Pankstr.
Bellermannstr.
Stettiner Str.
Grüntaler Str.
Behmstr.
Bf. Gesundbrunnen
Gesundbrunnen
Humboldthöhe 85
Volkspark Humboldthain
Sommerbad
Brunnenstr.
Swinemünder Str.
Ramlerstr.
Putbusser Str.
Rügener Str.
Gleimstr.
Gleimtunnel
Falkplatz
Max-Schmeling-Halle
Friedrich-Ludwig-Jahn-Sportpark
Mauerpark
Kopenhagener Str.
Korsöer Str.
Schwedter Str.
Schwedter Steg
Bernauer Str.
Eberswalder Str.
Oderberger Str.
Kremmener Str.
Voltastr.
Hussitenstr.
Gustav-Meyer-Allee
Technologie- und Innovationspark
TU-TIB
Demminer Str.
Ruppiner Str.
Vinetaplatz
Stralsunder Str.
Wolgaster Str.
Usedomer Str.
Ackerstr.
Max-Ulrich-Str.
Gartenpl.
St. Sebastians-K.
Lazarus-Krkhs.
Gedenkstätte Berliner Mauer
St. Elisabeth
Sophienkirch-gem.
Nordbahnhof
Am Nordbhf.
Naturkundemuseum
Invalidenstr.
Zionskirchpl.
Zions-K.
Kastanienallee
Veteranenstr.
Volkspark am Weinberg
Elisabeth-K. (Ruine)
Markthalle
Kultursenat
Rosenthaler Pl.
Torstr.
Rosenthaler Str.
Weinbergsweg
Werkst.d. Staatstheater
Brechthaus
Dorotheenstädtischer Friedhof
Deutsche Bischofskonferenz
Oranienburger Tor
Oranienburger Str.
Golgatha-K.
St. Adalbert-K.
Koppenpl.
Stilles Museum
VHS
Kulturhs. Mitte
St. Hedwigs-Krkhs.
Sophienk.
Neue Synagoge
Weinmeisterstr.
Hackesche Höfe
Neue Schönhauser Str.
Münzstr.
Fr. Mett-Sporthalle
Deutsches Theater
FDP
Archiv
Quartier
Linienstr.
Gormannstr.
Alte Schönhauser Str.
Joachimstr.
Teutoburger Pl.

134

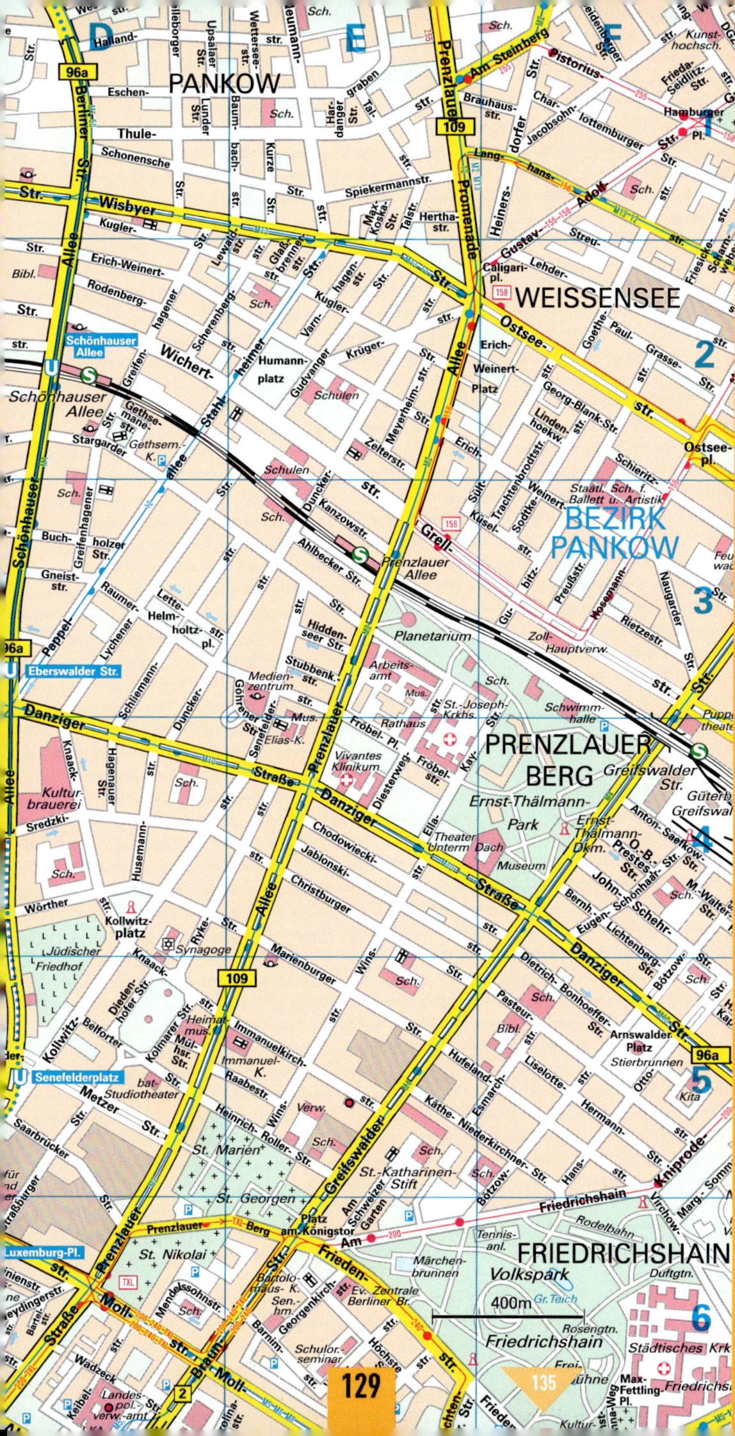
PANKOW
WEISSENSEE
BEZIRK PANKOW
PRENZLAUER BERG
FRIEDRICHSHAIN
Berliner Str.
Schönhauser Allee
Wisbyer Str.
Prenzlauer Promenade
Prenzlauer Allee
Ostsee-str.
Danziger Straße
Greifswalder Str.
Wichert-str.
Stahlheimer Str.
Humannplatz
Helmholtz-pl.
Kollwitz-platz
Planetarium
Ernst-Thälmann-Park
Ernst-Thälmann-Dkm.
Theater Unterm Dach
Museum
Kulturbrauerei
Jüdischer Friedhof
Synagoge
Heimat-mus.
Immanuel-K.
St. Marien
St. Georgen
St. Nikolai
Platz am Königstor
Am Friedrichshain
Volkspark Friedrichshain
Märchenbrunnen
Tennis-anl.
Gr. Teich
400m
Schönhauser Allee
Eberswalder Str.
Senefelderplatz
Luxemburg-Pl.
Ostsee-pl.
Arnswalder Platz
Stierbrunnen
Vivantes Klinikum
Rathaus
Arbeits-amt
Schwimm-halle
Zoll-Hauptverw.
Mollstr.
Friedenstr.
Landsberger Allee
Greifswalder Str.
Dietrich-Bonhoeffer-Str.
Kniprodestr.
Virchowstr.
Städtisches Krk.
Max-Fettling-Pl.
Bartolomäus-K.
Ev. Zentrale Berliner Br.
Schulor.-seminar
Landes-pol.-verw.-amt
96a
109
2
135

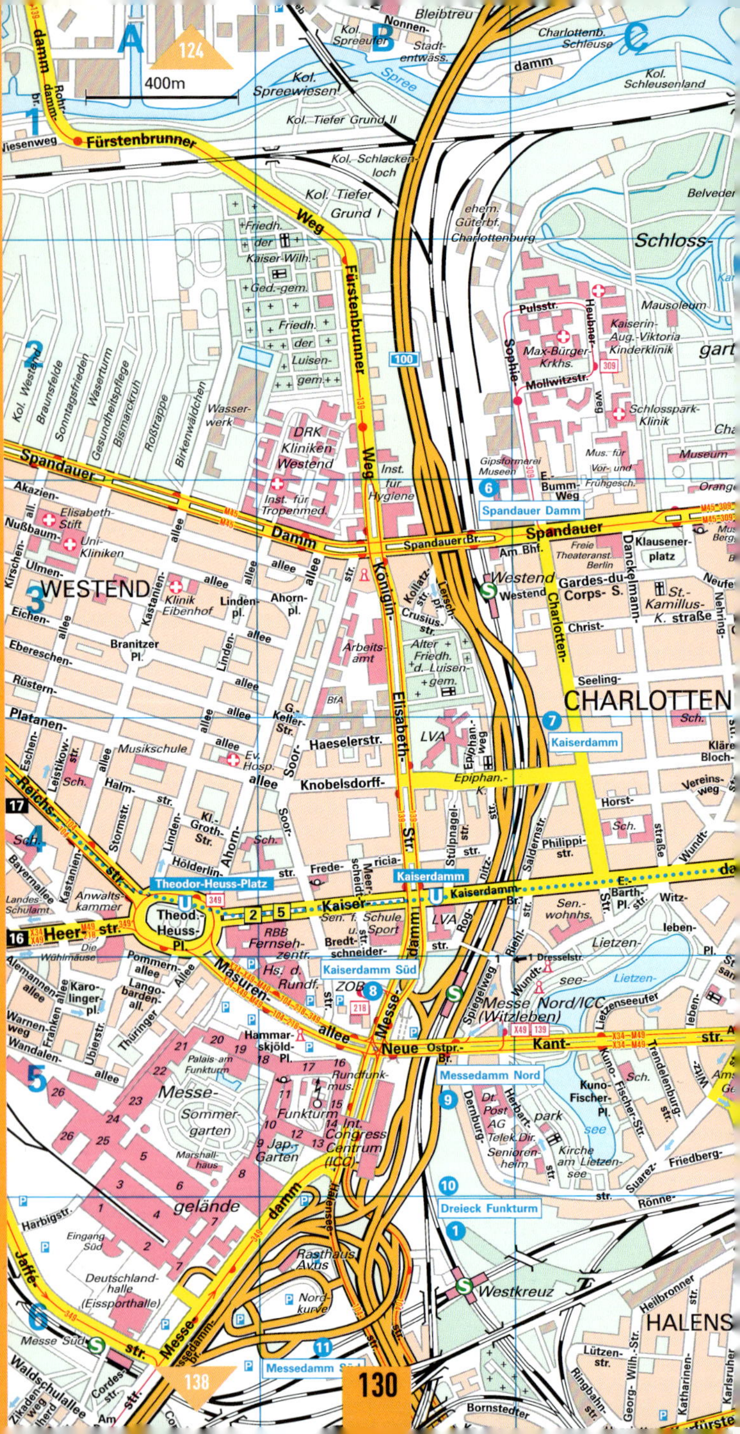
A
B
C
124
400m
Kol. Spreeufer
Nonnen-
Bleibtreu
Stadt-entwäss.
Charlottenb. Schleuse
damm
Kol. Spreewiesen
Spree
Kol. Schleusenland
Kol. Tiefer Grund II
Wiesenweg
Fürstenbrunner
Weg
Kol. Schlacken-loch
Kol. Tiefer Grund I
Belveder
ehem. Güterbf. Charlottenburg
Schloss-
Friedh. der Kaiser-Wilh.-Ged.-gem.
Friedh. der Luisen-gem.
Fürstenbrunner
Weg
Pulsstr.
Heubner-
Mausoleum
Kaiserin-Aug.-Viktoria Kinderklinik
Max-Bürger-Krkhs.
Sophie-
Mollwitzstr.
Schlosspark-Klinik
Kol. Westend
Braunsfelde
Sonntagsfrieden
Wasserturm
Gesundheitspflege
Bismarckruh
Roßtrappe
Birkenwäldchen
Wasser-werk
DRK Kliniken Westend
Inst. für Hygiene
Gipsformerei Museen
E.-Bumm-Weg
Mus. für Vor- und Frühgesch.
Museum
Spandauer
Damm
Akazien-allee
Elisabeth-Stift
Nußbaum-allee
Uni-Kliniken
Inst. für Tropenmed.
Spandauer Br.
Spandauer Damm
Spandauer
Am Bhf.
Klausener-platz
Freie Theateranst. Berlin
Ulmen-allee
WESTEND
Kirschen-allee
Klinik Eibenhof
Kastanien-allee
Linden-pl.
Ahorn-pl.
Königin-
Kollatz-str.
Lersch-pf.
Crusius-str.
Westend
Gardes-du-Corps-S.
Danckelmann-
St.-Kamillus-K.
straße
Nehring-
Eichen-allee
Eberesche-
Branitzer Pl.
Arbeits-amt
Alter Friedh. d. Luisen-gem.
Christ-
Charlotten-
Rüstern-allee
Seeling-
CHARLOTTEN
Sch.
Platanen-allee
BfA
Elisabeth-
G.-Keller-Str.
LVA
Epiphan.-weg
Kaiserdamm
Eschen-allee
Leistikow-str.
Musikschule
Ev. Hosp.
Soor-str.
Haeselerstr.
Knobelsdorff-
Epiphan.-K.
Klären Bloch-
Vereins-weg
Reichs-str.
Sch.
Halm-str.
Stormstr.
Linden-allee
Kl.-Groth-Str.
Ahorn-
Sch.
Str.
Stülpnagel-str.
Horst-
Sch.
straße
Wundt-
Bayernallee
Kastanien-allee
Hölderlin-
Frede-ricia-str.
Meer-scheidt-str.
Saldernstr.
Philippi-str.
Theodor-Heuss-Platz
Kaiserdamm
Kaiserdamm-Br.
E.-Barth-Pl.
Witz-leben-str.
Landes-Schulamt
Anwalts-kammer
Theod.-Heuss-Pl.
Kaiser-
Sen. f. Schule u. Sport
LVA
Sen.-wohnhs.
Heer-str.
Die Wühlmäuse
RBB Fernseh-zentr.
Bredt-schneider-str.
Rog-
Riehl-str.
Lietzen-
Pommern-allee
Hs. d. Rundf.
Kaiserdamm Süd
Dresselstr.
Lietzen-see
Alemannen-allee
Karo-linger-pl.
Lango-barden-all.
Masuren-allee
ZOB
Messe-
Spiegelweg
Wundt-
Messe Nord/ICC (Witzleben)
Lietzenseeufer
Warnen-weg
Franken-allee
Thüringer Allee
Hammar-skjöld-Pl.
Neue
Ostpr.-Br.
Kant-
str.
Wandalen-allee
Ubierstr.
Palais am Funkturm
Rundfunk-mus.
Messedamm Nord
Kuno-Fischer-Pl.
Kuno-Fischer-Str.
Trendelenburg-str.
Messe-Sommer-garten
Funkturm
Int. Congress Centrum (ICC)
Dernburg-
Dt. Post AG Telek.Dir.
Herbart-str.
park
see
Senioren-heim
Kirche am Lietzen-see
Suarez-
Friedberg-
Marshall-haus
Jap. Garten
gelände
damm
Halensee-
Dreieck Funkturm
Rönne-
Harbigstr.
Eingang Süd
Rasthaus Avus
Nord-kurve
Westkreuz
Heilbronner str.
HALENS
Deutschland-halle (Eissporthalle)
Jaffé-
Messe Süd
str.
Messedamm-Br.
Messe-
Messedamm Süd
Lützen-str.
Georg-Wilh.-Str.
Katharinen-
Ringbahn-str.
Karlsruher
Waldschulallee
Cordes-str.
Am
Bornstedter
138

125
139
CHARLOTTENBURG
Gaswerk Charlottenburg
Agentur für Arbeit
Sickingen-pl.
Jungfernheide
P+R
Am Bhf. Jungfern-
Dohrn-
Olbers-
Lambertstr.
Gauß-str.
Sickingen-br.
Sickingen-
Hutten-
Kol. Gerickeshof
Habsburger Ufer
Kol. Pretoria
Schulen
Landgericht
Brahe-
Fabricius-
G.-Adolf-K.
Schwarzer Weg
Verbindungskanal
Klarenbach-str.
Wiebe-
Osnabrücker Str.
Mierendorffpl.
Mierendorff-pl.
Kaiserin-Augusta-
Augusta-
Mindener
M.-Himmelf.
Mierendorffstr.
Nordhauser
Quedlinburger
Goslarer Pl.
Tauroggener
Bonhoeffer-ufer
Sommering-str.
Kraftwerk Charlottenburg (stillgelegt)
Wassersch.-Pol.
Darwinstr.
Spreebord
Schloss-Br.
Charlottenbgr.
Spree
Am Caprivi-Br.
Siemens-steg
Röntgen-Br.
BVG
Helmholtz
Dovestr.
TU
Luisen-platz
Eosander-
Eosander-pl.
Iburger Ufer
Sen.-wohnheim
Otto-
Kaiser-Friedrich-
Brauhofstr.
Herz-Jesu-K.
Lietzow
Alt-Lietzow-K.
Guericke-
Sch.
Alt. Luisen-Friedhf.
Einstein-ufer
March-Br.
Univ. der Künste
Physikal.-Technische Bundes-anstalt Berlin
Luisen-K.
Gierke-Pl.
Schalotte
Rich.-Wagner-Pl.
R.-Wagner-Pl.
Raths.
Standes-amt
Suhr-
Stadtbad
AOK
Cauer-
Fraunhofer-
Marchstr.
Tribüne-Theater
Haubach-
Auferst.-K.
Haus der Jugend
Zille-
Spielhagen-str.
Deutsche Oper Berlin
Deutsche Oper
F.-Fröbel-Haus
LZB
Allee
Ernst-Reuter-Pl.
Bismarck-
Bismarckstr.
Shakespeare-platz
Dritte Kirche Christi Wissensch.
Schillerth.
Hardenberg-
Sophie-Charlotte-Pl.
Windscheid-
Schiller-
Apost. Kath. K.
St.-Thomas-K.
Friedensbg.-Obersch.
Schiller-Gymn.
Renaissance-theater
Max-Lieberm.-Osch.
Goethe-park
Goethe-
VHS
Karl.-Aug.-Pl.
Trinitatis-K.
Synagoge
Senioren wohnhs.
Pestalozzi-
Deutsche Bundesbank Hauptverw.
Grundbuch-amt
Wilmersdorfer Str.
Kant-
Savigny-
Krumme
Stuttgarter Pl.
Charlottenburg
Sen.-wohnhs.
Niebuhr-
Haus der Familie
Savignyplatz
Schule
Mommsen-
Hinde-mithplatz
Kindertheater Charlottchen
Gervinus-
Sybel-
Damaschke
Dahlmann-
Lewishamstr.
Hub.-v.-Meyerinck Pl.
VHS Bibl.
W.-Benjamin-Pl.
George-Grosz-Pl.
Theater am Kurfürstendamm
Ku.-damm Karree
The Story of Berlin
Kurfürsten-
Droysenstr.
Jona-K.
Roscherstr.
Adenauer-pl.
Adenauerplatz
Leibniz-
Olivaer Pl.
Lietzenburger
Bundes-rechn.-hof
Lehniner Pl.
damm
Xantener
Pariser
Landes-versorgungs-amt
Dt. Inst. f. Intern. Politik u. Wissensch.

MOABIT
HANSA-
VIERTEL
400m
Turmstr.
Alt-Moabit
Ottoplatz
Kleiner Tiergarten
Birkenstr.
Perleberger Str.
Stromstr.
Lessingstr.
Beusselstr.
Gotzkowskybr.
Levetzowstr.
Hansa-Br.
Hansaplatz
Altonaer Str.
Bellevue
Schlosspark Bellevue
Akademie der Künste
Großer Stern
Tiergarten
Str. des 17. Juni
Bachstr.
Charlottenbgr. Br.
Technische Universität
Universität der Künste
Neuer See
Landwehrkanal
Zoologischer Garten
Hardenbergplatz
Aquarium
Europa-Center
Kaiser-Wilh.-Gedächtnisk.
Breitscheidpl.
Kurfürstendamm
Kurfürstenstr.
Tauentzienstr.
Wittenbergplatz
Kleiststr.
An der Urania
Urania
KaDeWe
Uhlandstr.
Augsburger Str.
Nürnberger Str.
Joachimstaler Str.
Kantstr.
Hardenbergstr.
Fasanenstr.
Theater des Westens
Käthe-Kollwitz-Museum
Literaturhaus
Lietzenburger Str.
Nollendorfpl.
Budapester Str.
Stülerstr.
Hofjägerallee
Klingelhöferstr.
Lützowufer
Herkulesbr.
Spree
Moabiter Br.
Lessingbr.
Holsteiner Ufer
Flensburger Str.
Händelallee
Bundespräsidialamt
Fasanerieallee
Lichtensteinallee
Corneliusbr.
Schillstr.
Keithstr.
Kalckreuthstr.
Wichmannstr.
Burggrafenstr.
Ansbacher Str.
Passauer Str.
Marburger Str.
Rankestr.
Los Angeles Pl.
Joachimst. Pl.
Steinplatz
Ernst-Reuter-Pl.
Einsteinufer
Franklinstr.
Helmholtzstr.
Wullenweberstr.
Solinger Str.
Klopstockstr.
Wegelystr.
Müller-Breslau-Str.
Hertzallee
Bremer Weg
Großer Weg
Tiergartenufer
Fontaneweg
Thomasiusstr.
Kirchstr.
Wilsnacker Str.
Lübecker Str.
Bremer Str.
Waldstr.
Wittstocker Str.
Emdener Str.
Erasmusstr.
Reuchlinstr.
Zwinglistr.
Agricolastr.
Dortmunder Str.
Bochumer Str.
Krefelder Str.
Elberfelder Str.
Essener Str.
Claudiusstr.
Schleswiger Ufer
Flotowstr.
Siegmundshof
Englische Str.
Cuxhavener Str.
Bartningallee
Siegessäule
Rauchstr.
Drakestr.
Dreysestr.
Schaperstr.
Fuggerstr.
Eislebener Str.
Meinekestr.
Nürnbgr. Pl.
Geisbergstr.
Urbanistik
LKA4
CDU
Klinik Hygiea
Gedächtniskirche
Die Stachelschweine
Inst. für Tropenmedizin
IHK
L.-Erhard-Haus
Heinr.-Hertz-Inst.
TÜV
Caritas-berg.-hm.
Sen.-wohnhm.
Stadtbücherei
St.-Laurentius-K.
BM des Innern
Oberverw.-gericht
Kaiser-Friedr.-Ged.-K.
Oswald-Schumann-Pl.
Berlin-Pav.
Hansatheater
Musikschule
St.-Paulus-K.
Markthalle
Arminiusstr.
Raths. Tiergarten
M.-Jacob-Pl.
St.-Ansgar-K.
Grips-Theat.
Sporthalle
Feuerwache
Technikerschule
Versuchsanst. für Wasserbau und Schiffbau
Unterschleuse
R.-Drawe-Institut
Bibl.
Theatersaal
Konz.-Saal
Oberfinanzdirektion
TU Berlin
Mus. für Fotografie
Oberverw.-ger. Berl.
Kurfürstendamm
Zoologischer Garten
Wittenbergpl.
Augsburger Str.
Uhlandstr.
Hansaplatz
Turmstr.
Birkenstr.
Nollendorf

126

140

D
E
F
1
2
3
4
5
6
127
141
Tennispl.
Rodelbahn
Fritz-
Schloß-
Park
Poststadion
Amts-gericht Tiergarten
JVA
Stadtbad
Seydlitz-platz
Geschichts-park
Senioren-heim
Heide-str.
Döberitzer Str.
Minna-Cauer-Str.
Friedhof
Museum für Gegenwart
Landes-sozial-gericht
BM für Wirtschaft und Arbeit
Invaliden-park
Orthopäd. Klinik
Museum für Naturkunde
Bundesamt für Geologie
BM für Verkehr, Bau- und Wohnungs-wesen
Neuen Tor
Bündnis 90 Die Grünen
Hannoversche Str.
R.-Koch-Pl.
Charité-Hochhaus
Invaliden-str.
Ladestr.
Humboldt-hafen
Charité Universitäts-medizin Berlin
Humboldt-Uni
Anatomisches Theater
Kammer-spiele
Deutsches Theater
Europapl.
Berlin Hbf. (Lehrter Bf.)
Hauptbahnhof
Washington-platz
Alexander-ufer
H.-Preuß-Br.
Kapelleufer
Charitépl.
Schumann-str.
Reinhardt-str.
Karl-pl.
Marienstr.
Alt-Moabit
Landesinst. f. gerichtl. u. soz. Medizin
LKA3
Quartier in Bau
Moabit
Rahel-Hirsch-Str.
Erhard-Ufer
1 E.-Herwegh-Str.
2 A.-Zahn-Harnack-Str.
3 I.-Schaeffer-Str.
4 Berta-Benz-Str.
Moltke-br.
Willy-Brandt-Str.
Botschaft Schweiz
Otto-von-Bismarck-All.
Konrad-Adenauer-Str.
Jak.-Miersch-Steg
Reinhardt-Schiffbauerdamm
Bds.-presse-Konf.
A.-Schreiber-Krieger-Str.
Marie-Elisabeth-Lüders-Haus (Dt. Bundestag)
Schiffbauerdamm
Marschallbr.
Gerhardt-str.
Fleming-str.
Ingeborg-Drewitz-Allee
Nord-br.
Kanzler-park
Spree
Bundes-kanzleramt
Paul-Löbe-Haus (DBT)
Reichstag
Alice-Berend-Str.
Süd-br.
Paul-
Joachim-
Karnatz-Allee
Haus der Kulturen der Welt
Platz der Republik
Reichstags-gebäude (DBT)
Fr.-Ebert-Pl.
Reichs-tag-
Jakob-Kaiser-Haus
Moabiter Werder
Bettina-von-Arnim-Ufer
Große Querallee
Carillon
Heinr.-v.-Gagern-Str.
Scheidemann-str.
Dorotheen-Haus (Deutscher Bundestag)
Unter den Linden
Luther-Br.
John-Foster-Dulles-Allee
Zelten-pl.
Simsonweg
Sowjetisches Ehrenmal
Grossfürsten-pl.
Yitzhak-Rabin-Str.
Platz des 18. März
Pariser Pl.
Brandenburger Tor
Akademie der Künste
Kleiner Stern
Straße des 17. Juni
Straßentunnel B96
Eisenbahntunnel in Bau
Behrenstraße
Bellevue-
Weg
Entlastungsstr.
Löwen-Dkm.
Goethe
Denkmal für die ermordeten Juden Europas
Hannah-Arendt-Str.
Cora-Berlin-Str.
Gertr.-Kolmar-Str.
Tiergarten
Rousseau-insel
Sternallee
Friedr.-Wilh. III
Ahorn-steig
Lessing
Landes-vertr. In den Min.-gärten
An der Kolonnade
Luiseninsel
Ahornsteig
1 I.-Beisheim-Pl.
2 Am Park
3 Berliner Freiheit
Lenné-str.
Kemper-Pl.
Henriette-Herz-Park
Hans-Bülow-S.
Voß-
Mosse-Palais
Musikinstr.-museum
Philharmonie
Bellevuestr.
Sony-Center
Arkaden
Potsdamer Pl.
Leipziger Pl.
Leipziger Str.
Bundesrat
LV-B.-Württemb.
Tiergarten-
Kunstgewerbe-museum
Kulturforum
Kunstbibliothek
Kupferstichkabinett
Gemälde-galerie
Kammer-musik saal
Matthäi-kirchplatz
Marl.-Dietrich-Pl.
Spiel-bank
Staats-bibl.
Fontane-pl.
E.-Berger-Str.
Abgeordnetenhaus von Berlin
Niederkirchnerstr.
Martin-Gropius-Bau
Europahaus
LV-Nordrh.-Westf.
LV-Bremen
Hiroshimastraße
Hildebrandstraße
Bundesamt für Kartogr. u. Geo.
Gedenkstätte Dt. Widerstand
BM der Verteidigung (2. Dienstsitz)
Stauffenberg-
Sigismund-
Hitzigallee
Neue Nationalgalerie
Wissenschafts-zentrum
Reichpietsch-ufer
Von-der-Heydt-Str.
Schöneberger Ufer
Bendler-Br.
General-Bds.-Anw.
Tilly-Durieux-Park
Gabriele-Tergit-Promenade
4 Potsd. Platz Arkaden
Landwehrkanal
Lützow-
Kultur-zentrum
Jugend-Gästehs.
Elisab.-Krkhs.
Potsdamer Br.
G.-C.-Marshall-Br.
Karlsbad
Am
Bissing-zeile
Mendelssohn-Bartholdy-Park
Köthener Str.
Dessauer Str.
Bern-burger Str.
Askanischer Pl.
Anhalter Bhf
Hafen-
Mendelssohn-Bartholdy-Park
Schöneberger Str.
Dkm. d. Anhalter Bf.
Magdebgr. Pl.
Arbeits-ger.
Schule
Derfflingerstr.
Genthiner
Kluck-
St.-Ludgerus-K.
Sch.
Wintergtn. varieté
Potsdamer Str.
Pohl-
Pohlstr.
Körnerstr.
Berlin-Kolleg
Flottwell-str.
Beach-volley-ball-platz
Schöne-berger Str.
Tempelhofer Ufer
Hallesches Ufer
Tiefbauamt
Tempodrom
Lapi-darium
Möckern-
Kurfürstenstr.
Zwölf-Apostel-K.
E.-Lasker-Schüler-Str.
Kurmärk. Str.
Bülow-
Kurfürsten-str.
Berufs-fachsch.
Finanzamt
Luckenwalder Str.
Gleisdreieck
Möckernbrücke
Anhalter Steg
133

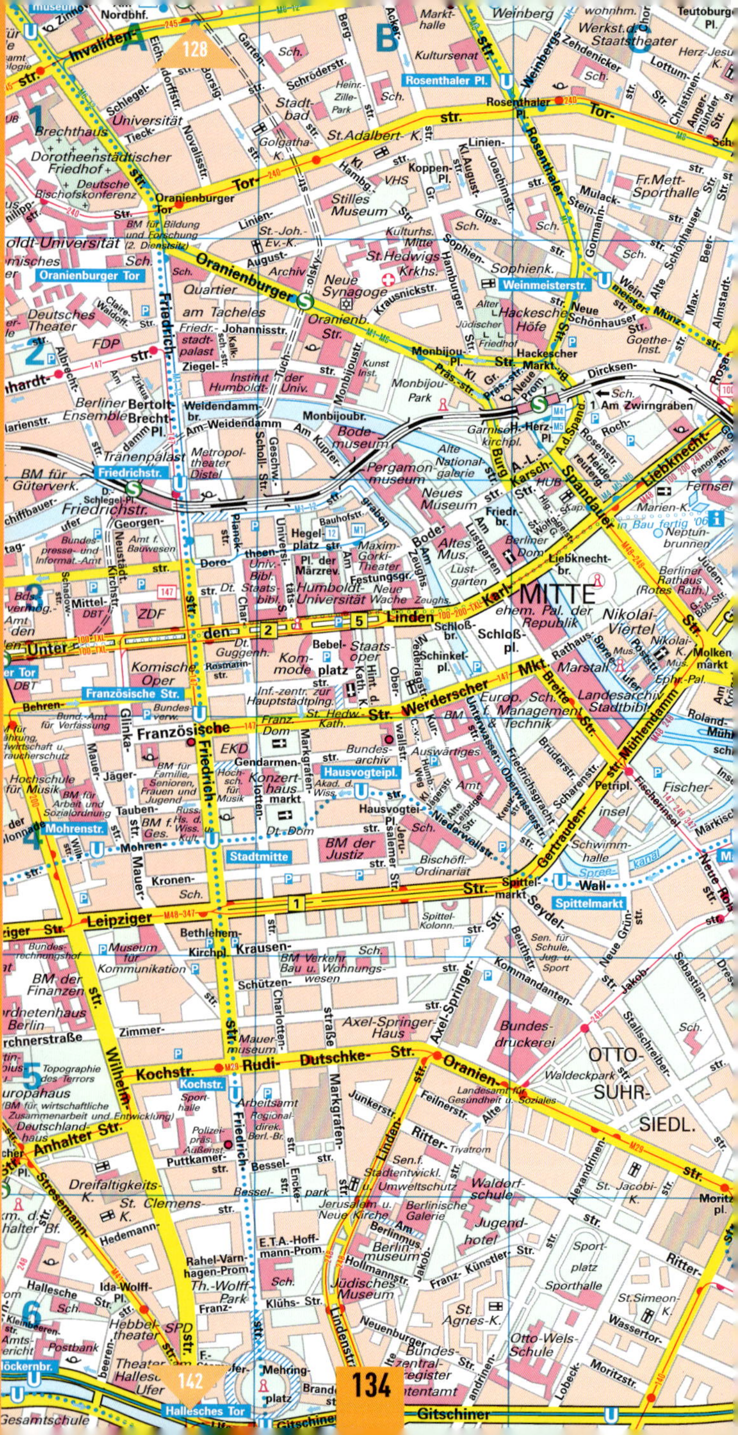

128
A
B
C
1
2
3
4
5
6
Nordbhf.
Invaliden-
str.
Markt-
halle
Kultursenat
Weinberg
Werkst.d.
Staatstheater
Teutoburger
Pl.
Zehdenicker
Lottum-
Rosenthaler Pl.
Schröderstr.
Heinr.-
Zille-
Park
Stadt-
bad
Schlegel-
Universität
Tieck-
Novalisstr.
Brechthaus
Dorotheenstädtischer
Friedhof
Deutsche
Bischofskonferenz
St.Adalbert-
K.
Tor-
str.
Rosenthaler
Pl.
Golgatha-
K.
Koppen-
Pl.
VHS
Linien-
Joachimstr.
Fr.Mett-
Sporthalle
Mulack-
Stilles
Museum
Gips-
Oranienburger
Tor
BM für Bildung
und Forschung
(2. Dienstsitz)
St.-Joh.-
Ev.-K.
Kulturhs.
Mitte
St.Hedwigs
Krkhs.
Sophien-
Sophienk.
Weinmeisterstr.
Oranienburger Tor
Oranienburger
August-
Archiv
Neue
Synagoge
Krausnickstr.
Quartier
am Tacheles
Hackesche
Höfe
Neue
Schönhauser
Goethe-
Inst.
Deutsches
Theater
FDP
Johannisstr.
Friedr.-
stadt-
palast
Oranienb.
Str.
Monbijou-
Pl.
Hackescher
Markt
Ziegel-
Institut
Humboldt-
Univ.
Kunst
Inst.
Monbijou-
Park
Dircksen-
Am Zwirngraben
Berliner
Ensemble
Bertolt-
Brecht-
Pl.
Weidendamm-
br.
Am Weidendamm
Monbijoubr.
Bode-
museum
Alte
National-
galerie
Garnison-
kirchpl.
H.-Herz-
Pl.
Rosenstr.
Heide-
reuterg.
Tränenpalast
Metropol-
theater
Distel
Friedrichstr.
Pergamon-
museum
Spandauer
Liebknecht-
BM für
Güterverk.
Friedrichstr.
Georgen-
Bauhofstr.
Hegel-
platz
Neues
Museum
Marien-K.
in Bau fertig '06
Neptun-
brunnen
Bundes-
presse- und
Informat.-Amt
Amt f.
Bauwesen
Doro-
theen-
Univ.
Bibl.
Pl. der
Märzrev.
Maxim-
Gorki-
Theater
Festungsgr.
Altes
Mus.
Lust-
garten
Berliner
Dom
Liebknecht-
br.
Berliner
Rathaus
(Rotes Rath.)
Mittel-
ZDF
Dt. Staats-
bibl.
Humboldt-
Universität
Neue
Wache
Zeughs.
Karl-
MITTE
ehem. Pal. der
Republik
Nikolai-
Viertel
Unter
den
Linden
Schloß-
br.
Schloß-
pl.
Dt.
Guggenh.
Kom-
mode
Bebel-
platz
Staats-
oper
Schinkel-
pl.
Rathaus-
Marstall
Molken-
markt
Komische
Oper
Französische Str.
Inf.-zentr. zur
Hauptstadtplng.
Werderscher
Mkt.
Europ. Sch.
f. Management
& Technik
Landesarchiv
Stadtbibl.
Behren-
Bund. Amt
für Verfassung
Französische
Franz.
Dom
St. Hedw.-
Kath.
Str.
Mühlendamm
Hochschule
für Musik
BM für
Familie,
Senioren,
Frauen und
Jugend
EKD
Gendarmen-
markt
Konzert-
haus
Bundes-
archiv
Hausvogteipl.
Auswärtiges
Amt
Petripl.
Fischer-
insel
Mohrenstr.
Mohren-
Tauben-
Dt. Dom
Hausvogtei-
Pl.
BM der
Justiz
Niederwallstr.
Bischöfl.
Ordinariat
Gertrauden-
Schwimm-
halle
Spree-
kanal
Stadtmitte
Kronen-
Wall-
Spittelmarkt
Leipziger
Str.
Spittel-
markt
Seydel-
Bethlehem-
Kirchpl.
Krausen-
Museum
für
Kommunikation
BM Verkehr
Bau u. Wohnungs-
wesen
Sen. für
Schule,
Jug. u.
Sport
BM der
Finanzen
Schützen-
Kommandanten-
Axel-Springer-
Haus
Bundes-
druckerei
Zimmer-
Mauer-
museum
OTTO-
SUHR-
SIEDL.
Topographie
des Terrors
Kochstr.
Rudi-
Dutschke-
Str.
Oranien-
Waldeckpark
Europahaus
(BM für wirtschaftliche
Zusammenarbeit und Entwicklung)
Deutschland-
haus
Arbeitsamt
Landesamt für
Gesundheit u. Soziales
Anhalter Str.
Polizei-
präs.
Puttkamer-
Bessel-
Ritter-
Tiyatrom
Dreifaltigkeits-
K.
St. Clemens-
K.
Sen.f.
Stadtentwickl.
u. Umweltschutz
Waldorf-
schule
St. Jacobi-
K.
Hedemann-
Jerusalem- u.
Neue Kirche
Berlinische
Galerie
Jugend-
hotel
Moritz
pl.
E.T.A.-Hoff-
mann-Prom.
Rahel-Varn-
hagen-Prom
Berlinmus.
Berlin-
museum
Hollmannstr.
Künstler-
Sport-
platz
Sporthalle
Ritter-
Hallesche
Ida-Wolff-
Pl.
Th.-Wolff-
Park
Jüdisches
Museum
St.Simeon-
K.
Hebbel-
theater
SPD
Postbank
Franz-
Klühs-
Str.
Lindenstr.
St.
Agnes-K.
Otto-Wels-
Schule
Wassertor-
Theater am
Halleschen
Ufer
Mehring-
platz
Bundes-
zentral-
register
Moritzstr.
142
Hallesches Tor
Gitschiner
Gesamtschule

129

Senefelderplatz
bat-Studiotheater
D
E
F
Metzer Str.
Saarbrücker Str.
Straßburger Str.
Raabestr.
Heinrich-Roller-Str.
Wins-str.
Verw.
Sch.
St. Marien
St. Georgen
Greifswalder Str.
St.-Katharinen-Stift
Käthe-Niederkirchner-Str.
Esmarchstr.
Bötzowstr.
Hans-Otto-Str.
Hermann-Str.
Kniprode-Str.
Virchowstr.
Marg.-Sommer-Str.
Kita
Friedrichshain
Rodelbahn
Prenzlauer Berg
Platz am Königstor
Am Schweizer Garten
Am Friedrichshain
Tennis-anl.
Märchen-brunnen
FRIEDRICHSHAIN
Volkspark
Duftgtn.
Luxemburg-Pl.
Prenzlauer Str.
St. Nikolai
TXL
Mendelssohnstr.
Linienstr.
Weydingerstr.
Bartelstr.
Mollstr.
Bartolomäus-K.
Sen.-hm.
Georgenkirchstr.
Friedenstr.
Ev. Zentrale Berliner Br.
Gr. Teich
Rosengtn.
Friedrichshain
Städtisches Krk.
Barnimstr.
Schulor.-seminar
Weinstr.
Höchste Str.
Verk.-Sch.
Büschingstr.
Lichtenberger Str.
Frei-lichtbühne
Max-Fettling-Pl.
Friedrichshain
Wadzeck
Keibelstr.
Landes-pol.-verw.-amt
LKA
Min. f. Umwelt Natursch. u. Reaktors.
Otto-Braun-Str.
Berolinastr.
Statist. Bundes-u. Landes-amt
Mollstraße
Kultur-samml.
Ernst-Zinna-Weg
Platz der Vereinten Nationen
Landsberger Allee
Matthiasstr.
Alexanderstr.
Alexanderplatz
Karl-Marx-Allee
Weydemeyerstr.
Rathaus Mitte
Sch.
Strausberger Str.
Friedrichsberger Str.
Pufendorfstr.
Diestelmeyerstr.
Kita
Kongress-halle
Jacobystr.
Schillingstr.
Weydemeyerstr.
Palisadenstr.
Fürstenwalder Str.
Schulweg
Sch. f. Schwerhörige
Pius-K.
Auferstehungs-K.
St.-Petrus
Dircksenstr.
Alexanderstr.
Landgericht
Neue Blumenstr.
Strausberger Pl.
Neue Weberstr.
Lebuser Str.
Koppenstr.
Ges.-Amt
Littenstr.
Magazinstr.
Gesundheits-zentrum
Rodewil
Klosterstr.
Waisenstr.
Feuer-wache
Stralauer Str.
Schillingstr.
Singerstr.
Ifflandstr.
M.-Planck-Obersch.
Singerstr.
Strausberger Pl.
Karl-Marx-Allee
FRIEDRICHSHAIN-
Kita
Sch. f. Sprachbeh.
Kommune
Schicklerstr.
Jannowitzbr.
Holzmarktstr.
Sportplatz
Lichtenberger Str.
Andreas-pl.
Rüdersdorfer Str.
Sen. f. Fin.
Jannowitzbr.
Märk. Pl.
Wallstr.
Märk. Museum
Köllnischer Park
Senatsverw. f. Stadtentwicklung
Kl. Markusstr.
Kl. Andreasstr.
Fr.-Engels-Obersch.
Kita
F.-Mehring-Pl.
Krautstr.
Lange Str.
Mehlbeerenweg
Schwimm-halle
Koppenstr.
Müncheberger Str.
Pariser Str.
Michaelbr.
Jannowitz Center
Andreasstr.
Sch.
H.-Stöhr-Platz
Am Wriezener Bahnhof
Runge-str.
Schultze-Delitzsch-Pl.
Jakobstr.
Schicklerstr.
Brückenstr.
Ohmstr.
Erich-Steinfurth-Str.
Lange Str.
Wriezener Karree
Köpenicker Str.
Deutsches Zentrum für Architektur, Planungs- u. Bauwesen
Am Ostbahnhof
Ostbahnhof
Heinrich-Heine-Str.
Michaelkirchstr.
Stralauer Platz
Schillingbrücke
P.-Thiede-Ufer
Andreas-K.
Straße der Pariser Kommune
Am Postbahnhof
Annenstr.
Schmidstr.
Michaelkirchstr.
Ober-stufen-zentr.
Bona-Peiser-Weg
Victoria-speicher
Spree
Spree-park
M.-v.-Rantzau-Str.
V.-Gert-Str.
Heinrich-Heine-Pl.
St. Michael-K.
Michaelkirchpl.
Melchiorstr.
Köpenicker Str.
St. Thomas-Gem.Hs.
Behala
Mühlenstr.
Rummelsburger Pl.
Engelbecken
Engeldamm
Bethaniendamm
Städt. Krkhs. Mitte
Dresdener Str.
A.-Döblin-Pl.
Waldemarstr.
Legiendamm
Leuschnerdamm
Adalbertstr.
Sen.-Freiz.-Hs.
Kunstamt Kreuzberg
Künstler-haus
St. Thomas-K.
Mariannenplatz
Wrangelstr.
Senioren-hm.
Sch.
Brommystr.
East-Side
Oranienplatz
Luckauer Str.
Garten-bauamt
Naunynstr.
Soz. Amt
-KREUZBERG
Muskauer Str.
Markthalle
400m
1 Wan
Oranienstr.
Prinzessinnenstr.
Oranien-Pl.
Ballhaus
Waldemarstr.
Eisenbahnstr.
Oberstufen-zentrum
Pfuelstr.
Theater Unart
Blinden-anstalt
Jugend-freizeitheim
Jerusalem Stift
Zeughofstr.
Sch.
Schlesische Str.
Museum Kreuzbg.
Stadt-bücherei
Heinrichpl.
Turnhalle
Manteuffelstr.
Pücklerstr.
Lausitzer Str.
Emmaus-K.
Reichenberger Str.
Görlitzer Bahnhof
Skalitzer Str.
Wassertor-Pl.
Kottbusser Tor
Feuer-wache
Wiener Str.
Wrangelstr.
Liebfrauen-K.
Lübbener Str.
Sch.
1
2
3
4
5

143

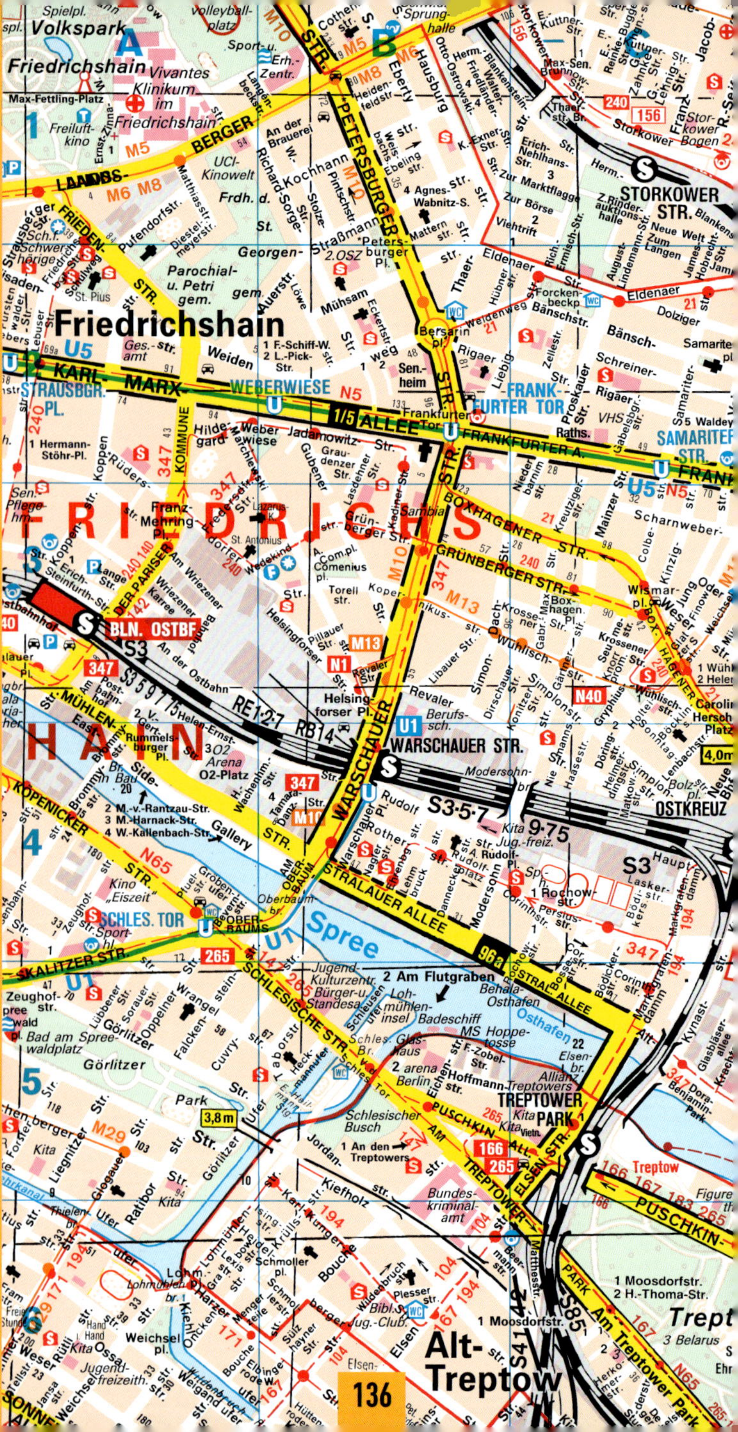

Volkspark
Friedrichshain
Vivantes Klinikum im Friedrichshain
Max-Fettling-Platz
Freiluftkino
LANDSBERGER ALLEE
UCI-Kinowelt
Frdh. d. St. Georgen-Gem.
Parochial- u. Petri gem.
PETERSBURGER STR.
Hausburg
Storkower Str.
STORKOWER STR.
Storkower Bogen
Zur Marktflagge
Zur Börse
Viehtrift
Eldenaer Str.
Forckenbeckpl.
Bänschstr.
Dolziger
Samariterstr.
Bersarinpl.
Weidenweg
Rigaer
Friedrichshain
Weiden
Strausberger Pl.
STRAUSBGR. PL.
WEBERWIESE
KARL-MARX-ALLEE
FRANKFURTER TOR
FRANKFURTER A.
SAMARITERSTR.
Schreiner-
Rigaer
Frankfurter Tor
Koppenstr.
KOMMUNE
Hildegard
Weberwiese
Jadamowitz-Str.
Graudenzer Str.
FRIEDRICHS
Franz-Mehring-Pl.
St. Antonius
Wedekind
Comenius pl.
Torell str.
BOXHAGENER STR.
GRÜNBERGER STR.
Scharnweber-
Wismarpl.
BLN. OSTBF
DER PARISER
Helsingforser Pl.
Revaler
Simon-Dach-Str.
Wühlisch-
Simplon-
Warschauer Str.
WARSCHAUER STR.
Helen-Ernst-Str.
O2 Arena
O2-Platz
MÜHLEN-
HAIN
RE1·2·7
RB14
S3·5·7
OSTKREUZ
KÖPENICKER STR.
Gallery
SCHLES. TOR
Kino „Eiszeit"
OBERBAUM
Oberbaumbr.
Spree
STRALAUER ALLEE
Rudolfpl.
Modersohnstr.
Rochowstr.
Persiusstr.
SKALITZER STR.
SCHLESISCHE STR.
Jugend-Kulturzentr.
Bürger-u. Standesa.
Lohmühleninsel
Badeschiff
2 Am Flutgraben
MS Hoppetosse
Osthafen
Elsenbr.
arena Berlin
TREPTOWER PARK
Görlitzer Park
Schlesischer Busch
PUSCHKIN-ALLEE
AM TREPTOWER
ELSEN STR.
Treptow
Bundeskriminalamt
Kiefholz
Karl-Kunger-Str.
Lohmühlen br.
Bouchéstr.
Jug.-Club
Alt-Treptow
Am Treptower Park
1 Moosdorfstr.
2 H.-Thoma-Str.
Weichsel pl.
Jugendfreizeith.
Sonnenallee
Zeughofstr.
Bad am Spreewaldplatz
Görlitzer
Wrangel
Falckenstein-
Cuvry-
Taborstr.
Liegnitzer
Glogauer
Ratibor
Thielen-Ufer
Weichsel
3,8 m
4,0 m

LICHTENBERG
Lichtenberg
Friedrichsfelde
Rummelsburg
Stralau
Victoriastadt
Hyperboloid-Projektion
Abstand zwischen 2 schwarzen Gitterlinien = 1 Kilometer
Ev. Krkhs. Königin Elisabeth Herzberge (KEH)
Herzbergstr.
Josef-Orlopp-Str.
Siegfriedstr.
Möllendorffstr.
Frankfurter Allee
B.-Lichtenberg
RB12·24·NE26
OE25,60
Nöldnerplatz
Rummelsburger Str.
Sewanstr.
Hauptstr.
Köpenicker Chaussee
Alt-Friedrichsfelde
Friedrichsfelde
Betriebsbf Rummelsbg.
Rummelsburger See
Liebesinsel
Kratzbruch
Insel d. Jugend
Spree
Kraftwerk Klingenberg
Stadion 1. Mai
Stadtpark
Gutspark
Finanzamt
BVG Betriebshof
Kinderkrkhs. Lindenhof
Bezirksamt
Magdalenenstr.
Güterbf. Lichtenberg
Rathaus
Amt f. Umwelt u. Natur
Stasi-Mus.
Bundesanstalt f. Arbeitsmed.
Tiefbauamt
Platz am Spreetunnel
Archenhold Sternwarte
Alt-Treptow
Park
1 Emma-Ihrer-Str.
2 Clara-Grunwald-Str.
3 Lina-Morgenstern-Str.
4 Alice- u. Hella-Hirsch-Ring
5 Paula-Fürst-Str.
6 Gisèle-Freund-Hain
7 Charlotte-Salomon-Hain
1 Dolgenseestr.
2 Mellenseestr.
1 Am Viehhof
2 Zur Waage
3 Zur Innung
RE 1·2·7
RB14
RE 3
S3
S5·7·75
S8·41·42
U5

A
B
C
1
3
4
5
6
130
144
Messe-
gelände
Funkturm
Rundfunk-
mus.
Int.
Congress
Centrum
(ICC)
Jap.
Garten
Marshall-
haus
Messedamm Nord
Dreieck Funkturm
Messedamm Süd
Kurfürstendamm
Westkreuz
Messe Süd
Harbigstr.
Eingang
Süd
Deutschland-
halle
(Eissporthalle)
Jaffé-
str.
Messe-
damm
Messedamm-
Br.
Rasthaus
Avus
Nord-
kurve
Halensee-
Dernburg-
Dt.
Post
AG
Telek.Dir.
Herbart-
Senioren-
heim
Kuno-
Fischer-
Pl.
Lietzen-
see
Kirche
am Lietzen-
see
Friedberg-
Suarez-
Rönne-
Heilbronner
HALENSE
Lützen-
str.
Ringbahn-
str.
Georg-Wilh.-Str.
Katharinen-
Karlsruher
Henrietten-
pl.
Kurfürsten-
damm
West-
fälis
Halensee
Seesener
J.-Sigismund-
Str.
Halberst.
Str.
Waldschulallee
Cordes-
str.
Am
Dorn-
busch
Zikaden-
weg
Am Vogelherd
Am
Fieder-
busch
Lärchenw.
Eich-
katzweg
Eichkamp-
str.
A V U S
Golf-
platz
Güterbhf.
Grunewald
des-
Werkstättenweg
Bornstedter
Kronpr.-
damm
Bor-
nimer
Str.
Ned-
litzer
Str.
Friedenthal-
Park
Halen-
see
Freibad
Jugendhm.
Rathenau-
Pl.
Storck-
winkel
Jgnd.-
hm.
Schwarzbchr.
Str.
Schwarzb.-
Br.
Friedrichs-
Gillweg
Marga-
rete-
str.
Trabener
Str.
Nier-
steiner
Str.
Erbacher Str.
Erdener
Str.
Wallotstr.
Umwelt-
Bundes-
amt
Schinkel-
str.
Senioren-
Hm.
Caspar-
Theodor-
Herbert-
str.
Sch.
Bismarck-
Pl.
Buntschuh-
str.
Kurfürstendamm
Theyß-
Viktoria-
Str.
Grieser
Pl.
Paulsborner
Rin-
telner
Str.
koenigs-
allee
Gneiststr.
Wissmann-
str.
Senioren-
hm.
Trabener
Lynar-Johanna-
Pl.
Herthastr.
Bismarck-
allee
Lynar-
str.
Klin. f. kosm.
Chirurgie
Mart.-Luth.-
Krkhs.
heim-
str.
Charlottenbrunner
Str.
Koenigs-
see
Koenigsallee-
Br.
Hertha-
see
Hertha-
str.
Schleinitz-
str.
Bismarck-
br.
Hasensprung
Winkler-
Diana-
see
DRK
Hosp.
E.-Seidel-
Krkhs.
Delbrück-
str.
Lassen-
str.
Hubertus-
see
Grunewald-
klinik
Humboldt-
str.
Warmbrunner
Wangen-
heim
Viktoria-
Hubertus-
Sportplatz
Kurt-Weiß-
Sporthalle
Kudowa-
brunner
Salz-
Hohe
Schwedler-
str.
Bismarck-
Grunew.-
K.
Sch.
GRUNEWALD
Koenigs-
allee
Taubert-
Hagen-
pl.
Feuer-
wache
Furtwängler-
str.
Delbrück-
str.
St.-Karl-
Borromäus-
K.
Hubertus-
allee
Carl-L.-
Schleich-
Prom.
Franzensbader
Str.
Reinerz-
str.
Auguste-
Viktoria-
Str.
Flinsbgr.
Pl.
Oberlin-
Seminar
Lan-
decker
Str.
Hohenzollern-
damm
Kranzer Str.
Sch.
Kreuz-
K.
Forckenbeck-
str.
Elgersbgr.
str.
Ilmenauer
Str.
Menzel-
str.
Klind-
worth-
stg.
Bilse-
str.
Taubert-
str.
Toni-
Werner-
str.
Lessler-
str.
Strauss-
Leo-
Blech-
Pl.
Dachsberg
Jos.-
Joach.-
Pl.
Berkaer
Str.
Nikisch-
str.
Grieg-
str.
Wissensch.-
zentrum
Reger-
str.
Hagen-
str.
B.-
Wieck-
Prom.
Rich.-
Brahms-
str.
Knaus-
str.
VJZ
Hubertusbader
Str.
Taunusstr.
Reuter-
pfad
berger
Teplitzer
Str.
Karls-
bader
Plö-
ner
Eger-
str.
Elster-
Pl.
Kissinger
Str.
Salvator-
K.
Kissinger
Pl.
Weinheimer
Tölzer
Davoser
Aug.-
Viktoria-
Str.
Städt.
Hosp.
Rathaus
Berkaer
Platz
SCHMAR
Spohr-
str.
Wild-
pfad
Rosen-
eck
Marien-
bader Str.
Ruhlaer Str.
Sulzaer
Str.
Reichenhaller
Kolbgr.
Pl.
Friedrichshaller
Sch.
Königsmarck
str.
Bernadotte-
str.
Kron-
berger
Tennis-
halle
Waldmeister-
str.
Eichhörnchensteig
Rob.-Stolz-
Anl.
Waldmeister-
str.
Hundekehle-
str.
Rheinbaden-
allee
Schellendorfer
str.
Selchowstr.
Breite
Str.
Cuno-
Neuap.
Dorfk.
Warnemünder
Str.
Misdroyer
str.
Kirchstr.
Saß-
nitzer
str.
Krampas-
pl.
400m
Hockey-
platz
Grune-
wald-
see
Jugenderholungs-
u. Tagungsstätte
Dünkelberg-
stg.
Rehkitz-
stg.
Clay-
allee
Miquel-
Lucius-
str.
Bernadotte-
Messel-
park
Heyden-
str.
stein-
str.

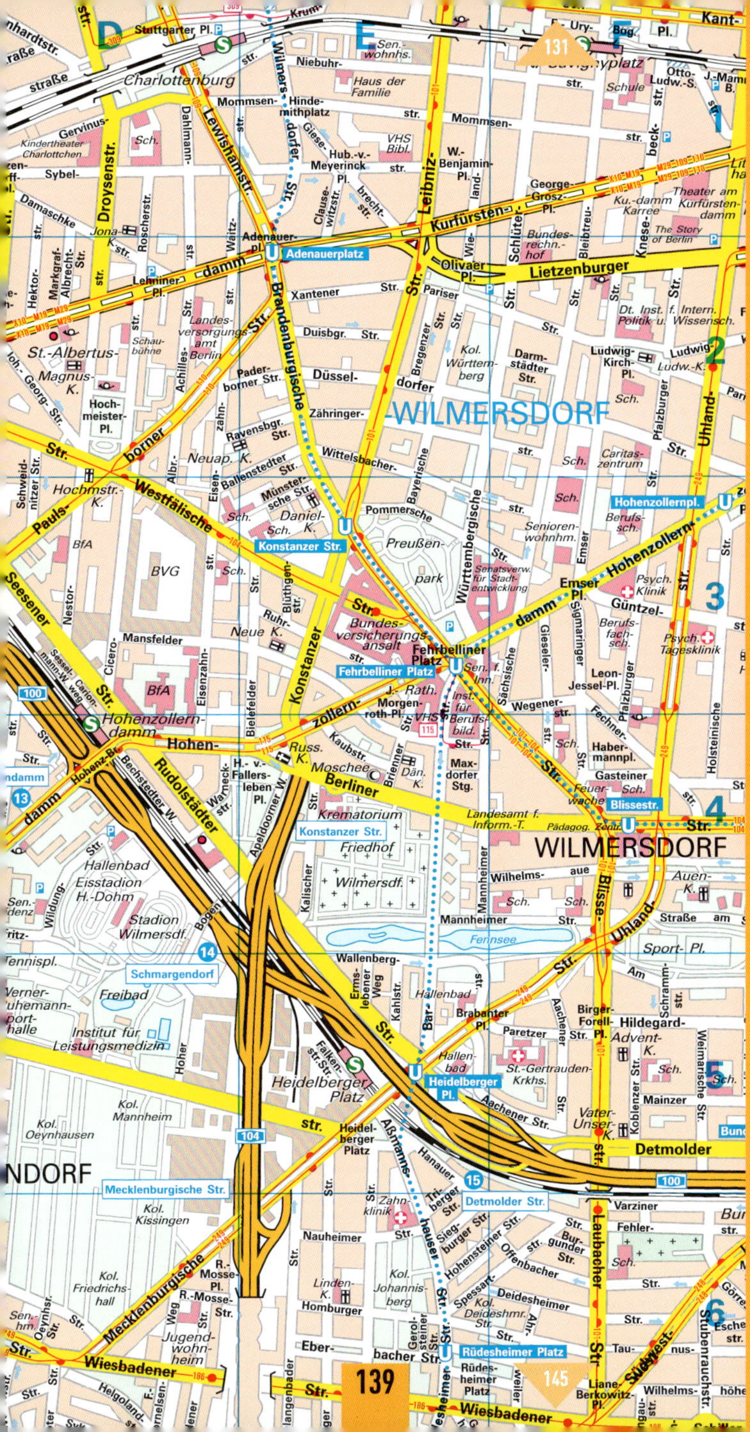

D
E
F
1
2
3
4
5
6
131
145
WILMERSDORF
WILMERSDORF
NDORF
Charlottenburg
Stuttgarter Pl.
Kant-
Niebuhr-
Haus der Familie
Sen.-wohnhs.
Savignyplatz
Schule
Otto-Ludw.-S.
J.-Mamm B.
Mommsen-
Hinde-mithplatz
Giese-
Hub.-v.-Meyerinck Pl.
VHS Bibl.
W.-Benjamin-Pl.
Gervinus-
Kindertheater Charlottchen
Sybel-
Damaschke
Droysenstr.
Dahlmann-
Lewishamstr.
Wilmersdorfer Str.
Clausewitzstr.
Leibniz-
Kurfürsten-
George-Grosz-Pl.
Ku.-damm Karree
Theater am Kurfürstendamm
The Story of Berlin
Bundesrechn.-hof
Adenauerplatz
Adenauer-pl.
Jona-K.
Roscherstr.
Lehniner Pl.
damm
Olivaer Pl.
Lietzenburger
Xantener
Pariser
Duisbgr.
Düssel-
dorfer
Bregenzer
Kol. Württemberg
Darmstädter Str.
Dt. Inst. f. Intern. Politik u. Wissensch.
Ludwig-Kirch-Pl.
Ludwig-
Ludw.-K.
Uhland-
Landesversorgungsamt Berlin
Schaubühne
St.-Albertus-Magnus-K.
Hochmeister-Pl.
Paderborner Str.
Zähringer-
Brandenburgische
Ravensbgr. Str.
Wittelsbacher-
Bayerische
Pfalzburger
Caritaszentrum
Sch.
Hohenzollernpl.
Berufssch.
Neuap. K.
Ballenstedter Str.
Münstersche Str.
Daniel-K.
Pommersche
Westfälische
Pauls-
Hochmstr.-K.
Schweidnitzer Str.
BfA
BVG
Konstanzer Str.
Preußen-park
Württembergische
Senatsverw. für Stadtentwicklung
Senioren-wohnhm.
Emser Pl.
Hohenzollern-
damm
Psych. Klinik
Güntzel-
Berufsfachsch.
Psych. Tagesklinik
Seesener
Nestor-
Mansfelder
Cicero-
Eisenzahn-
Ruhr-
Neue K.
Blüthgen-str.
Bundesversicherungsanstalt
Fehrbelliner Platz
Sen. f. Inn.
Sächsische
Gieseler-
Sigmaringer
Leon-Jessel-Pl.
Sasse-Carion-mann-W.
BfA
Hohenzollern-damm
Hohen-
zollern-
Konstanzer
Bielefelder
J.-Rath. Morgenroth-Pl.
VHS
Inst. für Berufsbild.
Wegener-
Fechner-
Haber-mannpl.
Gasteiner
Feuerwache
Blissestr.
Holsteinische
Hohenz.-Br.
Bechstedter W.
Rudolstädter
Warneck-str.
H.-v.-Fallersleben Pl.
Apeldoorner W.
Russ. K.
Moschee
Kaubstr.
Brienner
Dän. K.
Berliner
Max-dorfer Stg.
Landesamt f. Inform.-T.
Pädagog. Zentr.
Str.
Krematorium
Konstanzer Str.
Friedhof Wilmersdf.
Kalischer
Hallenbad Eisstadion H.-Dohm
Stadion Wilmersdf.
Bogen
Wildung-
Sen.-Residenz
Tennispl.
Schmargendorf
Wilhelms-aue
Mannheimer
Auen-K.
Straße am
Fennsee
Bisse-
Uhland-
Sport-Pl.
Wallenberg-
Ermslebener Weg
Kahlstr.
Hallenbad
Brabanter Pl.
Paretzer
Aachener
Birger-Forell-Pl.
Hildegard-
Advent-K.
Schramm-str.
Werner-Ruhemann-Sporthalle
Freibad
Institut für Leistungsmedizin
Hoher
Falkenstr.
Heidelberger Platz
Heidelberger Pl.
Hallenbad
St.-Gertrauden-Krkhs.
Koblenzer Str.
Mainzer
Weimarische Str.
Kol. Mannheim
Kol. Oeynhausen
str.
Heidelberger Platz
Aßmannshauser
Hanauer
Aachener Str.
Vater-Unser-K.
Detmolder
Bund
Mecklenburgische Str.
Kol. Kissingen
Nauheimer
Zahnklinik
Triberger Str.
Detmolder Str.
Varziner
Fehler-
Laubacher
Siegburger Str.
Hohensteiner Str.
Offenbacher
Burgunder Str.
Kol. Friedrichshall
R.-Mosse-Pl.
R.-Mosse-Str.
Mecklenburgische
Linden-K.
Homburger
Kol. Johannisberg
Spessart-
Deidesheimer
Kol. Deideshmr. Str.
Ahr-
Südwest-
Stubenrauchstr.
Görres-
Jugendwohnheim
Eber-
bacher Str.
Gerolsteiner Str.
Rüdesheimer Platz
Rüdesheimer Platz
Tau-
nus-
Oeynhstr.
Wiesbadener
Helgoland-
Langenbader
Wiesbadener
Liane-Berkowitz-Pl.
Wilhelms-
höhe
104
100
115
13
14
15
186
249

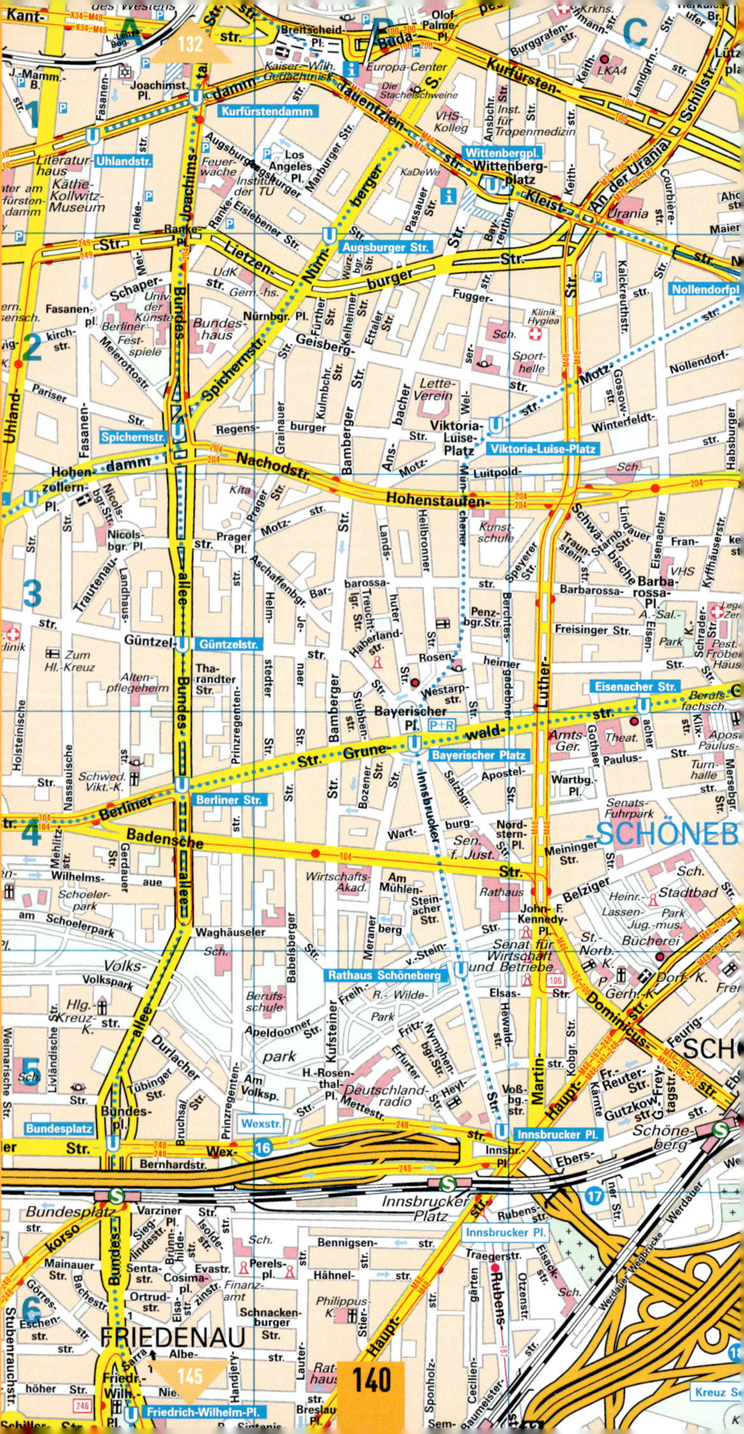

Kant-
Breitscheid-Pl.
Budapester
Olof-Palme-Pl.
Kaiser-Wilh.-Gedächtnisk.
Europa-Center
Die Stachelschweine
Burggrafen-str.
LKA4
Kurfürsten-
Joachimst. Pl.
Kurfürstendamm
Fasanen-
Tauentzien-
VHS-Kolleg
Inst. für Tropenmedizin
Schillstr.
Literaturhaus
Uhlandstr.
Käthe-Kollwitz-Museum
Feuerwache
Los Angeles Pl.
Institut der TU
Augsburger
Marburger Str.
KaDeWe
Wittenbergpl.
Wittenbergplatz
Kleist-
An der Urania
Urania
Courbière-str.
Keith-
Ranke-Pl.
Eislebener Str.
Lietzen-
Nürnberger
Augsburger Str.
Passauer Str.
Bayreuther
Maier
UdK
Gem.-hs.
Schaper-
Univ. der Künste
Berliner Festspiele
Bundeshaus
Nürnbgr. Pl.
Fürther Str.
Geisberg-
Kelheimer Str.
Ettaler Str.
Fugger-
Klinik Hygiea
Sch.
Sporthelle
Kalckreuthstr.
Nollendorfpl.
Fasanen-pl.
Meierottostr.
Spichernstr.
Bundes-
Lette-Verein
Motz-
Gossow-str.
Nollendorf-
Uhland-
Pariser Str.
Regens-
burger
Grainauer
Kulmbchr. Str.
Bamberger
Ans-bacher
Viktoria-Luise-Platz
Winterfeldt-
Habsburger
Spichernstr.
Hohenzollerndamm
Nachodstr.
Luitpold-
Hohenstaufen-
Kita
Prager Str.
Nicolsbgr. Str.
Nicolsbgr. Pl.
Prager Pl.
Lands-huter
Heilbronner
Münchener
Kunstschule
Speyerer Str.
Schwäbische
Traunsteinstr.
Bambg. Str.
Lindauer Str.
Eisenacher
Fran-
Kyffhäuserstr.
Barbarossa-
Barbarossa-Pl.
VHS
Trautenau-
Landhaus-
Aschaffenbg.
Bar-barossa-
Treuchtlgr. Str.
Penz-bgr. Str.
Berchtesgadener
Freisinger Str.
A.-Sal.-
Eisen-
Lega-Zentr.
Pest.-Fröbel-Haus
Güntzel-
Güntzelstr.
Zum Hl.-Kreuz
Altenpflegeheim
Tharandter Str.
Helmstedter
Jenaer
Haberland-str.
Rosen-heimer
Westarp-str.
Park
Schrader-Str.
Holsteinische
Nassauische
Prinzregenten-
Bayerischer Pl.
P+R
Grunewald-
Eisenacher Str.
Berufsfachsch.
Amts-Ger.
Theat.
Gothaer
Paulus-
Apos. Paulus-
Turnhalle
Merseburger Str.
Bayerischer Platz
Innsbrucker
Salzbgr.
Apostel-
Schwed. Vikt.-K.
Berliner
Berliner Str.
Bozener
Wartbg.-Pl.
Senats-Fuhrpark
SCHÖNEB
Badensche
Wart-burg-
Sen. f. Just.
Nordstern-Pl.
Meininger Str.
Mehlitz-str.
Gerdauer Str.
Wilhelms-aue
Schoeler-park
Schoelerpark
Wirtschafts-Akad.
Am Mühlen-
Steinacher Str.
Rathaus
Belziger
Sch.
Stadtbad
Heinr.-Lassen-Park
Jug.-mus.
Bücherei
John-F.-Kennedy-Pl.
Waghäuseler
Babelsberger
Meraner
berg
Senat für Wirtschaft und Betriebe
St.-Norb.-K.
Volkspark
Rathaus Schöneberg
Elsas-
Dorf-K.
Gerh.-K.
Dominicus-
Hlg.-Kreuz-K.
Berufsschule
Freih.-v.-Stein-
R.-Wilde-Park
Hewald-str.
Weimarische Str.
Livländische Str.
Durlacher
Apeldoorner Str.
park
Kufsteiner
Fritz-Elsas
Nymphenbgr. Str.
Erfurter
Kobgr. Str.
Feurig-
SCH
Tübinger Str.
Bruchsal.
Prinzregenten-
Am Volksp.
H.-Rosenthal-Pl.
Deutschlandradio
Mettestr.
Heyl-
Voßbg.-str.
Martin-Luther-
Haupt-
Fr.-Reuter-Str.
Gutzkow-str.
G.-Freytagstr.
Kärnter
Bundesplatz
Bundes-pl.
Wexstr.
Wex-
Innsbrucker Pl.
Schöneberg
Ebers-
Bernhardstr.
Innsbr.-Pl.
Bundesplatz
Varziner Str.
Innsbrucker Platz
Rubens-str.
Innsbrucker Pl.
Siegmundstr.
Brünnhildestr.
Isoldestr.
Sch.
Bennigsen-str.
Traegerstr.
Werdauer Wegbrücke
Werdauer
Mainauer Str.
Bachestr.
Senta-str.
Cosima-pl.
Evastr.
Perels-pl.
Finanzamt
Hähnel-str.
Rubens-
Otzenstr.
Sch.
Görres-
Eschen-str.
Ortrud-str.
Elsa-str.
Schnackenburger Str.
Philippus-K.
Stier-str.
Stubenrauchstr.
FRIEDENAU
Saarstr.
Albe-str.
Handjery-
Lauter-
Rathaus
Sponholz-
Cecilien-gärten
Friedr.-Wilh.-Pl.
höher Str.
Nie.
Friedrich-Wilhelm-Pl.
Bresl. Pl.
Sem-
Kreuz Sc

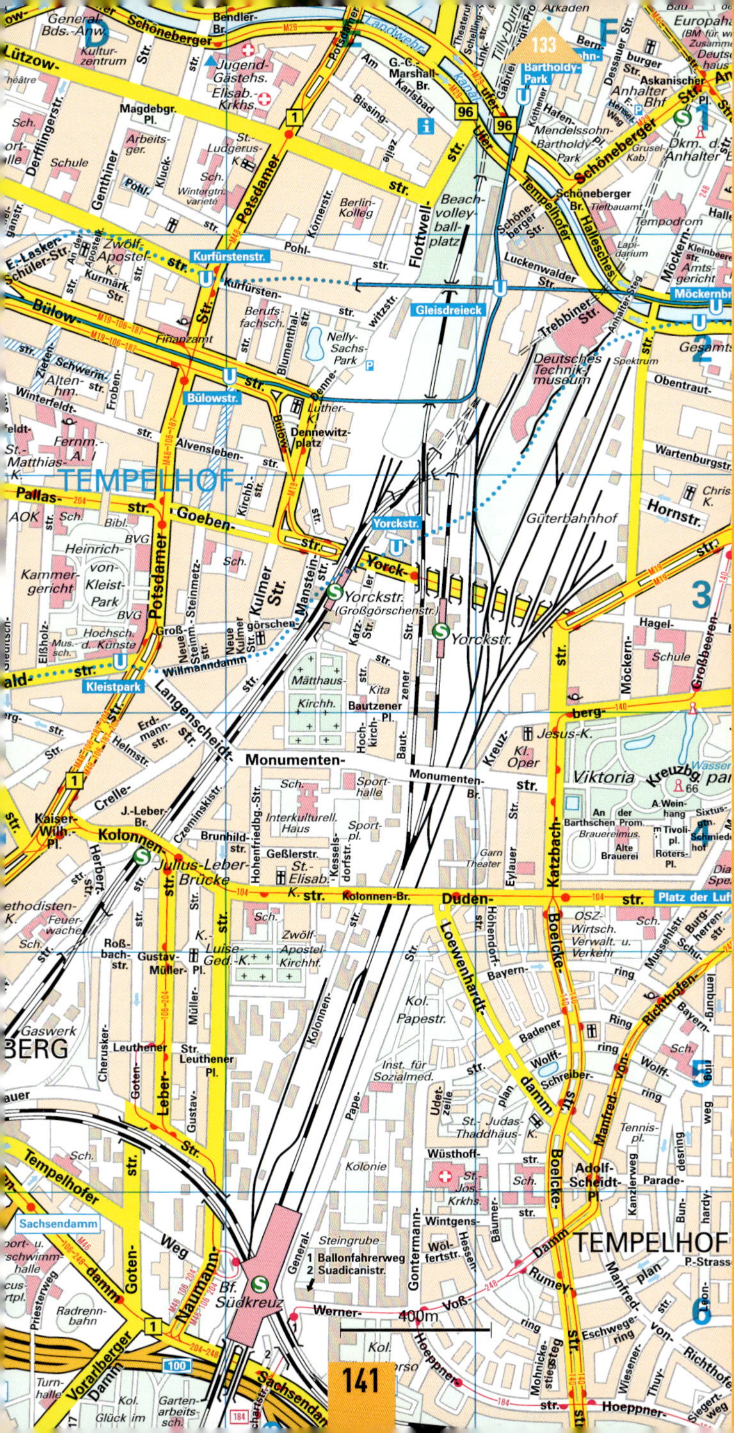
133
D
E
F
1
2
3
5
6
General-Bds.-Anw.
Schöneberger
Bendler-Br.
Landwehr
Lützow-
Kulturzentrum
Jugend-Gästehs.
Elisab.-Krkhs.
Magdebgr. Pl.
Arbeitsger.
St.-Ludgerus-K.
Potsdamer
Str.
Dörfflingerstr.
Schule
Genthiner
Potsd.
Kluck-
Wintergtn. varieté
G.-C.-Marshall-Br.
Karlsbad
Bissing-zeile
Gabriele-Tergit-Prom.
Link-str.
Schelling-str.
Theaterufer
Tilly-Durieux-Park
Arkaden
Mendelssohn-Bartholdy-Park
Hafen-
Köthener
Dessauer Str.
Bernburger Str.
Askanischer Pl.
Anhalter Bhf
Europahaus
Dkm. d. Anhalter Bhf.
Grusel-Kab.
Schöneberger Br.
Tiefbauamt
Tempodrom
Halleschеs
Tempelhofer Ufer
Schöneberger Str.
Luckenwalder Str.
Lapidarium
Möckern-
Kleinbeerenstr.
Amtsgericht
Möckernbrücke
Beach-volley-ball-platz
Flottwell-str.
Berlin-Kolleg
Körnerstr.
Pohl-
E.-Lasker-Schüler-Str.
Zwölf-Apostel-K.
Kurmärk. Str.
Kurfürstenstr.
Kurfürsten-
Gleisdreieck
Bülow-
Berufsfachsch.
Blumenthal-str.
Nelly-Sachs-Park
witzstr.
Trebbiner-Str.
Anhalter Steg
Gesamtschule
Deutsches Technikmuseum
Spektrum
Obentraut-
Finanzamt
Schwerin-
Alten-hm.
Zieten-
Winterfeldt-
Froben-
Bülowstr.
Denne-
Luther-K.
Dennewitz-platz
Alvensleben-
Fernm.-A.
St.-Matthias-K.
TEMPELHOF-
Wartenburgstr.
Pallas-
Goeben-
Kirchb.-str.
AOK
Sch.
Bibl.
BVG
Heinrich-von-Kleist-Park
Kammergericht
Güterbahnhof
Hornstr.
Chris K.
Yorckstr.
Yorck-
Manstein-str.
Kulmer Str.
Steinmetz-
Neue Steinm.-Str.
Neue Kulmer Str.
görschen-
Groß-
Hochsch. d. Künste
Mus.-sch.
Elßholz-
Kleistpark
Willmanndamm
Yorckstr. (Großgörschenstr.)
Katz-ler Str.
Hagel-
Schule
Großbeeren-
Langenscheidt-str.
Mätthaus-Kirchh.
Kita
Bautzener Pl.
Hoch-kirch-
Baut-zener
Jesus-K.
Kl. Oper
Kreuz-
berg-
Viktoria
Kreuzberg
Helmstr.
Erd-mann-str.
Crelle-
Monumenten-
Monumenten-Br.
Sportshalle
Interkulturell. Haus
Sport-pl.
Garn Theater
Eylauer
Katzbach-
An der Prom.
Barthschen Brauereimus.
A.Weinhang
Tivoli-pl.
Alte Brauerei
Roters-Pl.
Sixtus-gtn.
Kaiser-Wilh.-Pl.
J.-Leber-Br.
Kolonnen-
Czeminskistr.
Brunhild-str.
Hohenfriedbg.-Str.
Geßlerstr.
Kessels-dorfstr.
St.-Elisab.-K.
Julius-Leber-Brücke
Herbert-str.
Kolonnen-Br.
Duden-
Platz der Luftbrücke
Methodisten-K.
Feuerwache
Roßbach-str.
Gustav-Müller-Pl.
K.-Luise-Ged.-K.
Zwölf-Apostel-Kirchhf.
Loewenhardt-damm
Höhendorf-str.
Boelcke-str.
OSZ-Wirtsch. Verwalt. u. Verkehr
Bayern-ring
Mussehlstr.
Burgherren-str.
Schulen-
Richthofen-
Kol. Papestr.
Badener Ring
Gaswerk
BERG
Leuthener
Leuthener Pl.
Cherusker-
Goten-
Leber-
Gustav-Müller-
Inst. für Sozialmed.
Udet-zeile
Wolff-ring
Schreiber-
St.-Judas-Thaddhäus-K.
Manfred-von-
Tennis-pl.
Pape-
Kolonie
Wüsthoff-
St.-Jos.-Krkhs.
Adolf-Scheidt-Pl.
Kanzlerweg
Parade-
Bundesring
Tempelhofer
Sachsendamm
Sport- u. Schwimmhalle
Weg
Naumann-
Bf. Südkreuz
Steingrube
1 Ballonfahrerweg
2 Suadicanistr.
General-
Gontermann-
Wintgens-
Wölfertstr.
Hessen-
Bäumer-
TEMPELHOF
P.-Strasse
Rumey-
Radrennbahn
Priesterweg
Werner-
Voß-
400m
Hoeppner-
Kol.
Mohnicke-steig
Eschwege-ring
Wiesener-
Thuy-
Siegert-weg
Turnhalle
Vorarlberger Damm
Kol. Glück im Winkel
Gartenarbeits-sch.
Sachsendamm
Hoeppner-

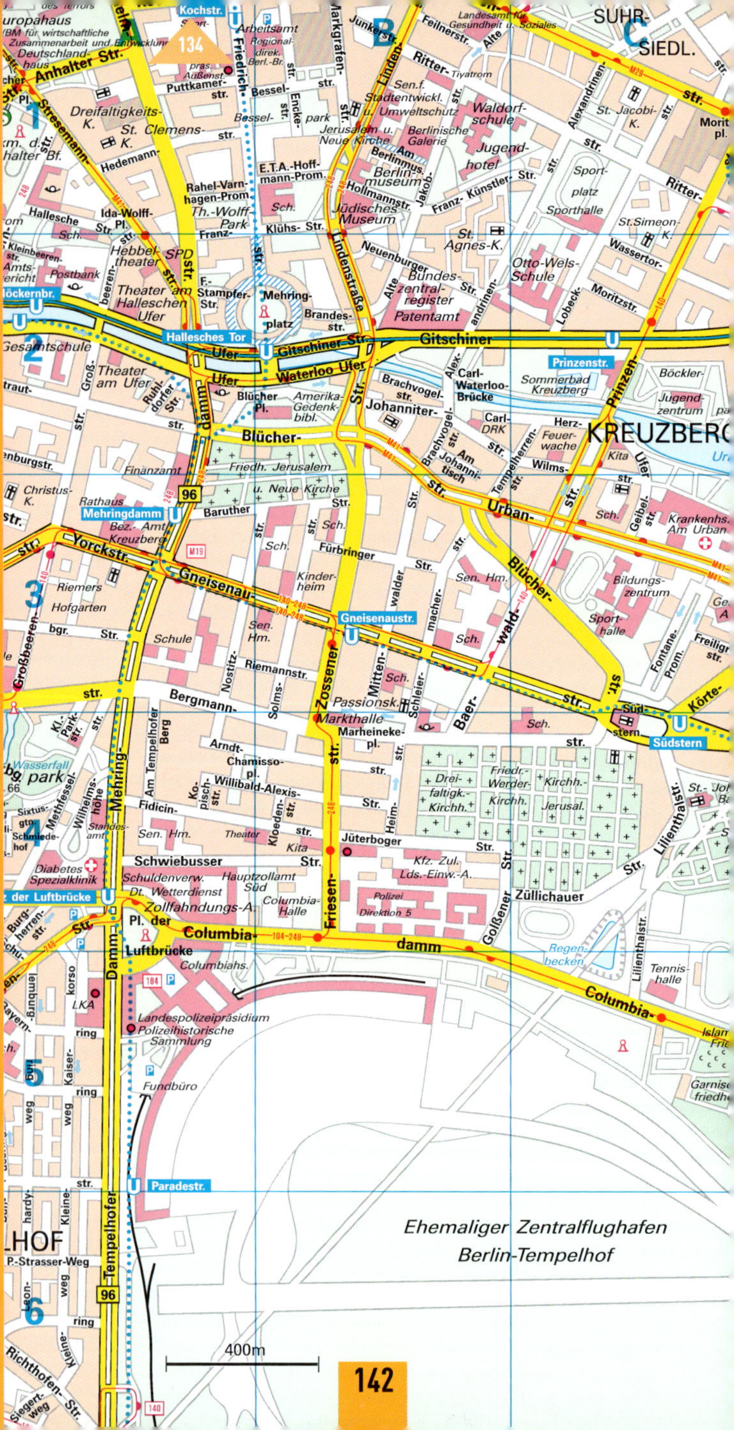
134
Kochstr.
Anhalter Str.
Stresemann-
Dreifaltigkeits-K.
St. Clemens-K.
Hedemann-
Puttkamer-str.
Bessel-str.
Enckestr.
Markgrafen-
Junkerstr.
Feilnerstr.
Alte
Landesamt für Gesundheit u. Soziales
SUHR-SIEDL.
Ritter-
Tiyatrom
Sen.f. Stadtentwickl. u. Umweltschutz
Waldorf-schule
Berlinische Galerie
Jugend-hotel
Jerusalem u. Neue Kirche
Am Berlinmus.
Berlin-museum
Hollmannstr.
Jüdisches Museum
Franz-Künstler-Str.
Alexandrinen-
St. Jacobi-K.
Moritz-pl.
Sportplatz
Sporthalle
St.Simeon-K.
Wassertor-
Moritzstr.
E.T.A.-Hoff-mann-Prom.
Rahel-Varn-hagen-Prom.
Th.-Wolff-Park
Franz-
Klühs-Str.
Lindenstraße
Ida-Wolff-Pl.
Hallesche Str.
Hebbel-theater
SPD
Postbank
Theater am Halleschen Ufer
F.-Stampfer-Str.
Mehring-platz
Brandes-str.
Neuenburger
Bundes-zentral-register
Patentamt
St. Agnes-K.
Otto-Wels-Schule
Lobeck-
Möckernbr.
Hallesches Tor
Gitschiner-Str.
Gitschiner
Prinzenstr.
Gesamtschule
Ufer
Waterloo Ufer
Theater am Ufer
Blücher-Pl.
Amerika-Gedenk-bibl.
Brachvogel-str.
Carl-Waterloo-Brücke
Sommerbad Kreuzberg
Böckler-
Jugend-zentrum
Johanniter-
Carl-DRK
Herz-
Feuer-wache
KREUZBERG
Kita
Blücher-
Friedh. Jerusalem
u. Neue Kirche
Finanzamt
Christus-K.
Rathaus
Mehringdamm
96
Baruther
Urban-
Krankenhs. Am Urban
Yorckstr.
Bez.-Amt Kreuzberg
Gneisenau-
Fürbringer
Kinder-heim
Riemers Hofgarten
Sen. Hm.
Bildungs-zentrum
Sport-halle
Gneisenaustr.
Schule
Riemannstr.
Zossener
Mitten-
Nostitz-
Solms-
Bergmann-
Passionsk.
Markthalle
Marheineke-pl.
Süd-stern
Südstern
Körte-
Am Tempelhofer Berg
Arndt-
Chamisso-pl.
Willibald-Alexis-
Fidicin-
Drei-faltigk.-Kirchh.
Friedr.-Werder-Kirchh.
Kirchh.-Jerusal.
Lilienthalstr.
Wasserfall
park
Mehring-
Wilhelms-höhe
Standes-amt
Sen. Hm.
Theater
Kita
Jüterboger
Kfz. Zul. Lds.-Einw.-A.
Schwiebusser Str.
Diabetes Spezialklinik
Schuldenverw.
Hauptzollamt Süd
Columbia-Halle
Polizei Direktion 5
Dt. Wetterdienst
Zollfahndungs-A.
Züllichauer
Golßener
Friesen-
Pl. der Luftbrücke
Columbia-
damm
Regen-becken
Tennis-halle
Columbiahs.
LKA
Landespolizeipräsidium
Polizeihistorische Sammlung
Fundbüro
Paradestr.
Tempelhofer
Damm
Ehemaliger Zentralflughafen
Berlin-Tempelhof
P.-Strasser-Weg
Richthofen-Str.
400m

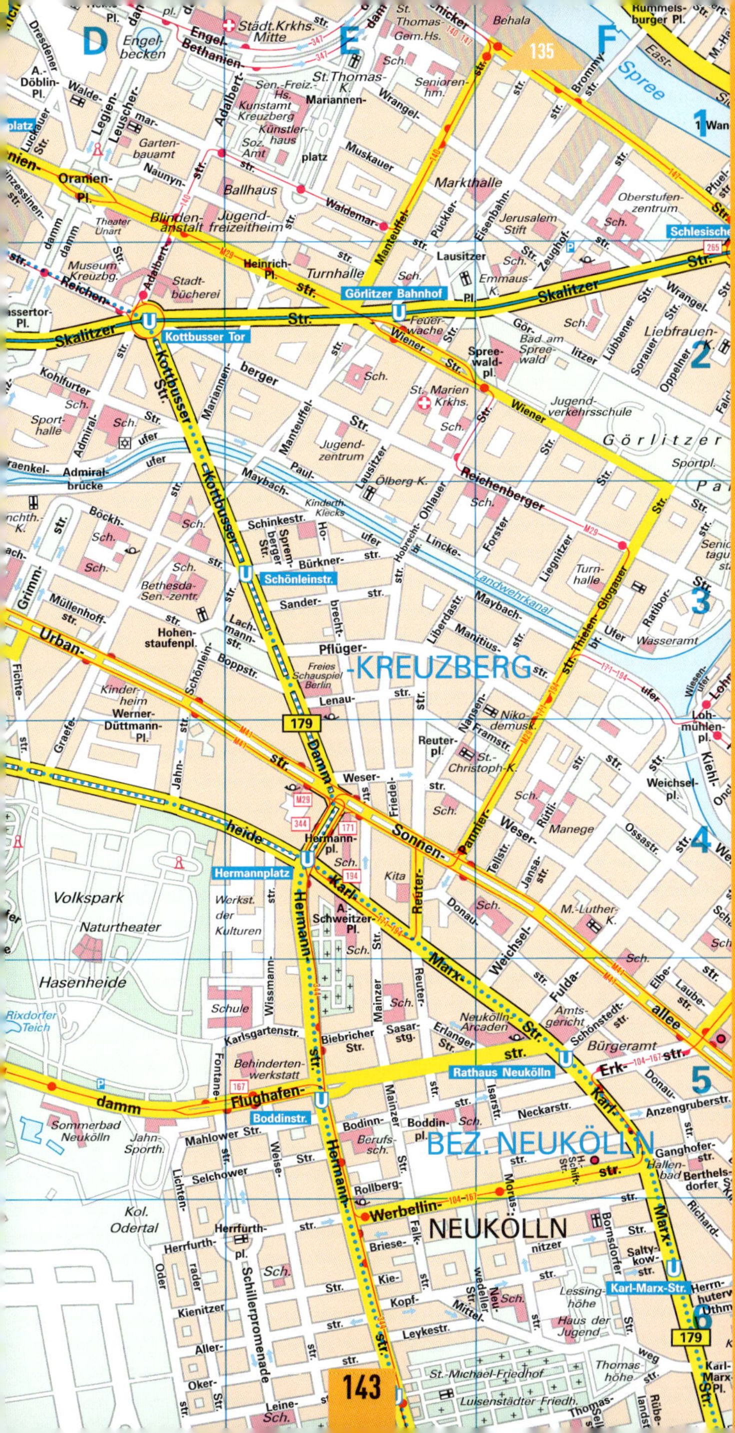

D
E
F
135
143
1
2
3
4
5
6
Städt. Krkhs. Mitte
Engelbecken
Engel-
Bethanien-
St. Thomas-Gem.Hs.
St. Thomas-K.
Mariannen-
Behala
Spree
Rummelsburger Pl.
Dresdener
A.-Döblin-Pl.
Walde-
Legien-
Leuscher-
Luckauer Str.
Kunstamt Kreuzberg
Künstlerhaus
Sen.-Freiz.-Hs.
Soz. Amt
Adalbert-
Garten-bauamt
Naunyn-
Senioren-hm.
Wrangel-
Muskauer
Markthalle
Oberstufen-zentrum
Oranien-Pl.
Ballhaus
Waldemar-
Theater Unart
Blinden-anstalt
Jugend-freizeitheim
Manteuffel-
Pückler-
Eisenbahn-
Jerusalem Stift
Schlesische
Heinrich-Pl.
Turnhalle
Museum Kreuzbg.
Stadt-bücherei
Reichen-
Görlitzer Bahnhof
Lausitzer
Emmaus-K.
Zeughof-
Skalitzer
Str.
Kottbusser Tor
Feuer-wache
Wiener
Spree-wald-pl.
Bad am Spree-wald
Görlitzer
Liebfrauen-K.
Lübbener
Sorauer
Oppelner
Kottbusser
Kohlfurter
Sporthalle
Admiral-
Mariannen-
berger
St. Marien Krkhs.
Jugend-verkehrsschule
Görlitzer
Sportpl.
Admiral-brücke
ufer
Paul-
Maybach-
Jugend-zentrum
Ölberg-K.
Reichenberger
Böckh-
Kinderth. Klecks
Schinkestr.
Sprenberger Str.
Ohlauer
Lincke-
Forster
Liegnitzer
Turnhalle
Hobrecht-
Bürkner-
Schönleinstr.
Bethesda-Sen.-zentr.
Müllenhoff-str.
Sander-
Landwehrkanal
Ratibor-
Grimm-
Hohenstaufenpl.
Lach-mann-str.
Pflüger-
Liberdastr.
Manitius-
Thielen-br.
Glogauer
Wasseramt
Urban-
Boppstr.
Freies Schauspiel Berlin
KREUZBERG
Fichte-
Kinderheim
Werner-Düttmann-Pl.
Schönlein-
Lenau-
179
Nansen-
Niko-demus-K.
Lohmühlen-pl.
Graefe-
Jahn-
Damm
Reuter-pl.
Framstr.
St.-Christoph-K.
Weichsel-pl.
Weser-
Friedel-
Hermann-pl.
Sonnen-
Pannier-
Rütli-
Manege
Ossastr.
heide
Hermannplatz
Karl-
Kita
Reuter-
Tellstr.
Jansa-str.
Volkspark
Werkst. der Kulturen
A.-Schweitzer-Pl.
Donau-
M.-Luther-K.
Naturtheater
Hasenheide
Wissmann-
Mainzer
Marx-
Weichsel-
Fulda-
Elbe-
Laube-str.
Schule
Rixdorfer Teich
Karlsgartenstr.
Biebricher Str.
Sasarstg.
Erlanger Str.
Neukölln Arcaden
Amts-gericht
Schönstedt-str.
Bürgeramt
allee
Behinderten-werkstatt
Fontane-
Rathaus Neukölln
Erk-
Donau-
damm
Flughafen-
Boddinstr.
Isarstr.
Neckarstr.
Anzengruberstr.
Sommerbad Neukölln
Jahn-Sporth.
Mahlower Str.
Weise-
Bodinn-
Boddin-pl.
Berufs-sch.
BEZ. NEUKÖLLN
Ganghofer-str.
Hallen-bad
Berthelsdorfer
Lichten-
Selchower
Rollberg-
Morus-
H.-Schlitt-Str.
Kol. Odertal
Herrfurth-pl.
Werbellin-
NEUKÖLLN
Bornsdorfer
Richard-
Herrfurth-
Briese-
Falk-
nitzer
Saltykow-str.
Oder
Schillerpromenade
Kie-
Lessing-höhe
Karl-Marx-Str.
Kienitzer
Kopf-
Mittel-
Neu-wedeller
Haus der Jugend
Leykestr.
Aller-
Thomas-höhe
St.-Michael-Friedhof
Oker-
Luisenstädter Friedh.
Leine-
Rübe-landstr.
Karl-Marx-Pl.

Hyperboloid-Projektion
Abstand zwischen 2 schwarzen Gitterlinien = 1 Kilometer
138
A
C
1
2
3
4
5
6
Forst Grunewald
Jugend-erholungs- u. Tagungs-stätte
Jugenderholungsstätte
„Chalet Suisse"
Clayallee
STEGLITZ
Dahlem
ZEHLENDORF
Lichter-
Domäne Dahlem
Freilicht-mus.
Podbielski-Allee
Dahlem-Dorf
Thielplatz
Oskar-Helene-Heim
Freie Universität
Lichterfelde West
Sundgauer Str.
Königin-Luise-Str.
Argentinische Allee
Saargemünder Str.
Thielallee
Unter den Eichen
Hüttenweg
Clayallee
Berliner Str.
Teltower Damm
Mühlenstr.
Finckensteinallee
Carstennstr.
Drakestr.
Altensteinstr.
Englerallee
Schorlemer Allee
Podbielskiallee
Rheinbabenallee
Pacelliallee
Dahlemer Weg
Botanischer Garten
Bundesarchiv
Parkfriedhf. Lichterfelde
Mus. Kunst u. Kulturen d. Welt
Archäolog. Inst.
Biol. B.-anst. f. Land-u. Forstw.
Bund. Inst. f. Verbr.sch.
BAM
Krkhm.
Reha. zentr.
Schweizerhofpark
Truman plaza
1 Churer Z.
2 Sittener Zeile
3 Reinacher Z.
4 Nidwaldener Zeile
5 Obwald. Z.
6 Waadter Z.
7 Locarnoweg
1 Fliednerweg
2 O.-Hahn-Pl.

Friedenau
Steglitz
KREUZ SCHÖNEBG.
FRIEDENAU
FEUERB. STR.
RATH. STEGLITZ
LANKWITZ
LICHTERFELDE OST
Friedhof
Stadtpark
Bäke-park
Hafen Steglitz
Teltow
Schloß-park
Stadion
Charité Campus Benjamin Franklin
SCHLOSS-STR.
SCHILDHORN-STR.
SAARSTR.
STEGLITZER DAMM
ALBRECHT-STR.
BIRKBUSCH-STR.
HINDENBURG-DAMM
SIEMENS-STR.
LEONOREN-STR.
KAISER-WILHELM-STR.
KÖNIGSBERGER STR.
MORGENSTERNSTR.
OSTPREUSSENDAMM
MÜNSTER-DAMM
THORWALDSEN-STR.
GRAZER DAMM
BUNDES-ALLEE
RHEIN-STR.
HAUPT-STR.
SÜDWEST-KORSO
LEPSIUS-STR.
W.-SCHREIBER-PL.
FR.-WILH.-PL.
TAN. GARTEN
Filandastr.
Klingsor-str.
103
140
DORF
elde

Hakenberg
Schlachtfeld
Linum
Kremmen
Ruppiner Kanal
Draisinenbetrieb
Sachsenhausen
ORANIENBURG
Germendorf
Nikolauskirche
Dechtow
Linumer Bruch
5 km
Kuhhorst
Flatow
Staffelde
Schwante
Ober-
Groß Ziethen
Leegebruch
Bärenklau
Vehlefanz
Kreuz Oranienburg
Tietzow
Dreieck Havelland
Oberkrämer
Deutschhof
Ländchen
Eichstädt
Karlsruh
Birkenwerder
Hohen Neuendorf
Ebereschenhof
Börnicke
krämer
Velten
Wolfslake
Marwitz
Hennigsdorf
Hertefeld
Kienberg
Grünefeld
Glien
Perwenitz
Dt. Tonstr.
Stolpe
Bergerdamm
Deutsche Alleenstraße
Paaren im Glien
-Glien
Bötzow
Stolper Heide
FROHNAU
Pausin
Wansdorf
Stolpe Süd
Am Weinberg
Schönwalde-
HERMSDORF
Lietzow
Havelkanal
Schönwalde Dorf
Falkensee
Schulzendorfer Str.
HEILIGENSEE
Nauen
Schönwalde
Schl. Tegel
Neukammer
Bredow
Brieselang
Tegeler See
Markee
Zeestow
FALKENSEE
KONRADSHÖHE
TEGELORT
Holzhauser Str.
Wernitz
Finkenkrug
Flughafen Berlin-Tegel
Neugarten
Seegefeld
SPANDAU
Wustermark
Berlin Spandau
Neuröhrbeck
Zitadelle
Elstal
Dallgow-
Flughafen Tegel
Heckerdamm
Hoppenrade
Döberitz
Dr. Charlottenbg.
Siemensdamm
Tremmen
Berlin-Spandau
STAAKEN
CHARLOTTENBURG
Spandauer
Etzin
Buchow-Karpzow
Havelkanal
Priort
Olympiastadion
Seeburg
Neu Falkenrehde
Falkenrehde
Kartzow
Finken-B.
Dr.-Funkturm
GATOW
Grunewald
Paaren
Potsdam-Nord
Satzkorn
Groß Glienicke
Luftwaffenmus.
Ketzin
Paretz
Uetz-
Marquardt
Fahrland
Hüttenweg
Jagdschl. Gr.
Schmergow
Sacrow-
KLADOW
Museum Dahlem
Neu Fahrland
Grunewald
Großer Wannsee
Leest
Paretzer-Kanal
Töplitz
Leest
Nedlitz
Sacrow
Spanische Allee
ZEHLENDORF
Grube
BORNIM
Phöben
Cecilienhof
WANNSEE
Museumsdorf Düppel
Kemnitz
BORNSTEDT
Schloss Sanssouci
Schloss Glienicke
Kleinmachnow
Derwitz
Golm
Eiche
Neues Palais
BABELSBERG
Zehlendorf
Teltowkanal
Phöben
Zern-see
ehem. Rathaus
Klein-machnow
Groß Kreutz
Plessow
Filmpark Babelsberg
Teltow
Stahnsdorf
Neu-plötzin
Werder (Havel)
POTSDAM
Geltow
Kl.-Ravens-B.
Drewitz
Ruhlsdorf
Glindow
Plötzin
Glindow-see
Templiner See
Babelsberg
Güterfelde
Petzow
Bergholz-Rehbrücke
P-Drewitz
Schenkenhorst
Dreieck Werder
Bliesendorf
Caputh
Philippsthal
Sputendorf
Schwielowsee
Krähen-B.
Wilhelmshorst
Nuthe-tal
Schwielowsee
Saarmund
Nudow
Langerwisch
Saarmund
Michendorf
Ludwigsfelde-Ost
Glindow
Ferch
Ferch
Michendorf
Fahlhorst
Ahrensdorf
Busendorf
Dreieck Nuthetal
Michendorf
Gröben
Ludwigsfelde
Ludwigsfelde-West
Neuseddin
Wildenbruch
Siethen
Fichtenwalde
Dreieck Potsdam
Seddiner See
Großer Seddiner See
Gröbener See
Siethener See
Fresdorf
Tremsdorf
Jütchendorf
Beelitz Heilstätten
Seddin
Kähnsdorf
Kleinbeuthen
Borkwalde
Beelitz Heilstätten
Oranier Route
Naturpark
Stücken
Mietgendorf
Großbeuthen
Thyrow
Schlunkendorf
Glau
Märkisch Wilmersdorf
Beelitz
Blankensee
Borkheide
Reesdorf
Nieplitz
Blankensee
Körzin
Beelitz
Schäpe
Schönefeld
Schönhagen
Trebbin

D
E
F
1
2
3
4
5
6
Schmachtenhagen
Stolzenhagen
Wandlitzsee
Wandlitz
Biesenthal
Lanke
Melchow
Sydower Fließ
Schönholz
Klobbicke
Tuchen
Märkische Eiszeitstraße
Liepnitzsee
Grüntal
Sydow
Lobetal
Danewitz
Beerbaum
Dt. Tonstr.
Zühlsdorf
Rüdnitz
Heidekrautbahn-Museum
Basdorf
Tempelfelde
Naturpark Barnim
Ladeburg
Albertshof
Beiersdorf
Mühlenbecker See
Summt
Mühlenbeck
Bernau-Nord
Bernau b. Berlin
Befestigungsanlage
Gorinsee
Schönow
Schönfeld
Schönwalde
Mühlenbecker Land
Zepernick
Börnicke
Willmersdorf
Schönerlinde
Kolonie Röntgental
Panketal
Bernau-Süd
Weesow
Dreieck Pankow
Glienicke/Nordbahn
Schildow
Elisenau
Hirschfelde
Oranier-Route
Buch
Schwanebeck
Birkholz
Birkholzaue
Löhme
Werneuchen
Schönerlinder Str.
B-Weißensee
Dreieck Schwanebeck
Seefeld
Lübars
Blankenfelde
Niederschönhausen
Bucher Str.
Blankenburg
Lindenberg
Neu Lindenberg
Blumberg
Berlin-Hohenschönhausen
Krummensee
Wegendorf
Pasewalker Str.
Buchholz
BERLIN
Ahrensfelde
Malchow
Mehrow
Altlandsberg
Pankow
Reinickendorf
Ski-Piste
Prenzl. Prom.
Weissensee
Eiche
Berlin-Marzahn
Seeberg-Dorf
Bruchmühle
Festplatz
Wedding
Prenzlauer Berg
Hohenschönhausen
Hönow
Seeberg
Planetarium
Zucker-Mus.
Beusselstr.
Marzahn
Hoppegarten
Neuenhagen
Fredersdorf-Vogelsdorf
Reichstag
Museumsinsel
Lichtenberg
Hellersdorf
Zoo
Brandenburger Tor
Gedächtnis-Kirche
Kreuzberg
Tierpark
Dahlwitz
Dt. Technikmus.
Treptow
Karlshorst
Mahlsdorf
Münchehofe
Berlin-Hellersdorf
Schulzenhöhe
Tasdorf
Sachsend.
A.-str.
Tempelh. D.
Britzer D.
Bln. Park-eisenb.
Wuhlhde.
Schöneiche
Rüdersdorf
Museumspark
Neukölln
Dr. Neukölln
Oberschöneweide
Fichtenau
Woltersdorf
Schöneb.
Oberlandstr.
Grade-str.
Spree
Schöneberg
Tempelhof
Späthstr.
Schön-blick
Kranich-Bge.
Blub
Johannisthal
Schloss Köpenick
Gr. Müggelsee
Rahnsdorf
Mariendorf
Johannisth.Ch.
Buckow
Stubenrauchstr.
Erkner
Lankwitz
Britz. Mus.-eisenb.
Adlershof
Wendenschloss
Müggel-Bge.
Müggelheim
G.-Hauptmann-Mus.
Rudow
Altglienicke
Grünau
Fangschleuse
Lichtenrade
Groß-Ziethen
Schönefd.-N.
Schönefd.-S.
Dreieck Treptow
Bohnsdorf
Karutzhöhe
Gosen
Freienbrink
Osdorf
Birkholz
Schönefeld
Waldeck
Seddinsee
Neu Zittau
Waßmannsdorf
Flughafen Berlin-Schönefeld
Schulzendorf
Schmöckwitz
Eichwalde
Wernsdorf
(Diepensee)
Waltersdf.
Waltersdf. Dr.
Waltersdorf
Einbeeren
Mahlow
Großbeeren
Selchow
Kiekebusch
Zeuthen
Zeuthener See
Oder-Spree-Kanal
Miersdorf
Rotberg
Diedersdorf
Blankenfelde
Glasow
Wildau
Dreieck Spreeau
Groß Kienitz
Schönefelder Kreuz
Königs Wusterhsn.
Niederlehme
Friedersdorf
Dahlewitz
Dannenreich
Genshagen
Rangsdorf
Brusendorf
Neue Mühle
Zernsdorf
Am Fichtenplan
Königs Wusterhausen
Jühnsdorf
Löwenbruch
Ragow
Krüpelsee
Kablow
Rangsdorf
Schenkendorf
Senzig
Bindow
Groß Machnow
Zeesen
Mittenwalde
Draisinenbetr.
Zeesener See
Bindow-Süd
Groß Schulzendorf
Naturpark
Körbiskrug
Blossin
Glienick
Bestensee
Gussow
Heidesee
Dolgenbrodt
Dabendorf
Telz
Gallun
Gräbendorf
Dolgensee
Nottekanal
Kolberg
Dahme-Heideseen
Nächst Neuendorf
Schünow
Langer See
Schöneiche
Pätz
Pätzer Vordersee
Prieros
Zossen
Am Kahlberg
Heimatmuseum
Horstfelde
Pätzer

This index lists a selection of the streets and squares shown in the Street Atlas

STREET ATLAS INDEX

STREET ATLAS INDEX

KEY TO STREET ATLAS

Autobahn Motorway (Freeway)	Autoroute Autostrada
Vierspurige Straße Road with four lanes	Route à quatre voies Strada a quattro corsie
Bundes-/Fernstraße Federal/trunk road	Route fédérale/nationale Strada statale/di grande comunicazione
Hauptstraße Main road	Route principale Strada principale
Fußgängerzone - Einbahnstraße Pedestrian zone - One way road	Zone piétonne - Rue à sens unique Zona pedonale - Via a senso unico
Hauptbahnhof mit Bahnhof Main railway with station	Chemin de fer principal avec gare Ferrovia principale con stazione
U-Bahn Underground (railway)	Métro Metropolitana
Buslinie - Straßenbahn Bus-route - Tramway	Ligne d'autocar - Tram Linea d'autobus - Tram
Information - Jugendherberge Information - Youth hostel	Information - Auberge de jeunesse Informazioni - Ostello della gioventù
Kirche - Sehenswerte Kirche Church - Church of interest	Église - Église remarquable Chiesa - Chiesa di notevole interesse
Synagoge - Moschee Synagogue - Mosque	Synagogue - Mosquée Sinagoga - Moschea
Polizeistation - Postamt Police station - Post office	Poste de police - Bureau de poste Posto di polizia - Ufficio postale
Krankenhaus Hospital	Hôpital Ospedale
Denkmal - Funk- oder Fernsehturm Monument - Radio or TV tower	Monument - Tour d'antennes Monumento - Pilone radio o TV
Theater - Taxistand Theatre - Taxi rank	Théâtre - Station taxi Teatro - Posteggio di tassí
Feuerwache - Schule Fire station - School	Poste de pompiers - École Guardia del fuoco - Scuola
Freibad - Hallenbad Open air -/ Indoor swimming pool	Piscine en plein air - Piscine couverte Piscina all'aperto - Piscina coperta
Öffentliche Toilette - Ausflugslokal Public toilet - Restaurant	Toilette publique - Restaurant Gabinetto pubblico - Ristorante
Parkhaus - Parkplatz Indoor car park - Car park	Parking couvert - Parking Autosilo - Area di parcheggio
Stadtspaziergänge Walking tours	Promenades en ville Passeggiate urbane

> OUR AUTHOR

An Interview With MARCO POLO Insider Christine Berger

Christine Berger has lived in Berlin for 20 years. As an author, she's always hot on the trail of the latest city trends.

Why do you live in Berlin?

Originally I came to Berlin to study journalism. Since then, the city has had me well and truly hooked.

What is it about Berlin that attracts you?

The free spirit and tolerance which go to make a true metropolis. Its creativity knows no bounds.

Where and how do you live exactly?

In the most attractive and exciting district in the city, Mitte, only five minutes' walk from the Hackescher Markt.

What do you do for a living?

I'm a travel guide author, working principally for MAIRDUMONT (Marco Polo and National Geographic Spirallo). I also work as a freelance journalist for various newspapers and magazines and I am music editor of the magazine Das Magazin. I also write novels (34, Loser) and run the literature platform 'Hörbar Berlin'.

Do you travel a lot in and around Berlin?

Yes, I do actually, thanks to my job. Wherever possible, I like to go by bicycle or on foot.

What do you do in your spare time?

I have two adolescent children. I also read a lot and go jogging, play tennis and swim.

Do you like Berlin cooking?

Berlin cooking is ideal for cold, rainy days; on days like that you need something hearty and filling to warm yourself up. My favourite dish is Currywurst from the organic stand, Wittys on Wittenbergplatz.

What don't you like about the people here?

Two things annoy me: ignorance and anonymity. Many people don't care about anything. That is the downside of the lack of social control.

Can you imagine returning to live in your home town some day?

My home town lies on the North Sea. It's a little naval base in which a huge container port is currently being built. The people, though, are very nice. In principle Berlin is now my home town. Whenever I'm away for longer than two weeks at a stretch, I get homesick.

NOTES

INDEX

This index lists all sights, museums and destinations plus the names of important people featured in this guide. Numbers in bold indicate a main entry, italics a photograph

> GET IN TOUCH

Dear reader,

We make every effort to ensure you get the most up-to-date information available for your trip. Although our authors have done their research very carefully, errors or omissions do sometimes occur. We regret that the publisher cannot be held responsible for the consequences of such mistakes.

We do, however, look forward to receiving your comments.

Please write to the editorial team at
MARCO POLO Redaktion,
MAIRDUMONT, Postfach 3151,
73751 Ostfildern, Germany
info@marcopolo.de

PICTURE CREDITS

Cover photograph: Brandenburger Tor (alamy images/Jon Arnold Images: Arnold)
Air Service Berlin CFH GmbH (106 centre right); alamy images/Jon Arnold Images: Arnold (1); C. Berger (154); Berliner Unterwelten e. V. (106 bottom right); Bildarchiv Berlin (3 centre); caro e. Carolin Graening (13 bottom); Farbrausch GmbH (107 bottom right); Fotolia.com: Penelope Berger (106 top left); R. Freyer (3 right, 5, 6/7, 11, 20, 20/21, 26, 33, 34/35, 46, 49, 50, 57, 60, 66, 72, 74, 77, 78/79, 80, 83, 84, 85, 88, 98/99, 99, 100/101, 103, 108/109, 111, 118/119); R. M. Gill (cover right, 53); J. Gläser (4 right, 63); HB Verlag: Specht (cover left, 2 right, 21, 39, 56, 70/71, 98, 105); Huber: Mehlig (16/17); ©iStockphoto: Mike Bentley (107 centre left), fabphoto (13 top), jean schweitzer (107 top left); JACKS – Beauty Department Berlin, Miriam Jacks: Marek Iwicki (14 bottom); G. Knoll (58/59, 64, 69, 90/91, 92, 97); Katja Krug (12 top); Laif: Babovic (36), Galli (87); Look: Wohner (2 l.), Wothe (8); QUCHNIA (15 centre); H. Schlemmer (54); Schnitzelei (107 centre right); SideSeeing Berlin (15 bottom); Sommer & Kohl, Berlin: Jens Ziehe (12 bottom); O. Stadler (3 l., 4 left); The Corner GmbH (106 left and centre); The Prop House GmbH: Joyce Knobloch (14 top); Jonas Weidemann/Daniel Gohlke (15 top); M. Weigt (cover centre, 22/23, 31, 41, 42/43, 44, 67); ydo sol (95); 103 Club GmbH & Co.KG (106 centre left)

6th (18th) German edition
Chief editors: Michaela Lienemann (Concept, Duty editor), Marion Zorn (Chief text editor)
Author: Christine Berger; Editor: Jochen Schürmann
Editor English edition: Jens Bey, Translator: Jane Riester
Programme supervision: Silwen Randebrock; Picture editor: Gabriele Forst
Scene/24hrs: wunder media, Munich
Cartography for the Street Atlas: © MAIRDUMONT, Ostfildern
Design and layout: Zum goldenen Hirschen, Hamburg; Title page/p. 1–3: Factor Product, Munich
Thanks to Berlin Transport Authority (Berliner Verkehrsbetriebe BVG), © Berliner Verkehrsbetriebe BVG

Printed in Hungary on paper bleached entirely without the use of chlorine

> DOS AND DONT'S

On the whole Berlin is a peaceable place, but there are a few things visitors should be wary of

The three-cups game

A group of mostly Eastern European men tempt unsuspecting onlookers into having a go at the three-cups game – an easy way to win money, they maintain. Here, three matchboxes are moved around at lightning speed, and the opponent must guess which one contains the ball. Generally, 50 euros are placed on each game – and lost for certain. Take note: don't be misled by supposed co-players or spectators; they are all part of the gang.

Driving in the city centre

If you are not exactly compelled to transport four suitcases, ten shopping bags and three poodles through the city, you can easily leave your car standing. The disadvantage of not knowing your way around, the countless traffic jams and lack of parking spaces – or the high charges when you do find one – are all factors which can rapidly take the fun out of your stay in Berlin. The reliable S-Bahn, U-Bahn and tram services plus the dense bus network give you optimum freedom of movement from A to B.

Buying smuggled cigarettes

Berlin is in many ways a city made for bargain-hunters; the prospect of purchasing cigarettes for half the regular price from a Vietnamese dealer in the eastern part of the city should still not be considered a lucrative offer, though. These are, after all, smuggled goods, and by buying them you are also committing an offence!

Dodging fares ...

... even unintentionally! Don't forget to validate your ticket in the machine! The inspectors in Berlin love their job: no telltale uniform, and conscientious to a T, they pounce on anyone travelling without a valid ticket on the U- or S-Bahn, for example. The penalty is 40 euros, after all. The best thing to do is to buy a weekly ticket or the 'Welcome Card' (see 'Back to Basics').

Taking a taxi without a map

Be prepared for the fact that not all taxi drivers know their way around the city or a particular district. Passengers often have to explain how to get somewhere, especially if it's on the outskirts. Ideally you should take a look at a city plan and check possible routes before you even embark on your journey.

Leaving bags unattended

Unfortunately, Berlin is a popular hunting ground for pickpockets.
These criminally-minded professionals regularly make good catches, especially at stations, on escalators and in crowds during big events. Don't carry your purse or wallet in your jacket or back pocket and always keep an eye on

S U Liniennetz *Routemap* B

Tarifbereich Berlin *Fare*

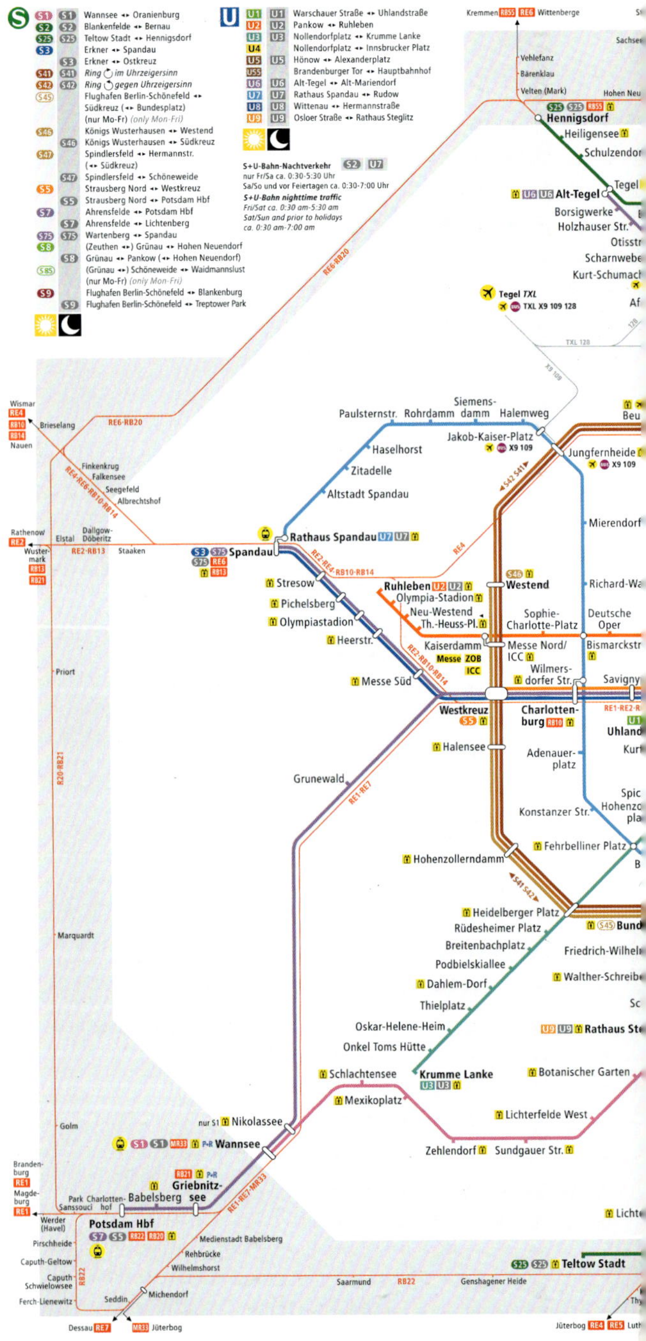